Camden District, S.C. Wills and Administrations 1781-1787 (1770-1796)

Abstracted by
Brent H. Holcomb, G.R.S.
and
Elmer O. Parker

Copyright 1978 by:
The Rev. Silas Emmett Lucas, Jr.

All rights reserved. No part of this publication may be reproduced,
stored in a retrieval system, transmitted in any form,
posted on to the web in any form or by any means
without the prior written permission of the publisher.

Please direct all correspondence and orders to:

www.southernhistoricalpress.com
or
**SOUTHERN HISTORICAL PRESS, Inc.
PO BOX 1267
375 West Broad Street
Greenville, SC   29601
southernhistoricalpress@gmail.com**

ISBN #0-89308-050-0

Printed in the United States of America

CONTENTS

Introduction

Abstracts of Camden District Wills and Estates in
    Kershaw County Court House, Camden, SC   Pp. 1-68

Abstracts of Camden District Wills transferred to
    Sumter County Court House, now in S. C. Archives Pp. 69-74

Illustrations

        Will of Leard Burns November 26, 1776
        Will of Alexander Pegan June 1, 1778

Index

The design on the front cover was copied from a watermark on paper in the file of Thomas Owen Apt. 54, Pck. 1885.

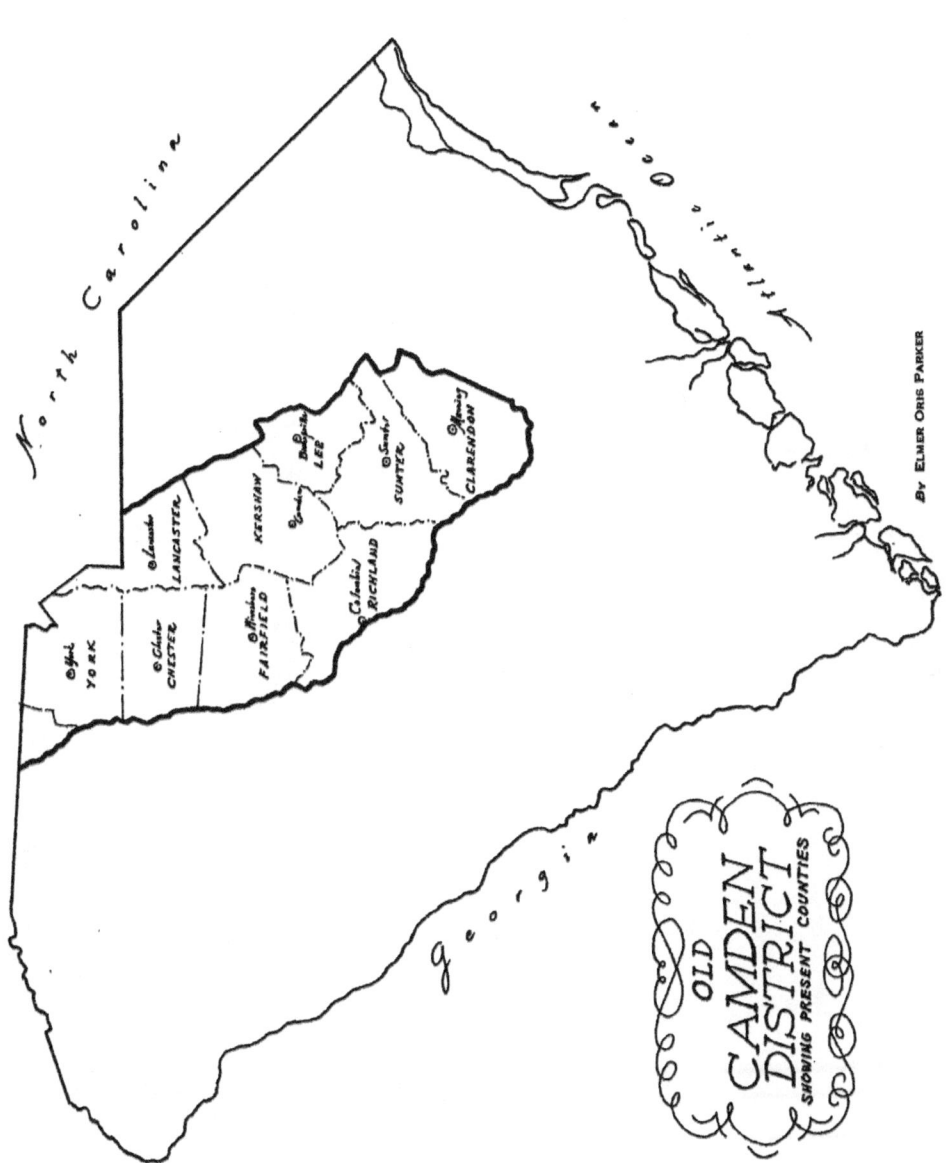

INTRODUCTION

   Camden District was formed in 1769, but there was no court of record for that district until much later. The seats of the Districts of 1769 were made courts of Ordinary by a proclamation of Governor John Rutledge 3 Nov 1781, when he appointed the following persons as ordinaries:
   Hezekiah Mayham for Charleston District
   William Harden for Beaufort District
   Charles Middleton for Orangeburgh District
   John Ewing Calhoun for Ninety Six District
   Wood Furman for Camden District
   Hugh Horry for Georgetown District, and
   Claudius Pegues for Cheraws District.
As can be seen in this volume some Camden District documents date from November of 1781. Wood Furman held the court at his house in the High Hills of Santee. He died February 10, 1783. The House Journal entry for 10 February 1783 shows that the Senate had elected the following ordinaries:
   Capt. Charles Lining for Charles Town District
   Colonel William Harden for Beaufort District
   Colonel Hugh Horry for George Town District
   Colonel Charles Myddleton for Orangeburgh District
   Colonel Henry Hampton for Camden District
   Mr. Claudius Pegues for Cheraws District, and
   Colonel John Thomas Jr. for Ninety Six District.
Henry Hampton held the court at his "plantation near Winnsborough" in present Fairfield County. This office was set up in Camden in 1784, and in 1785 Henry Beaumont appears as Deputy Ordinary. Camden District Court of Ordinary did not cease to exist in 1785, but continued until 1787 when courts of ordinary were set up in each county.
   The counties formed in Camden District were York, Chester, Fairfield, Richland, Lancaster, Clarendon, Claremont, and Salem. All of these counties have suffered some loss of records except York, Chester and Fairfield.
   The Camden District records themselves are quite varied and interesting. Some estate proceedings begun in Charleston were transferred to Camden District. Some records are found which are not easily explained, e. g., the estate of Samuel Davis of Prince William's Parish. The citate in any estate is a very important (and often overlooked) document in the estate packages. It helps to locate the decedent and may help to locate the place of burial. These are also helpful in locating churches and giving some locations for ministers. All documents found in the estate packages have been examined and abstracted.
   At some time twenty packages containing wills were transferred to Sumter Court House. These have also been abstracted and included here, as well as a few documents found in other counties relating to Camden District.
   There was at one time a Will Book No. 1, which is now lost. Will Book A-1 is extant and is located in the Office of the Probate Judge in Kershaw County Court House, where these Camden District papers are housed. This volume contains many of the wills and estate abstracted here as well as some for which the originals have not been found. This volume has been abstracted in its entirety in The South Carolina Magazine of Ancestral Research. This volume should be used in conjunction with the abstracts in SCMAR.
   My sincerest thank to my co-author, Mr. Elmer Oris Parker, without whose assistance this project would never have been even considered. No one has ever had a more able and helpful person with whom to work.

                              Brent H. Holcomb, G. R. S.
                              Columbia, South Carolina
                              April 19, 1977

ABBOT, JOHN   Apt. 1, Pck. 3
   [another John Abbott's estate is also contained in this package]
Administration Bond: WINIFRED ABBOT, Admx., WILLIAM DODD, ARTHUR RICHARD-
SON, & ISAAC JACKSON bound to WOOD FURMAN, Ordy of Camden District, for
₤ 14, 000 current money of S. C.(equal to ₤ 2000 sterling)...16 Apr 1782.
High Hills of Santee, Wit: JOSIAH FURMAN.
Inventory: 29 June 1782-13 July 1782. "The Hole Estate in one Lot ₤ 400"

ACRE, WILLIAM   Apt. 1, Pck. 6
   JACOB CURRY applied for Administration as Principal Creditor, 7 Nov
1782.
Citation published 8 Nov 1782 by JACOB GIBSON, Senr.
Administration bond: JACOB CUREY, Admr., BARNABY POPE and EDWARD McGRAUGH
(E), bound for ₤ 14, 000 S. C. currency to Wood Furman...3 Nov 1782.
Warrant of appraisement: to BARNABY POPE, LEWIS POPE, PETER CURRY, JACOB
GIBSON & BRYANT RAELY...3 Dec 1782. Sworn appraisers: 7 Jan 1783, PETER
CURRY, JACOB GIBSON JUNR., & BRYANT RAYLY sworn before BARNABY POPE, Esq.
Sale: 200 A sold to JACOB CURRY; other purchasers BAR'Y POPE, DUDLEY
CURRY, JACOB McGRAY. Total sale ₤ 46 :3:6.

ADDISON, THOMAS   Apt. 1, Pck. 22
   ESTHER ADDISON, widow, applied for administration as next of kin
22 July 1782.
Citation read at Fishing Creek [Meeting House], 4 Aug 1782 by JOHN SIMP-
SON, V. D. M.
Administration bond: ESTHER ADDISON, Admx., THOMAS GLAZE, & WILLIAM
STEWART bound to Wood Furman, for ₤ 14, 000 S. C. currency...28 Aug 1782.
Wit: RACHEL HAMILTON.
Warrant of appraisement: GEORGE WADE, WILLIAM McDOWEL, FREDERIC KIMBALL,
MIDDLETON McDONOLD, JAMES DENTON & THOMAS GARDINER...28 Aug 1782.
Sworn appraisers: MIDDLETON McDONALD, WILLIAM McDONALD, & THOMAS GARDINER,
sworn before JAMES SIMPSON, A Magistrate in Camden District, 25 Oct 1782.
Appraisement: ₤ 1089. 13. 9. 25 Oct 1782.

AGNEW, JOHN   Apt. 2 Pck. 24
   GEORGE AGNEW applied for Administartion 20 Dec 1783. "No return."
Administration bond: GEO. AGNEW, Admr., JOHN BARBER, bound to HENRY
HAMPTON, Ordy. of Camden Dist., for ₤ 3000 sterling...10 Jan 1784. Wit:
JNO. HARBIN.
Warrant of appraisement: 10 Jan 1784, to JOHN RICHMAN, SAMUEL ARMSTRONG,
JOHN CONAWAY, MECAGA PIKETT, & JAMES ARNETT.
Sworn appraisers: JOHN RICHMOND, JAS. ARNETT, & SAMUEL ARNETT, sworn be-
fore H. HAMPTON, J. Q., 11 Mar 1784.
Appraisement: 13 Mar 1784, Wit: JOHN CONNERY, Clerk.

ALLEN, JOHN   Apt. 2, Pck. 44
   ABRAHAM WIMBERLY, MARY ALLEN & WM. BREWER applied for administra-
tion...at my [HENRY HAMPTON's] plantation near Winnsborough...25 Feb 1785.
JNO. HARBIRT, Clk.
Citation published at Beaver Creek, by ROBT McCLINTOCK, 27[?] Feb 1785.
Warrant of appraisement to GLASS CASTON, JOHN RUTLEDGE, ROBERT MAHAFFEY &
HARRY HORTON...26 Mar 1785. Sworn before FREDK KIMBALL, J. P.
Administration bond: MARY ALLEN, WILLIAM BREWER, Admrs., ADAM THOMAS,
DANL HORTON bound for ₤ 3000 sterling...26 Mar 1785.
Inventory 23 ___ 1785...included slaves (named).
Sale not dated, purchasers not listed.
Estate of JOHN ALLEN in account with MARY HARRELL, admx. "for scooling
(sic) 2 children". Pd. FREDERICK KIMBALL, for JAS. McMANOS. "Boarding
3 children". Paid: JOHN RUTLEDGE, GLASS CASTON, LAWYER HUNT, WILLIAM
BREWER, WILLIAM NARRAMORE, THOMAS ROACH, ABRAHAM WIMBERLY, upon suit of
WALTER SHROPSHIRE, GEORGE MILLER, DANIEL AYRES, JOHN BOLDING, WILLIAM
BREWER, ARON LOCKHART, RICHARD KELTON, JNO HORTON for AMOS HORTON, DANIEL
HORTON, RUBIN COOK..
Receipts (Recd. of HOLODAY HARRELL) by JOHN MARSHALL, B. NAILEY(?), WM.
BREWER, DANIEL HORTON, JOHN TAYLOR.
[The widow MARY ALLEN apparently married HOLLADAY HARRELL.]

ANCRUM, GEORGE   Apt. 2 Pck. 47
   Administration bond: ROBERT LITHROW, Admr., JOHN MILLING, MINOR
WINN bound to HENRY HAMPTON...13 July 1785...before JENRY H. TILLINGHAST,
WARREN HALL. Warrant of appraisement (left blank)...13 July 1785.

ANDERSON, GEORGE Apt. 3 Pck. 52
        Administration bond: MARGARET ANDERSON (X), Admx., PHILIP WALKER, and JOHN WALKER (T), bound for L 3000 sterling...15 May 1783.
Estate appraised 14 June 1785 by JOHN STORMOND, BUCKNER HAGOOD, and SAMUEL ERWIN.

ANDERSON, ROBERT Apt. 3 Pck. 55
        MARGRET ANDERSON applied for letters of administration 1 May 1783. HENRY HAMPTON. Citation published by RALPH JONES.(no date).

ANDERSON, WILLIAM Apt. 3, Pck. 57
        DANIEL GREEN applied for adminstration 24 Apr 1783 to HENRY HAMPTON.
WILLIAM MARTIN, minister of the Gospel, read citation 11 May 1783 at Rocky Creek.
Administration bond: DANIEL GREEN and Robt STUART...15 May 1783.
Warrant of appraisement: ROBT STUART, RICHD GEATHER (GEATHER, GAITHER), ANDREW HEMPHILL, ALEXDR BRADY, JAS STENSON (STEVENSON)...15 May 1783.
Sworn appraisers before PHIL. WALKER, J. P. 5 July 1783.
Inventory L 22:14, 12 July 1783.

ANDREWS, THOMAS Apt. 3 Pck. 60
        FRANCES ANDREWS applied for administration as next of Kin to WOOD FURMAN...3 Dec 1782.
Citation read by DAVID STOCKTON, minister, 3 Dec 1782.
Administration bond: FRANCES ANDREWS, Admx., MIDDLETON McDONALD, JAMES DENTON, for L 14,000 S. C. currency...at High Hills of Santee...31 Dec 1782. Wit: JAMES SIMPSON.
Warrant of appraisement: JESSE TILLMAN, ROBT LEE, ROLLE CORNELIUS, JAMES DENTON, ROBT THOMSON & JOHN CASTON...3 Dec 1782.
Sworn appraisers: 11 Jan 1783, JESSE TILMAN, ROLLE CORNELIUS, JAMES DENTON.
WOOD FURMAN to JAMES SIMPSON, dedimus to qualify FRANCES ANDREWS as Admx. 11 Jan 1783.

ARD, JOHN Apt. 3 Pck. 63
    PHILIP REYLY applied for administration 14 Sept 1782 to WOOD FURMAN.
Citation read by JACOB GIBSON 29 Sept 1782. Letters of administration dated 14 Sept 1782.
Administration bond: PHILIP REYLEY, Admr. & HEMRY HAMPTON, for L 14, 000 SC currency. 14 Oct 1782. Wit: RACHEL FURMAN.
Warrant of appraisement: BRYANT REYLEY, BENJAMIN MAY, BARNABY POPE, ROBERT RAB, & WILLIAM WOODARD...14 Oct 1782.

ARRICK, FREDERICK Apt. 3 Pck. 64
        JOHN ARRICK applied for administration 29 June 1784 to HENRY HAMPTON.
Citation "duly read by me in the congregation of Winnsborough, July 11th, 1784. ROBT McCLINTOCK"
Administration bond: JOHN ARRICK, Admr., & THOMAS HILL for L 3000 sterling 12 July 1784. Wit: JOHN HAMPTON.

ARLEDGE, WILLIAM Apt. 3 Pck. 68
        JOSEPH ARLARGE (sic) applied for administration 6 Aug 1784 to HENRY HAMPTON.
Administration bond: JOSEPH ARLARGE, ISAAC ARLEDGE, & CLEMENT ARLEDGE, for L 3000 sterling18 Aug 1784. Wit: AMOS ARLEDGE.
Warrant of appraisement: BARTLET HINSON, ISAAC ARLEDGE, CHAS GAVIN, BENJAMIN PERRY & ISAAC GIBSON. 18 Aug 1784.
Sworn appraisers: 30 Aug 1784, ISAAC ARLEDGE, CHARLES GAVEN, BAT. HENSON, before CHARLES PICKETT, Esq.
Debts: JAMES LOVE, EPHRAIM POOL, JOSEPH THOMPSON, JAMES BISHOP, WILLIAM KITCHE, JOHN WRENS(?).
Appraisement: 2 Sept 1784. L 29-3-6.

ARRANT, CONROD Apt. 3 Pck. 73
        Dedimus from HENRY HAMPTON to ANDREW BASKINS, Esq., to examine witnesses and prove will. 26 Oct 1785. "no return"
Dedimus to JOHN MARSHALL to administer oaths to appraisers 29 Nov 1785. H. HAMPTON, Ordinary's Office, H. BEAUMONT.

Executors oath; MICHAEL MILLER, JOHN BAKER, 21 Dec 1786., JOHN MARSHALL, J. P.
Appraisers oath: BENJ. LADD, 22 Jan 1787(?).
Will of Coonrod Arrant of Craven County, Camden District, S. C....to wife ELIZABETH, ₺ 500...to son WILLIAM ARRANT, 100 A called the upper plantation ...to son PETER ARRANT, 100 A where I now live...daughter JANE...daughter MARY...3 youngest daughters ELIZABETH, HANNAH, & REBECCA...MICHAEL MILLER, JOHN BAKER, Exrs...31 Jan 1779...CONRAD ARRANT (SEAL), Wit: WILLIAM BOYD, JOHN MASTERS, JOHN BIRD.
Codicil: to child in my wife's womb an equal part. Proven 17 Nov 1785 by WILLIAM BOYD and JOHN MASTERS.

ARMSTRONG, JAMES Apt. 3 Pck. 72
   Bond: ISAAC BALL, admr., SAMUEL MOORE, REUBEN LACEY, securities 20 Aug 1782. Citation read at Flat Rock Meeting House July 28, 1782, by JAMES FOWLER, V. D. M.
Warrant of appraisement to: JOHN WALLACE, JAMES MITCHELL, PHILIP SANDIFORD, JAMES HETHERINGTON, THOMAS RAINEY, and SAMUEL RAINEY, 20 Aug 1782.
JOHN WALLACE, JAMES MITCHELL, and THOMAS RAINY sworn as appraisers 23 Oct 1782, by EDWD LACEY, J. P. Appraised value ₺ 87 14 8.

ATKINS, ELISHA Apt 4 Pck. 87
   ELIZABETH ATKINS & WM BROCKET applied for admn. 8 Oct 1782 to WOOD FURMAN. Citation certified by JNO SIMPSON, V. D. M.
Bond: ELIZABETH ATKINS, admx., WM BROCKET, FINY McCLANCHAN, & SAMUEL GAILY, securites. Wit: JOHN HARRIS, ROBT PATTON, 18 Oct 1782.
Another Bond witness by JAMES GREEN, 27 Dec 1783.
Warrant of appraisement to SAMUEL GALEY, PHINEHAS McCLENCHAN, ___ HUTE(?), ROBERT PATTON, HUGH WHITE, ISAAC McFADEAN.

ATKINS, JOHN Apt 4 Pck. 88
   Document: The widow before proving the will sold WM THERREL the old plantation & negro wench...The oldist of John Atkins sons got the will conceled it but having got a true coppe the Clark being Living with the other evidence the will is proved & recorded...the old widow being childish...her stepson buts(?) in the obligation. I, RICHARD ATKINS, son of JOHN ATKINS & the widow ATKINS living am ronged. Worthy Sr., please to give me advice.
   Will proved by JAMES GREER (no date).
ELIZABETH ATKINS, widow of ELISHA, after the death of her husband, (about two years ago) that JOSEPH ATKINS took a paper & said it was his father's will.
Dedimus from H. HAMPTON to JAMES KNOX to prove the will of JOHN ATKINS & qualify ESTHER GASTON. 26 Dec 1783.
RICHARD ATKINS admr. of JOHN, asserts that JOHN WALKER disposed of a negro girl, contrary to law, of JOHN's estate. 8 Sept 1784.
Appraisement, July 10, 1784, ₺-371 9 0., by SAMUEL ATKINS, JAS ROBINSON, JNO WALKER. Bonds on JAMES CRAFFORD, ARCHIBALD DAVYS, JOHN WHITE.

ATKINSON, HENRY Apt 4 Pkc. 89
   Bond: MARGARET ATKINSON (+), Admx., JNO MILLING & JNO BUCHANAN, securities, to HENRY HAMPTON, Ordy., ___ May 1787...estate of HENRY ATKINSON, Wit: JOHN HAMPTON. [No other documents in package]

AUSTIN, DREWRY Apt 4 Pack. 92
   Will of Drewrey Auston of Jacksons Creek in Camden District...to wife, 100 A that I live upon & horses, household furniture, etc., negro wench Hannah & cattle, to raise & support my children...to my eldest son WILLIAM AUSTON, 100 A on the creek below where I live betwixt my house & JOSEPH CHAPMAN, & negro Dick...to my son DAVIES, 100 A "on Buckhead in Georgia", negro girl Rose...to my eldest daughter CASIA, one negro girl... to my daughter NANCY...to my daughter BETTY..."to my wifes two sons", 100 A on Broad River, to daughter CASIA...wife ELISABETH AUSTON, CORNAL(sic) JOHN PHILLIPS, Exrs...13 Dec 1780...DRURY AUSTON, Wit: JAMES SLOAN, JAMES HENING, NATHEN AUSTON (A). Proved by JAMES HAYNAN, 2 Apr 1783, before H. HAMPTON, Ordy.
Admm. bond: ELIZABETH AUSTON & WILLIAM VININGHAM, 29 Sept 1783, Wit: FRA. PRINGLE. Inventory made by JOHN ROBERTSON, COL. HENRY HUNTER, ROBERT RAGG, 5 Dec 1783, before JOHN WINN.

BAGNALL, EBENEZER Apt 4 Pck. 94
    Will of EBENEZER BAGNALL, at present of Charles-Town...to my cousins EBENEZER BAGNALL, JOHN BAGNAL, ISAAC BAGNAL & REBECCA MARTIN & MARY TOBY, s 25 each...to friends JOHN BREADY & JOHN McCAMBRIDGE, L 10 sterling each...remainder to three of my nearest relations in the Kingdom of Ireland...L 150 sterling left in the hands of SUSANNA FLOOD, widow & 6,000 continental dollars due from MR. JOHN CHESNUT...friends JOHN CLEMENT & JOHN ADAMSON, both of Charlestown, Exrs...8 Aug 1781. EBR. BAGNELL (B), Wit: JOHN McCAMBRIDGE, JOHN BRADY, PETER DELCORE (+).
Camden, 26 Apr 1786, Both executors of Camden District, declined.
Will proved by JOHN McCAMBRIDGE, 31 May 1786, before J. ALEXANDER, J. P.
ISAAC BAGNALL, applied for letters of admn with the will annex't as nearest of kin...court of Ordinary to be held at Camden 17 May next...26 Apr 1786, H. HAMPTON, Ordinarys Office, H. BEAUMONT.
Published in St. Mark's Parish, 30 Apr 1786 by me, JOHN HUDDSON, V:D:M: Security WM MONTGOMERY & SAML MONTGOMERY, Magistrate JOHN DICKEY.
Dedimus to JOHN DICKEY to qualify ISAAC BAGNALL, 31 May 1786.
Warrant of appraisement: to EBENEZER BAGNALL, JOHN BAGNALL, ARTHUR WHITE, JOHN GAMBELL, THOMAS TOBIAS 31 May 1786.
Geo. Town District: Before JNO DICKEY, J. P. of said district, came ISAAC BAGNALL & made oath that there is [no?] personal estate to appraise. 3 Nov 1786.

BAILEY, ROBERT Apt 4 Pck. 100
    JOHN BAILEY applied for letters of admn. 26 Mar 1784. Citation read at Catholic Church on 28 Mar 1784. JN NEWTON.
Admn. bond: JOHN BAILEY & JAMES PEDEN, 26 Apr 1784, Wit: JNO HARBIRT.
Warrant of appraisement to JAMES PADIAN, DAVID McCALLEY, THOMAS McCALLEY, ROBERT STRONG & JAMES STRONG, 26 Apr 1784.
Appraisement: 1 March 1784, sworn 1 June 1784, DAVID McCALLA, THOMAS McCALLA, JAMES PEDEN before JAS. KNOX, J. P.
Buyers at sale: JOHN BAILLIE, JAMES HANNA, WILLM McCULLIG, GEORGE CHIREY, HUGH MCDONAL, THOMAS MCCALLA, BUCKNER HOWARD, JOHN MOORE, ROBERT STRONG, ALEXANDER BROWN, JAMES BANKHEAD, THOMAS STANFORD, THOMAS STEEL, JAMES KINGE, MAREY STANFORD, JOHN McWATTERS, CHRISTOPHER STRONG, WILLIAM MECALLUGH, JEAN BAILLIE, 2 July 1784.

BARKLAMS, JNO Apt 5 Pck. 126
    JOSEPH KERSHAW, Esq., applied for admn. on estate of JOHN BARKLAM as principal creditor...14 May 1785.
Citation read in the Congregation of Camden Sunday, 29 May 1785, JOHN LOGUE.
Admn. Bond: JOSEPH KERSHAW, admn., JOSEPH KIRKLAND & THOMAS BAKER, Securities to H. HAMPTON, 1 July 1785.
Warrant of appraisement to JAMES BROWN, FOULLER BRISBANE, JOHN CHESNUT, SAML MATHIAS & GEORGE GARTER.
Camden, 1 Feb 1785, there is no personal estate...unnecessary to qualify appraisers. JOSEPH KERSHAW.

BARNETT, JOHN Apt 5 Pck. 136
    MARGARET BARNETT applied for admn...28 Aug 1784. Citation read at Waxaw Church, Oct. 24, 1784, JAMES EDMONDS, V. D. M.
Appraisement: 10 Jan 1785 by JOHN FLEMING, JOHN HAGANS, ALEXR. CRAFORD [no other papers.]

BARNETT, WILLIAM Apt. 5 Pck. 138
    Will of WILLIAM BARNET of Camden District & Waxhaw Congregation ...to wife JANE, a sorrel mare, etc. & other items "which she brought with her"...to son ROBERT, Tract adj. ARCHIBALD COUSART & GEORGE M'KENNY on the main trading road from Charlotte to Charleston, 190 A...to son WILL, L 10 sterling...to son ANDREW, L 5 sterling...to daughter ANN, L 1 sterling... to daughter MARY, one young horse & pots I owned before I married my late espoused wife...to eldest son ROBERT, L 5...ANDREW BOYD SR. & ANDREW FOSTER, Esq., Exrs...9 Sept 1784...WILLIAM BARNET (X) (SEAL), Wit: ANDREW BOYD, ROBERT GUTHRIE, ROBT FINDLEY. Proven by ANDREW BOYD and ROBERT GUTHRIE 1 Oct 1784, JNO McCLENAHAN, J. P. ROBERT FINDLEY swears that he wrote the will...18 Jan 1785, before ANDREW FOSTER, J. P.
Dedimus to ANDREW FOSTER to prove will, 10 Jan 1785.
Warrant of appraisement: 28 Jan 1785, to JOHN ARNOLD BENDER[PENDER], JOHN KENNEDY, GEORGE WHITE, JOHN FOSTER & JOHN FLEMING. Sworn appraisers 20 Feb 1785, JOHN ARNOLD BENDER, JOHN KENNEDY, GEORGE WHITE & JOHN FOSTER.

Appraisement: 20 Feb 1785, before ANDREW FOSTER, J. P.

BARR, THOMAS Apt 5 Pck. 139
    ALEXANDER HENRY & JAMES CAMMELL applied for admn. as nearest of kin
...9 Apr 1783.
Citation read at the house of JNO VENABLE 22 Apr 1783 before a considerable collection of people...FPAS. CUMMINS, V. D. M.
Bond: JAMES CAMPBLE & ALEXR HENRY, 15 May 1783, Wit: JOSEPH CARRELL.
Warrant of appraisement: to ALEXANDER AKENS, WM PATRICK, ROBERT COWDEN, CHS RICHARDSON & JOSEPH PATERSON, 15 June 1783. Appraisement made by ALEXANDER EAKENS, WM PATRICK, ROBT COWDEN, 10 July 1783. Sale not dated, no buyers listed.

BEAM, JAMES Apt 6 Pck. 170
    WOOD TUCKER SR., applied for admn as next of kin...10 July 1782.
Citation 7 July 1782, CHRISTIAN THEUS.
Bond: WOOD TUCKER SR., WOOD TUCKER JR., & ROLING WILLIAMS, 5 Aug 1782. Wit: SAMUEL GOMERY, JOHN KNIGHT.
Warrant of appraisement to AMOS DAVIS, THOMAS TAYLOR, JAMES TAYLOR, DAVID WAISTCOST, RICHARD EVANS & ROBT LYEL, 17 Sept 1782. Appraisement: 9 Nov 1782, ROBERT LYELL, RICHARD EVANS, DAVID WESTCOTT.

BELL, JOHN Apt 6 Pck. 180
    Will of JOHN BELL of Camden District...to wife MARY, my best Feather Bed and Furniture...to my eldest son FREDERICK BELL, sl sterling...to WILLIAM RASOR BELL...to my eldest daughter PENELOPE STUCKEY, sl sterling ...to JOHN BELL, son of WILLIAM RASOR BELL...18 Oct 1786...JOHN BELL (+), Wit: WILLIAM DAMPUR, RICHARD HARDDICK (X), ELEAZAR SHARP. Proved by WILLIAM DAMPUR, 28 Nov 1786 before J. ALEXANDER, J. P.
Dedimus to ELIAS DUBOSE to admn. oath of appraisers, 5 Dec 1786.
Warrant of appraisement to ROBERT CARTER, WM RAZOR BELL, JACOB HUSK, ISAAC HUSK, WM DAMPIER, JONATHAN NEWMAN. Sworn appraisers: WILLM RASOR BELL, ISAAC HUSK, & JACOB HUSK, 25 July 1787 before ELIAS DUBOSE, J. P.
Warrant prolonged 3 months from 4 May 1787. H. BEAUMONT, Dep. Ordy.
Appraisement dated 18 Dec 1786.

BELL, VINCENT Apt 6 Pck. 183
    JAMES McCUNE applied for admn...26 June 1784. Citation read before ye Congregation of Fishing Creek on Sabbath, 19 July. WM. MARTIN, Rocky Creek. July 20, 1784.
Bond: JAMES McCOWN & ROBERT ELLISON, 22 July 1784, before JOHN HARBIRT.
[no other papers]

BETTICE, JAMES Apt 7 Pck. 205
    LUCY BETTICE and JOHN CHESNUT applied for admn...15 Aug 1783.
Citation read at Camden, 31 Aug 1783. RICHARD FURMAN.
Bond: JOHN CHESNUT, LUCY BETTICE & DOUGLAS STARKE...29 Apr 1784, Wit: ZACH CANTEY.
Warrant of appraisement, 29 Apr 1784 to SAMUEL BOYKEN, BURREL BOYKIN, WILLIS WHITAKER, ISAAC ROSS, JAMES CANTEY, & SAMUEL DENKINS.
Appraisement: 22 July 1785 by JAMES CANTEY, WILLIS WHITAKER, & SAMUEL DINKINS.

BISHOP, NICHOLAS Apt 7 Pck. 217
    Will of NICHOLAS BISHOP, Shoemaker...wife HANNAH, son HENRY, daughter DORCAS...son WILLIAM...daughter HANNAH...sons JAMES, NICHOLAS and JOHN (minor)...Ex. sons WILLIAM & NICHOLAS-..11 May 1778...Wit: HUGH WHITESIDE, WILLIAM JONES, PETER EOFF. Proven 21 Apr 1787. Estate appraised July 17, 1787 by DAVID HUNTER, JOHN PORTER, JOSEPH GASTON, Ł 30 9 10.
HANNAH BISHOP, widow, was appointed admx. and sworn 30 May 1787.
Purchasers at sale: WILLIAM MOORE, HUGH KNOX, WILLIAM WHITESIDE, DAVIN HUNTER, DOCTOR KNOX, RAFF McFADDEN, CHAS WALLIS, JAMES BISHOP, THOS WALLIS, JAMES PAGAN, JOHN PORTER, DAVID STREAN, JOSEPH GASTON, WM BISHOP, ABRAHAM WRIGHT, WILLIAM McELHENNY, HANNAH MILLER, DAVID BOYD, SAML McCOLL-UGH, NATHAN MOORE, MR. CONER(?), SAMUEL KNOX, JOSEPH MORROW. Ł 69 18 8.

BLAKE, WILLIAM Apt 7 Pck 225.
    CHARLES LEWIS applied for admn. on estate of WILLIAM BLAKE of Wateree Creek...court to be held at my house(WOOD FURMAN) 20 December next ...28 Nov 1781. Citation read 18 Dec 1781, RALPH JONES.

Bond: CHARLES LEWIS, MOSES KNIGHTEN & PETER BRUNSON...2 Jan 1782...Wit: THOMAS GARDNER.
Warrant of appraisement to JOHN KING, JOHN WATTS, FREDERIC BRIGGS, THOMAS STONE & JAMES YARBOROUGH, 2 Jan 1782, WILLIAM SIMMONS, J. P. Inventory made 2 Feb 1782, by CHARLES PICKETT, JOHN KING & JOHN WATT (X).
Buyers at sale (no date): JOHN KING, MOSES KNIGHTEN, FRANCES BLAKE widow, EPHRAIM PETTYPOOL, JOHN HOLZENDORF, CHARLES LEWIS, ISAAC GRAHAM, LARKIN CARDEN, THOMAS STARKS, JOHN OBSTANT(?).

BLISS, HENRY   Apt 8   Pck. 229
    Will of HENRY BLISS of Craven County, St. Mark's Parish...to son JOHN BLISS, negro (named)...to a child of ZILPHA HERRINGTON called SUSANNAH, a bay mare & heifer in case she will give up all obligations she has from under my hand...to my sisters Little Child called MARY MOORE...LEVI MOORE & SAMUEL MONTGOMERY, Exrs...23 Dec 1779...HENRY BLISS (SEAL), Wit: ROBERT CRAWFORD, JAMES GIBSON, JOSIAH SPRY. Proven 27 Nov 1784, by JAMES GIBSON.
Dedimus to prove will from WM. BURROWS, Ordinary of S. C., 4 Feb 1780, to WM. MARTIN, J. P. Sworn 14 Feb 1784, by WM MARTIN, J. P.
Warrant of appraisement to JOHN RAFFIELD, JOHN VIRTU, JAMES GIBSON, EBENEZER BAGNELL & ARCHIBALD CONNER. 27 Nov 1784. Sworn appraisers: JOHN RAFIELD, EBENEZER BAGNAL, JAMES GIBSON, ARCHIBALD CONNER, 27 Dec 1784.
Inventory dated 27 Dec 1784.

BOND, MOSES   Apt. 8   Pck. 231
    Will of MOSES BOND of Cravin County...to son ISOM, 300 A whereon I now live...to USLY, my wife, all estate during her widowhood & at her death to my children...Brother WILLIAM BOND & RICHARD JENKINS, Exrs...19 Dec 1771...MOSES BOND (+) (SEAL), Wit: CHRISTOPHER LOVING, DAVID HUDSON, ALSE BOND (Z), JOHN PRATT (stricken).
15 July 1783, This will was proved by ALCEY BOND. Grant letters testamentary with will annexed.
Bond: USLY BOND & ISOM BOND, Admrs. & JOS TIMMS & JOHN MAYFIELD, Security, 15 July 1783. Wit: RICHD WINN.
Warrant of appraisement to JOHN TERREY, JOS. TIMMS, JAS GOU, CHRIST. LOVING, & EDWD HENDERSON...15 July 1783
Inventory 10 July 1783: JOHN TERRY, JOSEPH TIMMS. Notes on JOHN STOW, JAMES FORE, JOHN McGOMERY, JESSY COFFEY.
Accts; JOHN JINKINS, BENJAMIN LOVE, WILLIAM LATHRUM, THOMAS HUMPHRIES, JOHN RODEN, JOB SELY, CHARLES HUMPHRIES, PATRICK McGRIFF; HIERS, a miller; JAMES TOMLINSON, EDWARD LACY, WILLIAM GOARD, ELIZABETH NANCE, WILLIAM GRISHAM, JOSEPH TIMMS, LEVI JOHNSON, THOMAS MOORE, CHARLES GILMORE, MYER MOSES, JAMES McNEEL, JOHN SADLER: Recd. of the Estate of THOMAS BAKER.
Wit: JOSEPH TIMMS, RICH BROWN.
Pursuant to Orders, return made...negro girl provd to be MR. BARTLEYS property. Note from JOHN MONTGOMERY April 20, 1787.
Last return Pd: USLY BOND, JOHN RODEN, EDWERD LACY, HUGH STROWD, DAVID HOPKINS, LEVY SMITH, JAMES GORE. Chester County 26 Jan 1796, USLEY BOND (X), before JOHN PRATT, J. P.

BOOTH, WILLIAM   Apt 8   Pck. 237
    Will of WILLIAM BOOTH of Craven County...to wife MARTHEW BOOTHE, all personal estate, at her death to my two sons GEORGE & WILLIAM BOOTHE, 1/4 part...1/4 part to sons HUGH & THOMAS...other 1/2 to her election... JOHN HUGHES, THOMAS KIRK, Exrs...25 Oct 1784. WILLIAM BOOTH (X), Wit: JNO DOWNING, WILLIAM SMILEY. Proven by both wit 9 Dec 1784 before H. HAMPTON, O. C. D.

BOWEN, GEORGE   Apt 8   Pck. 245
    ANN DOWNS of Camden, Spinster, applied for admn of estate of GEORGE BOWEN as Principal Creditor...1 Sept 1786.
Citation read to a full Congregation in the Meeting House, Swift Creek. Sept 1786. RICHARD SWIFT.

BRADLY, JOSEPH   Apt 10   Pck. 285
    Will of JOSEPH BRADLEY of Camden destrict...to wife SUSANAH, Bed & furniture...to son WILLIAM, plantation where I now live...my two youngest sons SION BRADLEY & WILLIAM BRADLEY, one negro man...for use of schooling each of them...to my two daughters SARAH BRADLEY & CHARITY BRADLEY... to son JOSEPH...to my daughter MARY LEWIS...COL JAMESCARY & ISAAC PIDGEON,

Exrs...11 Sept 1780...JOSEPH BRADLY (SEAL), Test: GEORGE WATTS, ISAAC
PIDGEON. Proven 15 July 1782 by WATTS, before WM. SIMMONS, J. P.
Bond: SUSANA BRADLY, HENRY MILY (M), ROBERT MILY, before THOMAS PEARSON,
   1783.
Warrant of appraisement: to ISAAC ROSS, WM SUTTON, JOHN MARTIN, BROWN
ROSS & DAVID MARTIN, 4 June 1783. Appraised by JOHN MARTIN, WILLIAM SUTTON,
& ARTHUR B. ROSS, 3 July 1783.
Inventory and appraisement of cattle 10 Oct 1784, JOHN FOUST (H), JACOB
FOUST, BENJAMIN ARENDALL. Buyers at sale, 10 July 1783: SUSANNA BRADLY,
BROWN ROSS, ZACH'H BARNS, WILLIAM SUTTON, JAMES LEWIS, THOMAS PEARSON.

BRADLEY, MATHEW   Apt 10   Pck. 286
          Dedimus to administer oath of admn. to ROGER WILSON & MARGARET
BRADLY, 13 May 1784, to WILLIAM MARTIN, Esq.
ROGER WILSON and MARGARET BRADLEY applied for admn. 13 Apr 1784. Citation
read 2 May 1784 "in my church".THOS REESE.
Bond: 17 June 1784, JAMES BRADLY and ROBERT CARTER, Securities. Wit:
WILLIAM MARTIN, J. P.
Warrant of appraisement: 13 May 1784, to JOHN HUGGINS, JOHN CASSELS,
ROBERT HAMILTON, THOMAS WILSON & JAMES CARTER.
Inventory 12 July 1784 by JOHN HUGGINS, JOHN CASSELS & THOMAS WILSON.

BRADLEY, THOMAS   Apt. 10   Pck. 288
          SARAH BRADLEY, widow of THOMAS BRADLEY & WILLIAM GORDON, her
Brother, applied for admn...22 Mar 1784. Citation read 27 Mar 1784 in
my church at Salem, THOS REESE.
Dedimus to ROGER WILSON, Esq., to qualify administrators, 2 Apr 1784.
Sworn 18 June 1784, ROGER WILSON, J. P.
Bond: SARAH BRADLEY, WILLIAM GORDON; and MOSES GORDON, security, 18 June
1784.
Warrant of appraisement: 2 Apr 1784, to ROGER BRADLEY, ROGER WILSON,
EPHRAIM PRESCOTT, SAMUEL BRADLY & JAMES BRADLEY. Inventory made 18 May
1784.

BRAZELL, JACOB   Apt 10   Pck. 310
          AVERILLA BRAZELL applied for admn...19 Feb 1787. Citation read
March 5, 1787 by LEWIS COLLINS.
An application for admn. by WILLIAM BRAZELL was begun but left incomplete.
Dedimus to ARTHUR BROWN ROSS to administer oath of AVERILLA BRAZELL, 22
May 1787. Appraisers: JOSIAH SCOTT, JACOB CHERRY, PAUL POWERS.
Bond: AVERILLA, relict of JACOB BRAZELL, admn; WILLIAM NETTLES, JACOB
Mack KINNY, securities, 18 May 1787. Inventory: 19 July 1787.

BRIDGES, THOMAS   Apt. 11   Pck. 321
          Will of THOMAS BRIDGES SENR of Camdon District, 28 July 1781...
to SARAH BRIDGES one young mare two years old past known by the Name of
the weel philey...also all my property that my mother now Hath in her
possession I give to SARAH BRIDGES at the death of My mother...to JAMES
SATTERFIELD, two cows and calves...to FEDRICK HAUCKINGS, one cow and calf
...to LEADY BRIDGES, one young Soril mare known by the Name of the
SATTERFIELD mare...unto RICHARD BRIDGES one Small white mare and yearling
...L 100 starling to be to the Support of the gospel of Jesus Christ and
the por Saints together with the Lords table...in the hands of Brother
JOSEPH CAMP, Mnr...to my well beloved wife ANN BRIDGES, one third of the
remainder of my Real and personal Estate...the other two thirds to her
during her lifetime and at her death to be divided amongst my Brothers...
my Brothers to wit: WILLIAM BRIDGES, JOHN BRIDGES, JAMES BRIDGES, BENJA-
MIN BRIDGES, JOSEPH BRIDGES...JOSEPH CAMP & wife ANN BRIDGES, Exrs...
THOMAS BRIDGES (SEAL), Wit: THOMAS CAMP, WILLIAM McBRAYER, MARTHA McBRAYER
(M). N. B. As my mother is old and may come to Be very helpless Therefore
I request(?) upon such cases that my Executors do out of my Estate admini-
ster to her if need requer.   Recorded Book No. 1, pp. 10 & 11.
Will proved 29 Jan 1782 by WILLIAM McBRYER, before WM McCULLOCH, J.P.,
ABRAHAM SMITH, J. P.
Receipts: "Recd of ANN Bridges..." 20 Mar 1782, WILLIAM BRIDGES (W), before
JOHN COPELAND.
Recd of ANN BRIDGES 4 Feb 1782, JOHN BRIDGES (+), Test: BENJAMIN WHORTER,
JOSEPH BRIDGES.
Recd of ANN BRIDGES 4 Feb 1782, JOSEPH BRIDGES. Test: BENJAMIN WHORTER,
THOMAS BRIDGES. Also similar receipts from BENJAMIN BRIDGES, WILLIAM
BRIDGES, JAMES BRIDGES.

Warrant of appraisement 9 Jan 1782 to WILLIAM COPELAND SR., THOMAS CAMP, WILLIAM McBRAYER, JAMES WILLSON & MOSES CAMP. Sworn: WILLIAM COPELAND, WILLIAM McBRIER, and THOMAS CAMP.
A memorandum of goods bequested out of the estate of THOMAS BRIDGES decd brothers & C.; to LYDE BRIDGES; to RICHD BRIDGES her son; JAMES SATTERFIELD. Recipts: Recd of ANN BRIDGES 23 Mar 1782, JELY DANEL, before JOHN COPELAND.

BROWN, GEORGE   Apt. 11   Pck. 334
Will of GEORGE BROWN of Craven County...to wife SARAH, personal estate...four children: REUBEN, my first born, SUSANNAH MILLS & ANES SPRADLEY & SARAH BROWN being all that are now living...to ANES SPRADLEYS daughter POLLY SPRADLEY; 100 A to son REUBEN already given by deed of gift ...ISREL MATHIS & FRANCES BOYKIN, Exrs...14 Feb 1786...GORGE BROWN (‡) (SEAL). Test: EDWARD PIGG. Proved by EDWARD PIGG, 3 June 1786, before J. ALEXANDER J. P. Warrant of appraisement not filled out.

BROWN, JAMES   Apt. 11   Pck. 340
JAMES BROWN applied for letters of admn on the estate of JAMES BROWN and MARY BROWN his widow both late of Camden District, 15 Feb 1782. Citation read in publick meeting 17 Feb 1782, SOLOMON THOMSON.
Bond: JAMES SMITH, Admr., GABRIEL GERALD & WILLIAM SMITH, sec., 2 June 1782, Wit: JEMIMA SMITH, JOHN SMITH.
Warrant of appraisement: to GABRIEL GERALD, ROBERT WHITE, WILLIAM WHITE, JOSEPH TERRY & JOHN DAVIS, 2 May 1782. Appraisers sworn: GABRIEL GERALD, ROBERT WHITE, & WILLIAM WHITE.
Sale: 16 nov 1781; Buyers: JAMES SMITH, RICHARD RIDGEL, DAVID PLAT, JAMES SMITH SR., JAMES SMITH JR., AMOS THAMES (HAMES?), WM MARTIN, ELIZ McLELON, JAS. McLELAN.

BROWN, JEREMIAH   Apt. 11   Pack. 341
ELIZABETH BROWN, widow and WILLIAM BROWN eldest son of JEREMIAH BROWN applied for admn...3 Sept 1782.
Citation read at High Hill Meeting House, 5 Oct 1782 by J. S. McCORMICK, Clerk.
Bond: ELIZABETH BROWN, WILLIAM BROWN, Admrs., & JAMES REMBERT & JACOB CHAMBERS, sec., 15 Oct 1782. Wit: JOHN WESBERY.
Inventory 23 Oct 1782 by JAMES REMBERT, JOHN WESBERY, JACOB CHAMBERS.
Sale 6 Nov 1782, (no buyers listed.)

BROWN, JOHN   Apt. 11, Pck. 343
SAMUEL BOYKIN applied for letters of admn. as near(est) of kin...30 March 1782. Citation read "in my congregation" 13 Apr 1782. JOSHUA PALMER.
Bond: SAMUEL BOYKIN, Admr., JOHN PLATT & JOHN COOK, sec., 22 Nov 1782. Wit: TOUSLAIN GENOT, ELISATH COOK.

BROWN, JOHN   Apt. 11   Pck. 344
Bond: MARY BROWN & SHAW BROWN, 4 June 1784.
Will of JOHN BROWN of Camden District...25 Jan 1784...to oldest son JOHN, 50 A to be run of the upper part of a track which I bought of SAMUEL MOON with 100 A formerly property of JOHN DOUGHERTY...to my younger son ROBERT, 100 A...to my wife MARY, bay mare & Negro Charles...other negroes (named)...JOHN LOWRY & ALEXANDER ARCHER, Exrs...JOHN BROWN (W) (SEAL), Wit: SHAW BROWN (U), WILLIAM HOMES (W). Proven by SHAW BROWN 4 May 1784, before JOHN LOWRY, J. P.
Paper: We have no objection to the widow Brown administering the estate... 100 A which the will specifies he bought of JOHN DOUHERTY Excepted as it doth not belong to the estate as yet, JOHN DOUGHERTY not being paid nor the right transferred...5 Apr 1784. JOHN LOWRY, ALEXANDER ARCHER.
Appraisers sworn 14 July 1784: HUMPHRYE BARNET, ALEXANDER ARCHER, SHAW BROWN.
Warrant of appraisement to HUMPHREY BARNET, ALEXANDER ARCHER, SHAW BROWN, THOMAS CHISM & MICHAEL BARNETT.
Inventory made 15 July 1784.

BROWN, MARK   Apt. 11   Pck. 350
SARAH BROWN applied for admn. as nearest of kin...5 Aug 1782.
Aug 11, 1782, Citation read in public meeting to ROBT CORTNA.
Bond: SARAH BROWN, Admx., THOMAS HOUSE, BURRILL BROWN & JAMES CLARK, sec., 13 Aug 1782. Wit: RACHEL HAMILTON.

Warrant of appraisement: to THOMAS HOUSE, BURRIL BROWN, JAMES CLARK, JOHN McCOY & WILLIAM BROWN SENR., 13 Aug 1782. Appraisers sworn 30 Aug 1782: THOMAS HOUSE, BURRIL BROWN, & JAMES CLARK.
Appraisement of estate of MARK BROWN of St. Marks Parish, 25 Sept 1782.
Sale, buyers: SARY BROWN, WILLIAM BROWN, (no date).

BROWN, WILLIAM Apt. 12 Pck. 368
  THOMAS BROWN applied for admn. as next of kin...7 Oct 1782.
Citation published in Camden District, Oct. 20, 1782 by CHRISTIAN THEUS, V. D. Minister.
Bond: THOMAS BROWN, Admr., JAMES McPHERSON & JAMES CAMPBELL, sex., 31 Oct 1782. Wit: JOSIAH FURMAN.
Warrant of appraisement: to PETER SMITH, JOHN BOYD, WILLIAM HOWELL, ROBERT LYELL, JAMES CAMPBELL & JAMES McPHERSON, 30 Oct. 1782. Appraisers sworn: 31 Jan 1783, before WM. MEYER, J. P.; PETER SMITH, WILLIAM HOWELL & JAMES McPHERSON.
[The following will is in the same package, but obviously is for a different BROWN.]
Will of THOMAS BROWN of Campbell County, Va., (late of South Carolina)...to wife PATIENCE...to son ELIJAH...to daughter MERYAN...to son WILLEY SPIERS...to son SAMUEL...to son JEREH...son ELIJAH BROWN, JESSE CRENSHAW & COL. EDWARD LEASEY, Exrs...10 Mar 1782. WM BROWN (LS), Wit: ROBERT RUTHERFORD, JAMES REID, ALEXANDER REID. Proven 2 May 1782 in Campbell Co., Va., by JAMES REID and ALEXANDER REID.

BROWN, WILLIAM Apt. 21 Pck. 369
  Dedimus to JOHN LOWRIE to admnister the oath of administration...4 June 1787. WM. BROWN, Admr.
Appraisers swron 21 June 1787: JAMES PERRY, JNO DICKSON, JACOB CHAMPION.
Warrant of appraisement: to JAMES PERRY, JNO DICKSON, JACOB CHAMPION, ISAAC MONCKS, WM WIMBERLY, Lancaster County.
Bond: WILLIAM BROWN, ROBERT LEE & WILLIAM TILMAN, 4 June 1787.
Inventory made 21 June 1787.
Buyers at sale: WM BROWN, MARY BROWN, NANCY BROWN, ESEBEL BROWN.

BRUMFIELD, WATSON Apt. 12 Pck. 377
  CHARLES BRUMFIELD applied for admn....22 Nov 1781.
Citation read at publick assembly, 25 Nov 1781, SOLOMON THOMSON.
Bond: CHARLES BRUMFIELD of Wake County, North Carolina, Admr., and JOHN WESTBURY & ROBT DEARINGTON of Camden Dist., S. C., sec., 15 Dec 1781.
Inventory 1 Dec 1781 by ROBT DEARINGTON, JOHN WESTBURY & ANTHONY LEE.
Notes on JOHN JENNINGS, HENRY CLARK.
Buyers at sale: CHARLES BRUMFIELD, SUSANA GOLDEN, ELISABETH BRUMFIELD, JOHN WHELER JR., ROBT MOOSES, RICHD SINGLETON, WM BROWN, MEMBRANCE WILLIAMS, JAS GOLDEN, EPHRAIM POOL, ISAAC JACKSON, GILBERT CROSWELL, ALBERT FORT, WM WILLIAMS, GEORGE SPAN, 14 Jan 1782.

BRUNSON, DAVID Apt. 12 Pck. 379
  WILLIAM & DANIEL BRUNSON applied for admn. as next of kin, 27 Nov 1784.
Citation read in Salem Church, 5 Dec 1784. THOS REESE.
Bond: WM BRUNSON JUN., DANL BRUNSON, admrs., JOHN NELSON & JOHN WEBB, sec. 10 Feb 1785
Dedimus to JOHN DICKEY to qualify appraisers. WM GILLAM, JNO LAFFERTY, DANIEL CONYERS, sworn. JOHN NELSON & JOHN WEBB also listed on warrant.
Dedimus to WILLIAM MARTIN to qualify admrs., 27 Jan 1785. Warrant of appraisement prolonged 28 Nov 1785. Inventory not dated.

BRUNSON, MATHEW Apt. 12 Pck. 381
  ANN BRUNSON applied for admn. as nearest of kin...22 Jan 1782.
Citation published 27 Jan 1782, RICHARD FURMAN.
Bond: ANN BRUNSON, BURRIL BROWN & THOMAS HOUSE, 12 Feb 1782.
Warrant of appraisement to JEREMIAH BROWN, THOMAS HOUSE, WILLIAM BROWN, GEORGE YATES & BURRIL BROWN, 12 Feb 1782.
Appraisers sworn 19 Feb 1782: JEREMIAH BROWN, THOMAS HOUSE, WILLIAM BROWN, GEORGE YATES. Inventory made 10 Apr 1782. Sale 12 Apr 1782, Only buyer: ANN BRUNSON.

BRYANT, JAMES Apt. 12 Pck. 384
  SAMUEL BOYKIN applied for letters of admn., 26 Feb 1785.
Citation published by LEWIS COLLINS, 10 Apr 1785.

Bond: SAMUEL BOYKIN, admr., WILLIAM BOYKIN & ZACHH. CANTEY, sec., 28 Apr 1785. Wit: FREDERICK BRIGGS.
Warrant of appraisement: to JOHN McKENNEY, WILLABY HARRISON, ISAAC LOVE, ROBERT MARTIN, ZACH NETTLES, & REUBEN HARRISON, 28 Apr 1785.
Appraisers sworn 16 July 1785: JOHN McKENNEY, ISAAC LOVE, ZACH NETTLES, & REUBEN HARRISON.

BULKLEY, JOSEPH   Apt. 12 Pck. 387
      Nuncupative will: JOSEPH McCAY & ARCHIBALD McDONALD, both of Camden, on the evening of the 12th instant heard the will....to JOHN McCAY, son of JOSEPH McCAY, of Camden, 5 guineas...remainder to DR. THOMAS BROWN ...15 Dec 1786. J. ALEXANDER J. P.

BURNS, JOHN   Apt. 12 Pck. 400
      JAMES BURNS, MARY BURNS & LAIRD BURNS applied for admm. April 3, 1782. Citation read at Fishing Creek, April 21, 1782, by JOHN SIMPSON, V. D. M.
MARY BURNS (X), bonded as amx., 23 May 1782, with PATRICK McGRIFF and JOHN MILES, sec. Wit: EDWD LACEY, J. P., JOHN ADAIR J. P. [future Gov. of Kentucky.]
JAMES BURNS refused to act as admr. JAMES MILES, WILLIAM GIVEN & JAMES HETHERINGTON appraised the estate, ₤ 594. 8. 6., exclusive of certain debts still due the estate by ANDREW McNIGHT, CHARLES BROCK, CHARLES ALLAN, DANIEL COLL, EDWARD BOX, ELIJAH WILLIAMSON, HENRY McNESS, JOSEPH CALLET, JAMES HARVEY, JOHN ROGERS, JOHN HOLMS, JOHN BRYANT, JOHN BELY, JOHN SIMMONS, JONATHON HOIL, JOHN SNIDDER (SNYDER), JAMES LINDLEY, JESSE JONES, JOHN CRUMY, LEWIS DEVAL, JOHN MCCAIN, MARGARET CAHUNE, MICHAEL DICKSON, PATRICK RYLY, PATRICK MEHON, THOS NEVILS, THOMAS COMS, PARMENAS JOHNSTON, ROBERT DENISON, ROBERT PARIS, WM BURTON, WM BOYD.
Purchasers at sale: COL EDWD LACEY, MARY BURNS, JOHN LOVE, COL. PATRICK McGRIFF. JAMES MILES, JAMES HETHERINGTON & WILLIAM GIVEN were sworn as appraisers by COL EDWD LACEY, 17 July 1782.

BURNS, LEARD   Pck. 12 Apt. 401
      Will dated 26 Nov 1770...to daughter MARY and her husband, 1 crown sterling...to son JOHN, 1 crown sterling...daughters; JANET, ANN and MARTHA. ...wife (not named)...son LEARD, two tracts I live on...Exors. son JAMES & ROBERT WALKER(son of ALEXANDER WALKER), Wit: AGNESS HUSTON (X), HENRY HUSTON(X). Proven before PHILIP WALKER, J. P. by HENRY HUSTON, 21 Jan 1784. Dedimus 19 Feb 1784, to WILLIAM BRATTON to qualify witness AGNESS HUSTON.
Sale 17 Aug 1784, by ROBERT WALKER, Exr. Estate appraised by JOHN FLEMING, JOSEPH TELFORD, WILLIAM McCAW, 16 July 1784.

BURNS, PATRICK   Apt. 12 Pck. 402
      JACOB GIBSON SENR applied for admm. in right of his wife SARAH, late widow of the deceased...24 Oct 1785.
Citation published 5 Nov 1785, JAS. MATHEWS.

Bond: JACOB GIBSON SENR, DAVID McGRAW SR & DAVID McGRAW JR...19 Nov 1785, Wit: WILLIAM WOODWARD.
Warrant of appraisement to: TO JESSE FORT, DANIEL WOOTON, HENRY CRUMPTON, RICHD YARBROUGH, JAS ANDREW, 19 Nov 1785. Appraisers sworn 24 Nov 1785: DANIEL WOOTON, RICHD YARBROUGH, JAS ANDREWS.
Inventory made 23 Nov 1785.
Sale: sold and Bought by JACOB GIBSON SR., 24 Nov 1786. Fairfield Co.
Notation:"for raising and schooling children."

BURNS, THOMAS   Apt. 12 Pck. 403
      JOHN ALLEN applied for admm. 19 Jan 1786. Citation read to the Congregation at Rocky Creek, 20 Jan 1786, by WILLIAM MARTIN, minister.
Bond: JOHN ALLEN of Rocky Creek, 9 Feb 1786, with JOHN McCOWN, sec. Wit: GINNINS ALLEN, JAMES McKOWN. Dedimus to ANDREW HEMPHILL, J. P. to qualify JOHN ALLEN, as admr. and SAMUEL ARWIN (X), JOHN DYE (X), & ZACHARY KITCHIN, qualified as appraisers, 6 Apr 1786, by ANDREW HEMPHILL.
Warrant of appriasement dated 9 Feb 1786.

BURNS, THOMAS   Apt. 12 Pck. 404
      JAMES PADIAN applied for letters of admm. 20 Sept 1783. Citation read 21 Sept 1783, JNO SIMPSON. Catholic [Church].

Warrant of appraisement, 15 Oct 1783: to ROBERT BAYLY, BUCKNER HEYWOOD, THOMAS STANFORD, CHRISTOPHER STRONG & SAMUEL DUNN "no return."

BURROUGHS, JAMES   Apt. 12 Pck. 405
          MARY BURROUGHS applied for admn., as next of kin 7 Sept 1782.
Citation published in Meeting, 21 Sept 1782. SOLOMON THOMSON.
Bond: MARY BURROUGHS, Admx., ABRAHAM PETTIPOOL SENR., & ABRAHAM PETTIPOOL
JR., sec., 4 Nov 1782. Wit: THOS ANDREWS.
Inventory made 23 Nov 1782 by LEOND. POWELL, THOMAS ANDREWS, BENJAMIN
WALLIS. Sale 25 Nov 1782. Buyers: MARY BURROUGHS, MR. DRURY FLETCHER.

BUSBY, JACOB   Apt. 13 Pck. 406
          Will of JACOB BURSBEY of District of Camden...to wife MARGET, all
my lands, negroes, cattle...wife and WILLIAM NUTTAWELL, Exrs...6 Feb 1781
JACOB BURSBY (J), Wit: EDWD LANE, MARYAN LANE (M), MARGET MINTZ (X). Prov.
15 Oct 1785 before JNO HARBIRT, J. P.
Warrant of appraisement to ADAM FREE, JOHN BUCHANAN, WILLIAM NELSON, CHAR-
NELL DURHAM, & LEWIS OWEN, 15 Oct 1785. Appraisers sworn 20 Oct 1785
before JOHN BUCHANAN, Esqr.: ADAM FREE, WILLIAM NELSON, LEWIS OWEN.
Inventory made 21 Oct 1785.

BUSER, GEORGE   Apt. 8 Pck. 236
          Dedimus to HENRY PATRICK, Esq., to prove will of GEORGE BOOSER, 18
Apr 1783.
Will of George Buser of Saxagotha Township in Barkley County, planter...
to wife MARGARET BUSSER, 146 A in Craven County between waters of Broad
[and Saluda], adj. CASPER KUNS, ADAM KUNS...to my father ULRICH BUSER,
my Hatt...to my Brothers JOHN ULRICH, JACOB, FREDERICK, CHRISTIAN, HENRICH,
RANDOLPH, CASPER BUSER, each ₤ 10...to my sister CATHRINE, feather bed...
CASPER KUN & JOHN ADAM MINICK, Exrs...14 Mar 1780...GEORG BUSER (SEAL),
Wit: CHRISTIAN THEUS, CHRISTIAN HAUSS (German signature), BARBARA MINICK
(X). Proven 22 Apr 1783 before HENRY PATRICK, J. P. by CHRISTIAN THEUS
& BARBARA MINICK.

BUTLER, JOEL   Apt. 13 Pck. 409
          JOHN OGLESVEE applied for admn. in right of his wife...13 Apr 1784.
Citation read 9 May 1784, JACOB GIBSON.
Dedimus to JOHN HARBIRT to qualify admr., 10 May 1784.
Bond: JOHN OGLIVIE, JAS OGILVIE & THOMAS PARROTT (T)...10 May 1784.
Warrant of appraisement to: HENRY CRUMPTON, JACOB GIBSON SR., THOMAS HAR-
BIRT, WILLIAM RABB & THOMAS PARROTT SEN. Sworn ____ 1784, before JOHN
BUCHANON, J. P.: THOMAS HARBIRT, WILLIAM RABB & THOMAS PARROTT SEN.
Appraised 8 June 1784.
Sale of JOEL BUTLER's estate, 8 June 1784, Only buyer: JNO OGILBIE.
On the same paper: Sale of WM PEARSON, 8 June 1784. Buyers: JNO OGILVIE,
JAMES BEARD, CHARNAL DURHAM, THOMAS MAY, THOMAS NILSON, ROBT RABB.

CANTEY, JOHN   Apt. 31 Pck. 429
          JAMES CANTEY applied for admn. as nearest of kin, 2 __ 1783.
Published in the Congregation of Camden after Devine Servies, Sunday 21
Sept 1783. JOHN LOGUE.
Bond: JAMES CANTEY, ZACHH CANTEY & JOHN CHESNUT, 29 Apr 1784, Wit: DERRILL
HART.

CANTEY, JOSEPH Apt. 13 Pck. 432
          Will of JOSEPH CANTEY of St. Marks Parish...to my son SAML CANTEY,
one Negro Chloe and Chest of drawers, one feather bed...to my daughter
MARTHA BAGNALL, one Negro Dinah, one Chest of Drawers, one feather bed...
the land hwereon I now live to be Equally divided between my sons MATHEW
& JOSEPH CANTEY...to ELIZABETH WOOD one prime horse saddle and bridle...
sons SAML CANTEY, EBENEZER BAGNELL & MATHEW CANTEY, Exrs...16 Aug 1781...
JOS CANTEY (SEAL), Wit: DAVID DAVIS, JOHN GODFREY, ALEXR ROBINSON.
Camden District: Nov 13, 1781: DAVID DAVIS and JOHN GODFREY proved will
before WILLIAM MARTIN, J. P.

CANTEY, WILLIAM Apt. 13 Pck. 434
          MARTHA CANTEY widow & JOSIAH CANTEY of Santee applied for admn.
9 Jan 1787. Citation published on the last Sabbath, RICHARD FURMAN, V. D.
M., 15 Jan 1787
Dedimus to WILLIAM McCONNICO to qualify admr., 30 Jan 1787

Bond: MARTHA CANTEY, JOSIAH CANTEY, admrs., & WILLIAM DUKES, sec., all of Santee River, 2 Feb 1787. Wit: ELIZABETH COULLIETTE, ALICE COOK.
Inventory 7 Feb 1787, of WILLIAM CANTEY SR., by PATRICK BROCK, LEVY MOORE, & JACOB KINGSWOOD.
Sale, 1 March 1787. Buyers: WILLIAM CANTEY, ELIZABETH CANTEY, MRS. MARTHA CANTEY, WILLIAM RICHBOURGH, JAMES CANTEY, JOSIAH CANTEY, ARTHUR CLEMONDS, BRINKLEY CORBET, RICHARD SINGLETON, RICHD G. DENNIS, WILLIAM BRADLEY

CARRELL, SAMUEL Apt. 14 Pck. 445
    MARGARET CARROLL & JOSEPH CARROLL applied for admn. as nearest of kin 9 Apr 1783. Citation read at dwelling house of JOHN VENABLE, 22 Apr 1783 by FRAS CUMMINS, V. D. M.
Bond: JOSEPH CARROLL & MARGARET CARROLL, admr., ALEXANDER HENRY, sec., 15 Mar 1783.
Inventory made 23 May 1783, by JONATHAN FITCHETT, JAMES NICHOLS & WILLIAM HENRY.

CARTER, HENRY Apt. 14 Pck. 449
    Dedimus to MALCOLM CLARK, Esq., to prove will 5 Dec 1785. Proved by DAVID JOYNER 8 Dec 1785.
Will of HENRY CARTER of Camden District...to son JOHN CARTER, 3 guineas... to son JOSEPH CARTER, 2 guineas...to daughter MARY JOYNER, s 1 sterling... to son BENJAMIN CARTER, s 1 sterling...to wife BARBARA CARTER & daughter RACHEL DAY, all horses & cattle...Exrs., RICHARD BROWN & WILLIAM FOX... I have made deeds of gift to my sons GEORGE & ROBERT CARTER...1 Nov 1785 ...HENRY CARTER (+), Wit: JOSEPH JOYNER, DAVID JOYNER (+), PETER CLYNE (P).
Inventory by JOSEPH McCORD, ROBERT WESTON, R. M. CAMPBELL.

CARTER, JACOB SENR. Apt. 14 Pck. 450
    Will dated 23 Dec 1779, proved before PHILIP WALKER, J. P. by CHARLES MILLER 23 May 1781 & before WOOD FURMAN, Ordinary, 20 Dec 1782. ...wife HANNAH, dwelling house and land on east side of Charles Town Road, called the South Fork Road...son JACOB...son JOHN...daughter MARTHA... daughters MARY, LYDIA, and HANNAH...Exrs.: sons-in-law WILLIAM MILLER, & GEORGE ADAMS, and they to be guardians to son JACOB...Wit: CHARLES MILLER, ANN MILLER (X), JOHN DICKSON.
Estate inventoried by WILLIAM WYLIE, THOMAS McDILL, CHARLES MILLER.

CASKEY, JOHN Apt. 14 Pck. 456
    Will of JOHN CASKEY of Craven County, otherwise Chester, Camdin District...to wife ESTER CASKEY, 100 A where I now live...to my daughter ISEBELL...all remainder of 350 A divided among my four sons...to daughter MAREY CASKEY, negro Keat & tools...ARCHIBALD COULTER & ANDREW GRAHAM, Exrs. ...19 Sept 1785...JOHN CASKEY (SEAL), Wit: DAVID GRAHAM, ANDREW GRAHAM, JOHN GRAHAM. Proven 16 Aug 1786 before H. HAMPTON. Inventory made 21 Sept 1786 by JAMES BROWN, DAVID McQUISTON, DAVID GRAHAM.

CASON, CANNON Apt. 14 Pck. 457
    Dedimus to JOSEPH MICKLE & ISAAC LOVE, Esq., of Camdin District to prove will 22 Oct 1779, WM BURROWS, Ordinary of South Carolina(dedimus from Charleston Court of Ordinary). Sworn 21 Jan 1780, before ISAAC LOVE, J. P.
Will of CANNON CASON of Prov. of S. C. in Craven County and Parish of St. Marks...to my son WILLIAM CASON, 100 A whereon he now lives...to my wife 100 A whereon I now live and three negros, stock, etc...at her deceased to be divided among all my children...to son CANNON CASON, 100 A...to son WILLIS CASON, negro Jacob...to son WHITEHURST CASON, negro Dave...to son LABAN CASON, negro Beck...to daughter WINNEFRED CASON...to daughter JEAN CARDIN...to daughter ANNE PAGE...WILLIAM CASON and RALPH JONES, Exrs...14 Sept 1779...CANNON CASON (CC) (SEAL), Wit: MEKNZAY MATTECKS (X), ELIZABETH MATTECKS (E), BENJAMIN BELL. Recorded in Book No. 1 fo. 75 p WOOD FURMAN.

CASSELL, WILLIAM Apt. 14 Pck. 458
    JOHN CASSELS applied for admn. 24 Mar 1785.
Citation published in MR. PALMERS Congregation 16 Apr 1785 pr me JNO McKRAY, Clk.
Bond: JOHN CASSELLS, Admr., GEORGE BYRD & WM BYRD, Sec., 28 Apr 1786.
Wit: ROBT CARTER.
Inventory made 16 May 1785 by GEORGE BYRD, WM BYRD, EPHRAIM PRESCOTT.

CASITY, THOMAS   Apt. 14 Pck. 459
　　　　Will of THOMAS CASSETY of the Province of South Carolina...to wife MARTHA CASSETY, household furniture & house where I now live with 20 A about the house & 20 A planting land...to son PETER CASSETY, silver watch ...to son JESSE CASSETY, 300 A of high land on Jacks Creek surveyed jointly between me and WILLIAM RICHARDSON, but titles made to RICHARDSON...my part I give to my son THOMAS (?)...to son CHARLES CASSETY, 200 A near Rafting Creek...to sons HUGH & JAMES CASSETY, 3 tracts of River swamp land which Part I planted this present year...to son ROBERT CASSETY, equal value...daughter NAOMI...7 Nov 1780...THOMAS CASSITY (T) (SEAL), Wit: JOHN MALONE, WILLIAM SANDERS, CHARLES SPEARS. Proven 9 Oct 1782.
Warrant of appraisement: to WILLIAM SANDERS, JOHN WHEELER, JOHN MOORE, JOHN MALONE, JOHN MAY & CHARLES McGINNIS...9 Oct 1782. Appraisers sworn 22 Oct 1782, before BURL BOYKIN, J. P.: WILLIAM SANDERS, JOHN MALONE, & CHARLES McGINNIS.
Inventory dated 29 Oct 1782, due from JOHN CHESNUT, ROBERT LEWIS.

CASTLES, HENRY   Apt. 14 Pck. 460
　　　　JOHN LEE applied fro admn. as nearest of kin in right of his wife...10 Sept 1785.
Sept 25, 1785, Citation read immediately after Public Worship, THOMAS H. McCAULE, V. D. M.
Bond: JOHN LEE (‡), WILLIAM ROTTONBURY (⌒)...1 July 1785. Wit: JOSH(?) M. KELLY.

CENTER, NATHAN   Apt. 14 Pck. 471
　　　　Dedimus to ROBERT GOODWYN & JOHN FAIRCHILD to prove will...16 Jan 1783. Proven same date.
Will of Nathan Center of Camden District...to wife MARTH[A] CENTER, negro Tanzy...to daughter ELIZABETH CENTER, Negro girl Rouse...to son NATHAN CENTER, negro Dick...to son JOHN CENTER, negro Sam...to son WILLIAM CENTER, negro Phraim...wife to have plantation...to my children as they come of age...21 Dec 1782...N CENTER (SEAL), Wit: SOLOMON PETERS, ELIZABETH JACKSON, LUCY HOWELL.
Inventory made 8 Mar 1783.
Warrant of appraisement: to RICHARD EVANS, JOHN BOYD, ETHAN HEATH, FREDERICK HEATH & JESSE DANIEL...16 Jan 1783.
Appraisers sworn 20 Jan 1783, before R. GOODWYN, J. P.: RICHARD EVANS, ETHAN HEATH, FREDERICK HEATH.

CHANDLER, SAMUEL   Apt. 14 Pck. 475
　　　　THOMAS CHANDLER & SAMUEL CHANDLER applied for letters of admn. on estate of SAMUEL CHANDLER of Lynches Creek...6 Nov 1786. Citation read at Church of SALEM on 12 Nov 1786, THOS REESE.
Bond: THOMAS CHANDLER, SAMUEL CHANDLER, admrs., JOHN BIGGOT SENR., & PETER FITZPATRICK, all of Lynches Creek, se....7 Dec 1786, before ELIAS DUBOSE, JUNR.
ELIAS DUBOSE qualified admrs., 22 Dec 1786.
Warrant of appraisement 5 Dec 1786 to ROGER WILSON, JOHN CARSON, EPHRAIM PRESCOTT, GEORGE BOND & WILLIAM BOND. 22 Dec 1786, sworn: ROGER WILSON, EPHRAIM PRESCOTT, & GEORGE BOND.
Inventory made 1 Jan 1787.

CHAPPELL, ELIZABETH   Apt. 15 Pck. 476
　　　　Will of ELIZABETH CHAPPELL, 29 March 1782...son JOHN (under 21) ...CHARLOTTE RIVES...Exr., TIMOTHY RIVES...Wit: THOS HARBIRT, JAMES BAIRD, MARY DAILY (X). Proven 27 Oct 1782.
Sworn appraisers: JAMES DANIEL, WILLIAM DANIEL, LEWIS POPE, 2 Nov 1782.
Estate appraised 3 Nov 1782, for ₤ 932. 19. 3. Purchasers at sale, 4 Nov 1782: JOHN MILES, HICKS CHAPPELL, ISAAC LOVE, JACOB CURRY, WILLIAM WILLINGHAM, HENRY GREGORY, THOS HUTCHISON, THOS BAKER, BARNABY POPE, COL. JOHN WINN, JAMES BEARD, LABUN CHAPPEL, THOS JEFFREYS, LEWIS POPE, JAMES KINCAID, ROBT RABB, JOHN COOK, OSBORN ASHLEY, FRANCIS BRISNO, WM. DANIEL JOHN FRIDAY, ANGEL STOCKMAN, BENJAMIN BUSBY, WM. SCOTT.

CHAPPELL, HENRY   Apt. 15 Pck. 477
　　　　Will of HENRY CHAPPELL, 11 Nov 1779...wife ELIZABETH...son HICKS, son LABAN, son ROBERT, son JOHN, son HENRY, daughter ELIZABETH SNEADE, daughter MARTHA LOVE...Exrs.: wife ELIZABETH, ISAAC LOVE, LABAN CHAPPELL. Wit: BEN GRUBB, WM WILSON, HENRY WELLS. Dedimus to HENRY PATRICK

J. P. to examine the witnesses and prove will, 16 Dec 1779. Will proved 9 May 1783.

CHERRY, MOSES   Apt. 15   Pck. 483
Bond: ELIZABETH CHERRY (O), admx., SAMUEL TORBERT, THOS WORD & FRAME WOODS, sec. Wit: NATHL HENDERSON, RICHARD ADDIS. Citation read in Bullocks Creek Church, 5 Jan 1783 by JOSEPH ALEXANDER V. D. M.
Estate appraised by THOS WOODS, GEORGE BLACK, JOHN WILSON, THOS WORD. Purchasers at sale: WIDOW CHERRY, SAMUEL TORBERT, JOHN LOVE, DRURY GOINS, FRAME WOODS, ROBERT ELIOT, VARDRY McBEE, MERRY McGUIRE, JAMES JOHNSON, THOMAS WOODS, JACOB BARNETT, DANIEL GIVENS, ADAM MEEK. Listed: "one bond on ASCHIBLE SHEARRER in Virginia for Pensilvana monne." ₤ 200 and "one note on WILLIAM THOMSON for 6 dollars" ₤ 2 8 0. Total sale ₤ 693. 11. 4.

CHESNUT, SAMUEL   Apt. 15   Pck. 493
JANNET CHESNEY & JAMES CHESNEY appl. for admn. Citation read at Wateree, 26 June 1785, by THOMAS H. McCAULE.
JANE CHESNUT, Bond 1 July 1785, with WILLIAM MARTIN, WILLIAM JOHNSTON, sec. Test: JAMES KNOX, J. P.
Warrant of appraisement: to JAMES BROWN, ROBERT STRONG, THOMAS McDILL, WM. MAFFET & JAMES STRONG, 1 July 1785. Sworn 17 Aug 1785: WILLIAM MAFFET, ROBERT STRONG and JAMES BROWN.

CHICK, REUBEN   Apt. 15   Pck. 494
URIAH GOODWYN & FRANCIS GOODWYN applied for admn...9 Nov 1785. Citation published by JOSEPH REES, 13 Nov 1785.
Bond: 3 Feb 1786, FRANCIS GOODWYN, admr., JOHN MOORE, WM HOPKINS, sec., Wit: JOEL McLEMORE, GREEN RIVES. Admr. qualified 12 Feb 1786.
Dedimus to WILLIAM MYER to qualify admr., 3 Feb 1786.
Warrant of appraisement: to WILLIAM HOPKINS, JAMES HOFF, JOEL McLEMORE, ROBERT LYSLE & THOMAS HUTCHINSON 3 Feb 1786.
Inventory made (no date), by JOEL McLEMORE, WILLIAM HOPKINS, THOS HUTCHINSON.

CLARKE, JAMES   Apt. 16   Pck. 507
MARY CLARK applied for admn. as next of kin...22 Jan 1782. Citation published 27 Jan 1782, RICHARD FURMAN.
Inventory 4 Apr 1782 by THOMAS HOUZE, JEREMIAH BROWN, WILLIAM BROWN. Sale 10 Apr 1782, MARY CLARKE, only buyer.

CLARKE, WILLIAM   Apt. 16   Pck. 515
ELIZABETH CLARK, widow, applied for admn. on the estate of her deceased husband WILLIAM CLARK, 1 Sept 1786.
Swift Creek, Sept 1786. Citation read to a full Congregation in the Meeting House. RICHD SWIFT.
Bond: ELIZABETH CLARK, NATHANIEL CARY & FIELDING WOODROOF, 12 Oct 1786. Wit: MARY BREWTON, H. BEAUMONT.

CLEMMONS (CLEMENTS), WILLIAM   Apt. 16   Pck. 520
Will dated 30 June 1784, probated 14 Feb 1786...Children: ARTHUR, MARTHA, KATHRINE, SARAH, WILLIAM, JAMES, CHRISTIAN, DAVID and MICHAEL (in his 7th year)...wife MARTHA...Exers: wife MARTHA, sons ARTHUR and WILLIAM CLEMMONS. Wit: JOHN McFADDIEN, JOHN GRAHAM, ROBERT GRAHAM... WILLIAM CLEMMONS (X). Proved by JOHN GRAHAM in Georgetown District before JOHN DICKEY, J. P.
MARTHA CLEMMONS qualified as Extx. before JOHN DICKEY, 3 Apr 1786. Estate appraised by CHARLES CANTEY, JOSHUA HILTON and JESSE HILTON 3 Apr 1786, for ₤ 386 17 0. JONAS WOODS and JOHN RIDGELL were also appointed but did not serve.

CLINTON, PETER   Apt. 16   Pck. 522
MRS. FRANCES CLINTON appeared before JOSEPH HOWE, J. P. of New Acquisition Dist., 17 Nov 1783, and stated that she was incapable of acting as admx. of her decd. husband's estate and prayed that her relations JAMES CAMPBELL & JAMES BEARD be permitted to administer the estate.
JAMES CAMPBELL & JAMES BEARD appl. for admn. 20 Apr 1784. Citation read by FRANCIS CUMMINS, V. D. M. [probably at Bethel M. H.]. JAMES CAMPBELL and JAMES BEARD were bonded 20 May 1784 as admrs.
[Capt. PETER CLINTON commanded a company in COL. THOMAS NEEL'S Regiment of S. C. Militia during the Cherokee War of 1776.]

COATS, WILLIAM Apt. 17 Pck. 537
          Dedimus to JOHN HITCHCOCK Esq. to prove will 16 Dec 1783.
Will of WILLIAM COATES of South Carolina, Damden District....to my daughter ANNE STARKES one Cow...to my daughter PRISILLA COATS one feather bed the same now in her possession...to my son BARTON COATES, one horse, saddle, etc...to my son WILSON COATES one bay horse, saddle, bridle... to son BENJAMIN COATES one horse valued to Ł 5 starling when he comes of age...remainder of estate to wife FRANCES COATES...15 June 1783...WILLIAM COATES (SEAL), Wit: JAMES FORE, POLLEY COATES, ELISHA GORE
Warrant of Appraisement directed to JOHN COLVEN, JOHN COCKRELL, JOHN PRATT, WILLIAM TRUSSELL & JOHN GRESHAM, 16 Dec 1783. JOHN PRATT, WILLIAM TRUSSELL & JOHN GRESHAM sworn 13 Beb 1784. Inventory made 14 Feb 1784. FRANCES COATS took the oath of Extx, 13 Feb 1784.

COLEMAN, HENRY Apt. 17 Pck. 539
          [see also GALLMAN, HENRY]
Bond: JACOB FOUST & CHRISTIAN KINSELLER, 3 Sept 1783, Wit: FRA. PRINGLE
Warrant of appraisement 3 Sept 1783 to JAMES TAYLOR, BENJN. GRUBB, STEPHEN CURREY, HENRY GREGORY & JOHN MAY.
BENJN. BRUGG, STEPHEN CURREY, & JOHN MAY sworn 6 Sept 1783 before TIMO RIVES, J. P.

COLLEDON, MARTHA Apt. 17, Pck. 540
          SAMUEL ERVIN applied for admn. as nearest of kin, 1 May 1785.
Citation read in my church 15 May 1785. TH. McCAULE.
Bond: SAMUEL ERVING of Santee River and JAMES BROWN SR. of Camden, 13 Jan 1786. Wit: ELEAZAR ALEXANDER.
Dedimus to ROBERT McKELVEY to administer the oath of admn. 13 Jan 1786
Warrant of appriasement to DANIEL CAIN, PETER KIRK & PHILIP COUTURIER, 13 Jan 1786. Inventory made 4 May 1786.

COLNEY, DANIEL Apt. 17 Pck. 551
          JOHN HERONS applied for admn, 2 Aug 1784. Citation published by JOSEPH REES (no date).
Bond: JOHN HERON, FRANCIS GOODWYN & JN. HAMILTON, 21 Sept 1784. Wit: WM MEYER, J. P.
Dedimus to WILLIAM MYER to qualify admr., 24 Aug 1784. Admr. qualified 21 Sept 1784.
Warrant of appraisement 24 Aug 1784, to FRANCIS GOODWYN, JOHN HAMILTON, JOHN HOPKINS, ISAAC RAFORD, ARTHUR HOWELL & JONATHAN DUNCAN.
Sworn, FRANCIS GOODWYN, JNO HAMILTON & JOHN HOPKIN. Inventory not dated.

COMBEST, JOHN Apt. 17 Pck. 553
          JOHN SERVICE, planter, applied for admn. on estate of JOHN COMBEST, late of Rocky Creek, planter, 16 Aug 1786. Citation read at Fishing Creek 25 Aug 1786, by JOHN SIMPSON.
Bond: JOHN SERVICE, admr., JOHN WINN & JOHN MILLING, sec., 12 Sept 1786, Wit: WM. C. PINCKNEY, JOHN CAMPBELL.
Estate appraised by MICHAEL DICKSON, JAMES BISHOP & ROBERT MORRISON, 17 Sept 1786, for Ł 50 8 4.

COOK, JOHN Apt. 17 Pck. 563
     6 May 1784, JOHN DURER made oath before FREDK. KIMBALL, J. P. that he never received any instrument of writing of JOHN FIELDS of Charleston but he remembers very well in discourse the will of JOHN COOK....
Bond: ELIZABETH RUGELEY, admr. cum testo annexo & WILLIAM COOK, 9 June 1784.
Will of JOHN COOK, late of Camden District & now of Charlestown...to wife ELIZABETH COOK, 2 negroes (named)...to son JOHN COOK, large Bible & rifle...to daughter MARY MASCALL, negroes (named)...to son WILLIAM COOK, negroes (named)...to daughter ELISABETH COOK, negroes (named)...to grandson JOHN SAMUEL AUGUST, negroes (named)...HENRY RUGELEY & HENRY MASCALL, Exrs...21 June 1782...JOHN COOK ▓. Wit: JOHN FIELDS, JAMES HARRIS. Prov. 14 May 1784.
Before JOHN GALBRAITH, J. P., MISS HESTER CUMMINS said that she often saw the will of JOHN COOK SR at MRS. ADAMSONS house in Charleston & MRS. RUGELEY, daughter of sd. JOHN COOK & she read it several times...14 Dec 1784.
JOHN ADAMSON, FIELDING WOODROOF, appraisers.
JESSE COOK appointed to transact business by HENRY RUGELEY, 2 Aug 1785. Inventory made 3 Aug 1785.

COPPLY, PATRICK   Apt. 18 Pck. 581
    ELIZABETH COPPLY (widow) applied for admn, 16 Nov 1784.
Citation read 24 Nov 1784, SAML KENNEDY, Min of ye Gospel.

COUSART, RICHARD   Apt. 18 Pck. 587
    Warrant of appraisement, 4 Nov 1783, directed to NATHAN BARR, JOSEPH LEE, ROBERT DUNLAP, JOHN WHITE, & SAML DUNLAP JR. Appraisers sworn 24 Nov 1783, before ROBERT MONTGOMERY, J. P.: NATHAN BARR, JOHN WHITE, SAML DUNLAP JR. Inventory made 9 Nov 1783.
Will of RICHARD COUSART, 5 Oct 1779...of St. Marks Parish, Camden District ...to daughter CHATHRINE NUT, negro Sal & large chest...to daughter JANE LOVE, negro Sam...to son ARCHIBALD COUSART, 115 A on Gils Creek...to son NATHANIEL COUSART, Negro Sampson...to son JAMES COUSART, 350 A, et. al...to daughter LETTIA DUNLAP, negro wench...to JAMES COUSARTS son RICHARD COUSART 100 A on Gils Creek next to the plantation I formerly lived on...to NATHANIEL COUSARTS Son RICHARD, negro Philip & 100 A on Gils Creek... RICHARD COUSART (SEAL), Wit: JOHN COUSART, NATHAN BARR, ROBERT DUNLAP. Prov. 26 July 1783 by NATHAN BARR.

CRAIG, JOHN   Apt 18 Pck. 588
    Will of JOHN CRAIG of Wattree Creek, fairfield County...to JENNET BONNER daughter of JOHN BONNER, Roan Mare and Colt and two Guineas in money...to my Cuzen(sic) WILLIAM CRAIGE my Loom...Cuzen JOHN BONNER, Exr. 9 Aug 1785...JOHN CRAIG (X) (SEAL), Wit: WILLIAM LOWRY, SAMUEL CORRY, ROBERT DUNLAP (R). Prov. by SAMUEL CURRY and ROBERT DUNLAP.
JOHN BONNER took oath of Exr. 29 Mar 1786, before JAMES CRAIG, J. P. Dedimus to JAMES CRAIG to Qualify Executor, 4 Jan 1785(sic).
Warrant of appraisement, 4 Jan 1785(sic) to ANDREW YOUNG, JOHN HOUSTON, JOHN WATSON, JOSEPH KINKAIRD & WILLIAM LOWRY.
Appraisers sworn 29 Mar 1786: JOSEPH CATHCART, A YOUNG, & J HOUSTON. Inventory made 29 Mar 1786.

CRAWFORD, JAMES   Apt. 18 Pck. 590
    Will of JAMES CRAWFORD, late of County Antrim, in the Kingdom of Ireland, Camden 26 Oct 1789...Inventory of his goods, etc. to be transmitted to ARTHUR HARPER, merchant in Elliott Street, Charleston. Ex: ISAAC ALEXANDER and HUGH McDOWELL of Camden...anything after debts are paid to be transmitted to JAMES DAVIDSON, merchant in the town of Antrim, in County Antrim, Ireland. Wit: JOHN MEREDITH BROWN, JOHN SIMS. Estate inventoried by WM TATE & ROBERT HENRY, 7 Dec 1789, for L 44 12 1. Estate sold 12 Dec 1789, for L 47 19 3. Purchasers: ISAAC ALEXANDER, JOHN ADAMSON, MORDECAI LION, JOHN PLATT, JOHN SANGSTER, PETER OSGOOD, JOHN SIMS, NICHOLAS ROBINSON, ALEXANDER GOODALL, JOHN HOLZANDORF, EDWARD MORTIMER, RICHARD KING, SOLOMON STANSBURY, FREDERICK ROBINSON, JAMES WILLIAMS.

CROFT, EDWARD   Apt. 18 Pck. 597
    ELIJAH BROWN applied for admn. 30 May 1783. Citation read at Fishing Creek, 1 June 1783 by JOHN SIMPSON.
Bond: ELIJAH BROWN, Admr., JOHN McWHORTER, Sec., Wit: NIMROD MITCHELL.
Estate appraised 22 March 1784 by WILLIAM LEWIS, JOHN FERGUSON, JOHN GILL & SAMUEL PORTER.

CROFT, HENRY   Apt. 18 Pck. 598
    Will of HENRY CROFT, tailor, 29 Jan 1781, prov. 8 Mar 1781...wife [not named]...son JOHN, daughter ELIZABETH, son ABIAH, daughter REBECCA, daughter RACHEL, son MOSES, son JESSE (youngest)...Ex: son JOHN & friend JOEL ADAMS, Wit: WILLIAM SCOTT, MARTHA COOK, MARY HIXONS.
Estate appraised 3 Jan 1787 by JOHN BISWELL, PHILIP PARTRIDGE, WILLIAM WESTON.
ABIAH CROFT bonded 27 Oct 1786 as admr. with THOMAS BROWN & WILLIAM SCOTT, sec. Wit: RICHARD BROWN, JOHN SULLIVAN.

CULP, HENRY   Apt 18 Pck. 602
    WILLIAM McKINNEY & PETER CULP bonded 15 May 1783 as admr., with PHILIP WALKER & WILLIAM ELLIOTT as sec. Wit: RALPH JONES.
Estate appraised by WILLIAM McFADDEN, ROBERT MARTIN & GEORGE NEELY 6 June 1783 for L 644 11 3. Purchasers at sale: AUGUSTIN CULP, GEORGE NEELY, SAMUEL McCANCE, HUGH McCLURE, JAMES KNOX, JOHN McKINNEY, BENJAMIN CULP, JAMES ROBINSON, PETER CULP, JOHN STEEDMAN, JOHN McCAMMON and JACOB COOPER.

CROSBY, HANAH   Apt. 18 Pck. 600
    THOMAS CROSBY applied for admn. as next of kin, 25 Apr 1785.
Citation not returned.
ELIZABETH VAWN made oath that she heard HANNAH CROSBY say she would give
JOHN BROSBY as much pewter as she had given the other children, 23 June
17--.
 Appraisers sworn 23 June 1785 before AMOS DAVIS, J.P.: HENSON DAY, JOHN
HARBEN, NATHAN JAGGARS. Sale, 12 Aug 1785. Buyers: WM CROSBY, JOHN
CROSBY, JOHN HAVEN(?), JAMES GATER, JOHN GWINN, THOS CROSBY, JAMES GLENN,
RICHARD CROSBY.

CUNNINGHAM, JNO   Apt. 18 Pck. 607
    ANN CUNNINGHAM applied for admn. as nearest of kin, 13 Dec
1783. Citation read 28 Dec 1783, Fishing [Creek], JOHN SIMPSON.
Bond: ANN CUNNINGHAM; JNO McMICHAEL sec., 27 July 1784.
Warrant of appraisement to JAMES SIMRAL, ALEXANDER McWHORTER, THOS Mc-
MURRAY, WILLIAM BERRY, ARCHIBALD BARRON(?), 27 July 1784.
Appraisers sworn before WM.HILL, J. P.: THOS McMURRAY, JAMES SIMRAL &
ALEXANDER McWHORTER.

DABNEY, JAMES   Apt. 19 Pck. 618
    JOHN OWEN applied for admn. on estate of JAMES DABNEY as principal
creditor, 7 Nov 1782. Citation pub. 17 Nov 1782, by RALPH JONES.
Bond: JOHN OWEN (X), admr., WM ROBERTSON & JAMES ANDREWS, sec., 7 Dec
1782, Wit: WILLIAM SIBLEY, BENJAMIN OWENS.
Appraisement 15 Jan 1783. Buyers at sale, 15 Jan 1783: JOHN OWIN(S),
JACOB CARRELL, JACOB LEWIS, GEORGE HARSSOM, WM SIMMONS, ANDREW PATTERSON,
WM SMILEY, SAMUEL BOWAN (ROWAN?), WM ADDERSON.
Warrant of appraisement to WM ROBERTSON, JOHN WOODARD, PHILIP RAFORD,
JAMES NELSON, WM. SIMONS, JACOB LEWIS, & JAMES HIGH, 7 Dec 1782.
Appraisers sworn: JAMES HOY, & JACOB LOEWIS before WM SIMMONS, J. P.
WILLIAM SIMMONS sworn before JACOB RICHMAN, J. P. (no date).

DALE, JOSEPH   Apt. 19 Pck. 622
    GEORGE HARRISON applied for admn. 11 Sept 1786, and citation read
in church at Jackson's Creek, 11 Sept 1786 by THOS. H. McCAULE.
JOHN WINN, M[inor] WINN, and JOHN MILLING of Fairfield County objected to
the appointment of GEORGE HARRISON as a "Very improper person to administer the Estate...." 30 Sept 1786.
Bond: GEORGE HARRISON 16 Nov 1786, admr., EDWARD McGRAY, DAVID ANDRAS,
sec. Test; MADDON (or MADDOX) LEGGE, ROBT TABB, JNO BELL, & J. WINN.

DANCER, PETER   Apt. 19 Pck. 624
    HENRY DANCER & CHARLES PINIGAR applied for admn., 8 Aug 1783.
Citation read "three Difrent Sundays" by J. G. BAMBERG, M. o. g.
Bond: HENRY DANCER & CHARLES BINNICKER, 15 Sept 1783, Wit: RICHARD WINN.
Warrant of appraisement to TIMOTHY REAVES, Esq., JAMES TAYLOR Esq., JACOB
BOOKTER, SENR., JOHN GUIGER, & CHRISTIAN KENSLER, 15 Sept 1783. All
sworn before TIMO. REEVES, Esq., 14 Sept 1783.
Appraised 22 Oct 1783 by JOHN GEIGER, CHRISTIAN KENSLER, JAMES TAYLOR.
Sale, 23 Oct 1783, purchasers: JOHN SURGEONER, JAMES TAYLOR, CASPAR KUHN,
JOHN TURNIPSEED, WIDOW DANCER, ULRICK BEARD, JOSEPH KENNERLY, HENRY DAN-
CER, JOHN DANCER, BENJAMIN ARNOLD, CHARLES BINNICKER.

DARGAN, WM.   Apt. 19 Pck. 628
    KEMPT STROTHER applied for admn, 31 Mar 1786. Citation published
"in my congregation" Sunday 2 Apr 1786, JACOB GIBSON.
Bond: KEMP T. STROTHER: HENRY HUNTER & HUGH MILLER, sec., 8 Apr 1786,
Wit: HENRY CALDWELL.

DAVIS, AMOS   Apt. 19 Pck. 631
    Will of AMOS DAVIS of Fairfield County...to son JOHN DAVIS, planta-
tion 150 A & 238 A adj. where I now live & negro Ben...to son ELNATHAN
DAVIS, negro Rose...to child my wife SARAH DAVIS is now pregannt with...
THOMAS LEWIS & wf SARAH DAVIS, Exrs...6 Dec 1785...AMOS DAVIS (SEAL),
Wit: W. HOGAN, MOSES ARNOLD, MARY ARNOLD (X).
Appraisers sworn 12 Jan 1787 before ANDERSON THOMAS J. P.:THOMAS CROSBY,
JAMES THOMAS, NATHL HARBIN.
Appraisment made by THOMAS CROSBY, JAMES THOMAS NATHL HARBIN and WILLIAM
HARBIN, 20 Jan 1787. Sale: 20 Jan 1787, buyers: SARAH DAVIS, WILLIAM
HALL, WILLIAM HOGAN, THOMAS LEWIS.

Will of AMOS DAVIS proven by WILLIAM HOGAN 14 Nov 1786 before RICHARD WINN, J. P.
Dedimus to admn. oath of Exr. 6 Jan 1787, administered by JNO BUCHANAN, 30 Mar 1787 in Fairfiled Co. Warrant of appraisement 6 Jan 1787,(not filled out.)

DAVIS, EDWARD   Apt. 19 Pck. 634
Will of EDWARD DAVIS, Craven County, St. Mark's Parish, May ye 14, 1770...all land, & living to wife NELLY during her "wider hood"...to my daughter WEHERFOR DRADEN, land where I now live...WILLIAM CANTEY, attr... to son HENSON, negro Gay...to son ROZURE, 100 A on S side Little Linches River...to son MASON, negro Frank...to daughter ESTER, negro Sam...wife, Sole Extx...EDWARD DAVIS (X) (SEAL), Wit: N. S. ROBINSON, PATRICK McKAIN, JACOB HOLLY, WINNEFOR DAIVS (X). Proven by NICHOLAS ROBINSON 16 Oct 1786, before ISAAC ALEXANDER, J. P. for Lancaster County.

DAVIS, ELIJAH Apt. 19 Pck. 635
AMOS DAVIS applied for admn, 9 Mar 1782, Citation published 17 March 1782, ISRAEL SEYMORE.
Bond: JOHN BARCLAY, AMOS DAVIS, ROBT BARCLAY, WILLIE BARCLY, 19 Aug 1782, Wit: JOHN KITCHEN.
Appraisement: 5 Oct 1782 by THOMAS DUKE, NATHL HARBEN, PETER ACKER; CAPT. AMOS DAVIS, Admr. Sale: 15 Oct 1782, no buyers listed.

DAVIS, JOHN Apt. 19 Pck. 638
[N. B. There are two or three estates for persons named JOHN DAVIS in this file.]
JOHN BARCLAY & AMOS DAVIS applied for admn, __ Mar 1782. No return on citation "GLASS CASTON, 25 Mar 1782"
Bond: JOHN BARCLAY, AMOS DAVIS, Admrs., ROBT BARCLAY, WM BARCLY, sec.,on estate of JOHN DAVIS JUNR., 19 Aug 1782.
Appraised 26 Apr 1785 by C. B. BRADFORD, THOS PARROT SEN (X), JAMES OGILVIE.
Sale: 23 May 1785, Buyers: JAMES DAVIS, AMOS DAVIS, ROBERT RABB, JNO GREGG, THOMAS PARROT.

Will of JOHN DAVIS of Camden District...to son JONATHAN DAVIS, s 1 sterling...to son AMOS DAVIS, tract whereon he now lives, 150 A 7 negro Harry ...to daughter RACHEL PRITCHARD, L 30 sterling...to grandson JOHN DAVIS, son of JOHN DAVIS, L 30 sterling...to son JAMES DAVIS, Plantation where I now live, 250 A & Known as ENGLEMANS old place & 200 A on Sandy River known as DAVIS' old place & 150 A on Rockey Creek, adj. where ABRAHAM MAYFIELD now lives...sons AMOS & JAMES, Exrs...JOHN DAVIS (SEAL), Wit: C. D. BRADFORD, CHARLES SIMON. Proven by CHS. D. BRADFORD, before H. HAMPTON.
JAMES DAVIS applied for letters of admn. on the estate of JOHN DAVIS not mentioned in his will, 13 Apr 1785. [Citation torn off]
Warrant of appraisement: 21 Apr 1785 to JAMES OGILSVIE, JOHN OGLESVIE, CHARLES D. BRAFORD, THOMAS PARROTT & ROBERT HANCOCK.
Sworn appraisers: CHARLES DARNELL BRADFORD, THOMAS PARROT SENR (T), & JAMES OGILVIE, 26 Apr 1785, before PHIL. PEARSON, J. P.
Administration bond, wit by JOHN OGILVIE.

WILLIAM HENDERSON Esqr., applied for admn. on estate of JOHN DAVIS 9 Apr 1785. Citation pub 17 Apr 1785, RICHARD FURMAN.

DAVIS, ROSHER Apt. 19 Pck. 649
DACEY DAVIS, Widow, applied for admn on Rosher Davis, late of Lynches Creek, planter...26 Aug 1786. Published in the Congregation, after divine Service, on Sunday 24 Sept 1786. JOHN LOGUE.
Bond: DACEY DAVIS, Admx., JOSEPH KERSHAW & WILLIAM NETTIES, sec., 30 Sept 1786. Wit: JAMES PEIRSON.

DAVIS, SAMUEL Apt. 22 Pck 779
Dedimus to STEPHEN BULL of Sheldon & BENJA. GARDEN, Esquires to admn. the oath of administration unto WILLIAM DAVIS of Prince Williams Parish, admr. of SAMUEL DAVIS, late of Parish aforesd, 18 Feb 1775.
[Why is this in Camden District?]
[For more information, see my Probate Records of SC, Vol II, Letters of admn., Vol. 00]

DAVISON, SAMUEL Apt 41 Pck. 1476
    [in same package as estate of ROBERT LOVE]
Return for 1787, dated 1 Jan 1788, shows advances made to the widow (not named), to JOHN GULLICK, in right of his wife REBEKAH, and to WILLIAM DAVISON.

DEAN, WILLIAM Apt. 19 Pck. 654
    DOCTOR THOMAS BROWN applied for admn. on estate of WILLIAM DEANS, late of Camden, Carpenter, 28 Sept 1786. Citation read in the Congregation of Camden, Sunday 1 Oct 1786, JOHN LOGUE.
Bond: 25 Nov 1786, WILLIAM LANG, JOHN HARKER sec., Wit: ROBERT DAVIS.

DENTON, JAMES Apt.20 Pck. 671
    MARY DENTON, Widow, applied for admn, 1 Dec 1784. Citation read in publick assembly of Cedar Creek on 5th Inst. Sunday JOHN NEWTON.
Bond: MARY DENTON, Admx; PATRICK GLAZE, GIDEON GLAZE, sec., 24 Mar 1785, Wit: JNO HARBIRT

DOHERTY, BRYANT Apt. 21 Pck. 715
    ROBERT MUNSON applied for admn., 3 Mar 1787. Citation read in the Congregation of Camden, 18 Mar 1787, JOHN LOGUE

DORRITY, JERVAIS Apt 21 Pck. 718
    ABRAHAM GIBSON & CHAS. PICKETT applied for admn., 1 Sept 1784. Citation published by RALPH JONES 8 Sept.
Bond: ABRAHAM GIBSON (X), CHAS. PICKETT; CHARLES LEWIS, sec., 15 Sept 1784. Wit: JOHN HARBIRT.

DOWD, CALEB Apt 21 Pck. 725
    SUSANNA DOWD applied for admn., 27 Jan 1785. Citation published by RALPH JONES 10 Feb.
Bond: SUSANNA DOWD (S); ISAAC LOVE, DARLING JONES, sec., 25 Feb 1785. Wit: J. HARBIRT.
Warrant of appraisement to ALLEN DAVIS, JAMES SCOTT, HENRY MYLEY, THOMAS VAUGHAN & ALEXANDER STEWARD, 25 Feb 1785.
Sworn: JAS SCOTT (X), THOS VAUGHAN, ALLEN DAVIS (D), before JNO LOWRY, J.P. Inventory made 8 Mar 1785.

DOWNEY, JOHN Apt 21 Pck. 726
    MARGARET DOWNEY applied for admn. as next of kin 11 June 1785. Citation read to Congregation at Rocky Creek, 19 June 1785 by WILLIAM MARTIN.
Bond: MARGARET DOWNEY (X), 27 1785, admx., JOHN CARSON, JAMES CRAFFORD, sec. Wit: JAMES KNOX, J.P.

DOWNS, WILLIAM Apt. 21 Pck. 727
    Letters of admn. to ANN DOWNS, 23 Apr 1783.
Bond: ANN DOWNS, WILLIAM WYLY & MARY DOWNS, 23 Apr 1783. Wit; RICHARD WINN.
Warrant of appraisement to WM. WYLEY, WM BOND, JOHN BELTON, DANIEL O QUINN, & SAML BOYKIN. Sworn appraisers, 3 July 1783, before WILLIAM LANG, J. P.: WM WYLEY, JOHN BELTON, DANIEL O QUINN.
Estate appraised 3 July 1783.
Accounts: 1786--Sept 5: 2 tracts of Land on Hanging Rock sold by the Sheriff. To Judgment of Suit obtained by ANDREW LESTER. To MR. HUGH RUTLEDGE, for defending suit.

DOYLE, THOMAS Apt. 21 Pck. 728
    JOHN THOMSON applied for admn. as greatest creditor, 4 Sept 1784. "Oct 24, 1784 read as ordered at the Waxaw Chruch. JAMES EDMONDS V D M"

DUBBERTS, FREDERICK Apt 22 Pck. 741
    FED. DAWSEN & JONES BEARD appleid for admn. as friend and Creditor, 4 Apr 1783. Citation published 21 Apr, Pr me RALPH JONES.
Bond: FEDRICK DAWSEN & JONAS BEARD, 28 Apr 1783, Wit: TIMO RIVES. Dedimus to admn. oath to JONAS BEARD directed to TIMO REEVES, Esq., 21 Apr 1783. Admd. oath on 28 Apr 1786.

DUKE, ROBERT Apt 22 Pck. 746
    Will of ROBERT DUKE of Camden District, 10 Dec 1784...to son THOMAS DUKE, ₴ 1 sterling....to daughter RACHEL CRIM, ₺ 30 sterling...to sons

MOSES and AARON DUKE, plantation where I now live on Twenty five mile Creek...to wife NANCY DUKE, wench Jude...all remainder to be held until MOSES Comes to the age of 21...then to be divided among my six youngest children...to my youngest son JESSE DUKE, L50 A on Sawneys Creek...tracts near the mouth of Fishing Creek & near CAREYS old saw mill...MOSES DUKE & WILLIAM SIMMONS, Exrs...ROBERT DUKE (SEAL), Wit: WILLIAM SIMMONS, PETER CRIM, MOSES DUKE. Prov. 28 Jan 1785 before JOHN HARBIRT.
Bond: GEORGE WADE & FREDERICK KIMBALL, 30 Apr 1784. [GEORGE WADE, admr. with the will annexed?]

DUNCAN, JAMES Apt. 22 Pck. 748
Will 6 Dec 1782, proven 7 June 1783...wife MARGARET, son ROBERT, son WILLIAM, daughter MARY DUNCAN and the "Babe now in the womb"...Ex. brother JOHN DUNCAN, and JOSEPH RATCHFORD, my Brother in Law. Wit: WM. McLEAN, JOSEPH JEWEL, THOMAS DUNCAN (X).
Dedimus to WILLIAM HILL 15 May 1783, to qualify the witnesses.
[N. B. JOSEPH RATCHFORD was a Lt. under COL. JAMES HAWTHORN of New Acquisition in 1781. JAMES DUNCAN served as a horseman under CAPTAINS THOMPSON, HENDERSON and GARRISON. His widow MARGARET assigned his indent to FRANCIS ADAMS of York County.]

DUNCAN, PATRICK Apt. 22 Pck. 749
Will 20 Oct 1776, prov. 22 May 1783...son THOMAS, son JAMES, daughter MARGARET DUNCAN, son JOHN, son ROBERT, son WILLIAM; sons in law JAMES KERR, JNO ALEXANDER, JNO GARVAN, JAMES LUSK, granddaughter MARY GARVAN; daughter JEAN KERR, MARY LUSK, RACHEL ALEXANDER & granddaughter VIOLET DUNCAN...Ex: JNO DUNCAN, WILLIAM WATSON and cousin CHAS. MOORE, overseer...Wit: WILLIAM WATSON, ANDREW BARRY, CHAS. MOOR.
Proved by CHARLES MOORE and ANDREW BARRY in Ninety Six Dist., before JOHN THOMAS JUNR., 22 May 1783, per dedimus to JOHN THOMAS JUNR, J. P. by HENRY HAMPTON, Ordy. of Camden Dist.
Purchasers at sale: JOHN KENSLER, JAMES DUNCAN, WILLIAM RATCHFORD, JOHN DUNCAN, MATTHEW SMITH, JOHN ALEXANDER, MARY RUSK, JOHN GREEN, ____ WATSON SAMUEL WATSON, J. Q. takes receipts from children: THOMAS DUNKIN (X), MARY RISK (X) [LUSK], and MARGARET DUNCAN (X), 21-27 Nov 1783.

DUNN, SAMUEL Apt. 22 Pck. 760
ELIZABETH DUNN, widow, and CHRISTOPHER STRONG applied for admn. 8 Feb 1786, and citation "read in Publick" 12 Feb 1786, by JNO SIMPSON, [V. D. M.]

ELDEN, THOMAS Apt 23 Pck. 788
JAMES DENLY applied for admn., as Near[est] of Kin, 3 Dec 1782. Citation published 15 Dec 1782, CHRISTIAN THEUS, V D Minister.
Bond: JAMES DENELY, admr., WILLIAM McGRAY & DANIEL McLANE (+), sec., 28 Dec 1782, Wit: RACHEL FURMAN.
Warrant of appraisement to BENJAMIN EVERT, LAGROVE YOUNG, ALEXDR McGREW, JOHN SOJOURNER & WILLIAM TAYLOR, 28 Dec 1782. Sworn: BENJA. EVERIT, LeGROS YOUNG, and ALEXR McGREW.

ELKINS, DAVID Apt. 23 Pck. 793
ANN ELKIN by JOHN ARMSTRONG applied for admn. as next of kin, 9 Sept 1782. Citation pub. 21 Sept pr RALPH JONES.
Bond: ANN ELKIN (X), Admx., ISAAC LOVE & WILLIAM ELKINS, sec, 7 Oct 1782, Wit: JOSEPH WRIGHT, REUBIN IVEY.
Appraisement of estate of DAVID ELKINS of Colonals Creek made 21 Dec 1782 by JOHN ARMSTRONG, THOS MUSE(?), THO. VAUGHAN.

ELKINS, WILLIAM Apt. 23 Pck. 798
SARAH ELKINS applied for admn. 16 Aug 1783. Citation read 15 Sept by RALPH JONES.
Bond: SARAH ELKINS, admx., ZACHARIAH NETTLES or RICKETS, sec., 17 Sept 1783, Wit: R. WINN.

ELLIOTT, DANIEL Apt. 23 Pck. 801
WILLIAM ELLIOTT applied for admn., 11 Apr 1783. Citation read at Fishing Creek, 13 Apr 1783 by JOHN SIMPSON, V. D. M.
Bond: 15 May 1783, with PHILIP WALKER and JOHN WALKER sec.
Sworn appraisers: NICHOLAS BISHOP, DAVID PORTER, JOSEPH GASTON, JOHN PORTER and JOHN McFARLAN, 15 May 1783. Estate appraised 20 May 1783 by JOHN PORTER, DAVID PORTER & JOHN McFARLAN, L 1488 15 0.

ELLIOTT, THOMAS   Apt. 23 Pck 806
         Will of THOMAS ELLIOTT of Twelve Mile Creek in Camden District,
29 Nov 1781, prov. by JOHN McCULLOH, who wrote the will and swore that
THOMAS ELLIOT expired before signing the will....son JAMES, Unborn child,
wife JEAN, daughter MARY, daughter JANE...Extx: wife JEAN and brother
JOHN ELLIOTT and friend ROBERT CROCKETT.
Estate appraised by WM PORTER, CHARLES MILLER JUNR., ARCHD. COUSART, ROBT
CROCKETT JUNR., certified before ANDW FOSTER, J. P. [Since the will was
not signed, there were no witnesses·]

ENSMINGER, PETER   Apt. 24 Pck. 825
         FREDERICK ENCEMINGER applied for admn. as nearest of kin, 13
Apr 1783. Citation"Published according to Law Pr Me RALPH JONES"

FARIS, JOHN   Apt. 24 Pck. 843
         ELIZABETH FARIS applied for admn. as nearest of kin, 30 Apr 1784.
Citation read in the Presbyterian Church at Jackson's Creek, 16 May 1784,
by T. H. McCAULE, V. D. M.
Bond: ELIZABETH FARIS (X), Admx., ARCHIBALD PAUL (X), sec. Wit: JNO
HARBIRT.
Estate appraised by ALEXANDER ROSBOROUGH, WALKER AKINS, 15 June 1784, for
Ł 23 15 6.

FARRELL, WILLIAM   Apt 24 Pck. 844
         Bond: MIDDLETON McDONALD, WILLIAM McDONALD & ELEANOR FARREL,
Adm. of WILLIAM FARRELL, late of Hanging Rock, planter, 18 Oct 1786. Wit:
ROBERT REID, R. H.(?) SCOTT.
Appraisers sworn 18 Oct 1786 before JOS. LEE, J. P.: FREDERICK IMBALL,
GEORGE WADE, GLASS CASTON.
Inventory of Estate of COLO. WILLIAM FARRELL "Negroes in MR. JOHN
HOLZENDORFS" 28 Dec 1786.
Sale: 28 Dec 1786; MIDDLETON McDONALD, only purchaser.

FELDER, JOHN   Apt. 24 Pck. 848
         JOHN RAEGON applied for admn. 21 Dec 1782. Citation read in
congregation at halfway swamp Meeting, 29 Dec 1782, GABRIEL GERRALD.
Bond : JOHN RAEGAN, ADAM SNELL SENR., ADAM SNELL JUNR., 18 Jan 1783, Wit:
PETER CASSITY
Inventory of JOHN FELDER of St. Mark's, Craven Co...appraised by WILLIAM
CANTEY, EDWARD BROUGHTON & JOSEPH TERRY, 17 Mar 1783.

FERGUSON, JAMES   Apt. 24 Pck. 849
         MARY FERGUSON, widow of JAMES FERGUSON   applied for admn.,
24 Feb 1785. Citation read "before ye Congregation at Sharon Meeting
House on Fishing Creek," 12 Mar 1785 by WILLIAM MARTIN, Minister.
MARY FERUGSON (X), bonded as admx., with SAMUEL EORGUSON & ROBT FARGUSON
sec., Wit: PHILIP WALKER, Esqr.
Estate inventoried 30 Apr 1785 by WILLIAM WILEY, THOMAS DUGAN, ROBERT
MARTIN for Ł 133 11 8 sterling, or Ł 9 3 5 old currency.

FERGUSON, WILLIAM   Apt. 24 Pck. 850
         Will 26 Jan 1775, wife MARY, her youngest son HENRY SMITH,
brother JOHN FORGURSON, SARAH SMITH, CATHERINE SMITH. Extx: wife MARY.
...WILLIAM FORGUESON (X). Wit: WM. BROWN, PATIENCE BROWN (X), SARAH
SMITH (X). Proven by SARAH SMITH (now SARAH MILLS) before JOHN ADAIR,
J. P. (no date given). SARAH MILLS (X) renounced her legacy before
P. WATERS, J. Q. 31 Aug 1785. Dedimus to EDWD LACEY & JOHN ADAIR J.P.
to qualify witnesses, 2 Sept 1784.

FETHERSTONE, WILLIAM Apt. 24 Pck. 851
         GEORGE WADE applied for admn. as greatest creditor, 3 Nov
1783. [No citation returned]
Bond: GEORGE WADE, admr., FREDERICK KIMBALL sec., 13 Apr 1784: Wit:
ZACH CANTEY.

FISHER, WILLIAM   Apt. 24 Pck. 854
         SARAH FISHER, widow, applied for admn. as nearest of kin, 8 May
1782. Citation read of Rocky Creek, 14 May 1782 by JOHN SIMPSON, V. D.
M.
Bond: SARAH FISHER 10 June 1782, admx., ROBIN STEWART & DANIEL STEWART,
sec.

Estate appraised by ROBT STEWART, MIDDLETON McDONALD & JAMES HOUZE(HOUSE) 14 Aug 1782, for ₤ 2042. JAMES DENTON and GEORGE WADE also appointed but did not serve as appraisers.

FLEMING, ALEXANDER Apt. 24 Pck. 851
    ROBERT FLEMING & WILLIAM FLEMING applied for admn. as nearest of kin, 8 Dec 1783. Citation read at Fishing Creek 14 Dec 1783 by JNO SIMPSON.
Warrant of appraisement 30 Dec 1783 to JOHN ANDERSON, ARCHIBALD STEEL, WM. SAVAGE, THOS BLACK & DAVID PORTER.
Dedimus 30 Nov 1783 to WM BRATTON, J. P. to qualify ROBT FLEMING as admr. Qualified 4 Jan 1784.
Estate appraised by CAPT THOS BLACK, CAPT. JNO ANDERSON, ARCHD. STEEL & DAVID PORTER for ₤ 829 5 10., certified before COL. WM. BRATTON.

FLINTON, JACOB Apt. 24 Pck. 867
    JAMES HUEY applied for admn. 15 May 1783. Citation read "in my meeting" 23 May 1783, by THOS WILLIAMS.
    THOMAS JENKINS applied for admn 11 May 1786, and citation read 17 May 1786 in public congregation by STEPHEN JOHNSON.
Bond: THOMAS JENKINS, 30 June 1786 as admr., WALTHAL BURTON, DANIEL PRICE sec., before DD. HOPKINS, JOHN PRATT.
Dedimus to DAVID HOPKINS, J. P. to qualify THOMAS JENKINS as adm. & swear PETER SEALY, AMBROSE NIX, & JOHN LYDA as appraisers. All sworn 24 July 1786.
THOMAS JENKINS certified 19 Aug 1786 "There is no property of JOSEPH FLINTHAM to be appraised--there is ₤ 1700 owing to him by THOMAS FLETCHALL who administered on his father's estate and never paid it, also a tract on Sandy River, the South fork containing 100 acres, another on Owens Creek containg 200 acres which PHILIP PARSON lives on."

FORD, THOMAS Apt. 25 Pck. 875
    STEPHEN PRITCHETT applied for admn. as greatest creditor, 11 Oct 1784. Citation read to congregation at Rocky Creek, 21 Oct 1784, by WM MARTIN, minister.
Bond: STEPHEN PRITCHETT, admr., JOHN KITCHIN sec., 23 Oct 1784.
Estate appraised by THOMAS DYE & THOMAS GATER (GEATHER), for ₤ 23 19 3.
Warrant of appraisement directed to abvoe and JOHN LOTT, JOHN DYE, JOSEPH ROBINSON.
Purchasers at sale: STEPHEN PRITCHELL, ZACHARIAH RAFE, WM FORD, BENJAMIN MORRIS, JOHN STORMAN, THOMAS DYE, JOHN DYE, JAMES MORRIS, CHARLES LEWIS, THOMAS STROUD, MARY FORD, JOHN WINN, WM. STORMAN, ABRAM MILLER, THOMAS McCAULEY.

FORTUNE, JOHN Apt. 25 Pck. 876
    ANNE FORTUNE applied for admn. as nearest of kin, 7 Apr 1783.
Citation published 21 Apr 1783, RALPH JONES.
Camden District: Before me JOHN BUCHANAN Esqr., personally appeared MARY McCREARY who saith that a will made by JOHN FORTUNE was left in her care for a considerable time...to his son WILLIAM FORTUNE, s 5...to his eldest daughter MARY wife of ROBERT McCREARY s5...to daughter JENNY, ₤ 5...to daughter ELIZABETH, ₤ 100...to sons MARK & RICHARD, ₤ 100...to grandson WILLIAM, son of WILLIAM, one Cow and calf...to granddaughter ELIZABETH, daughter to MARY, ₤ 10...to wife ANN, all household furniture & ₤ 100... land on heads of Jackson Creek to be sold & will was witness by WILLIAM SIMMONS, Esqr., WILLIAM SAUNDERS & ROBERT DUKES...14 Jan 1784, JOHN BUCHANAN, J. P.
Before JOHN SMITH J. P. appeared WILLIAM SIMMONS who maketh oath that he was at a Mill Belonging to JOHN DOUGHARTY & there met JOHN FORTUNE who desired him to witness as will and this was _____ 1776, sworn 24 Aug 1778. Also same oath made by WILLIAM SANDERS.

FOWLER, WILLIAM Apt. 28 Pck. 973
    FRANCIS GOODWIN JUNR. applied for admn. as Principal Creditor, 11 June 1782.
Citation Published in Cambden District 16 June 1782 by CHRISTIAN THEUS, V D Minister.

FRANKLIN, JOHN Apt. 25 Pck. 878
    BRYAN RAELY applied for admn. as nearest of kin, 30 Oct 1782.

S. C. Camden District, St. Marks Parish, Broad River, 10 Oct 1782, published citation, JACOB GIBSON, M. G.
Warrant of appraisement to BARNABY POPE, HENRY HUNTER, DAVID McGRAGH, JACOB GIBSON, LEWIS POPE, JOHN ROBERSON, 22 Nov 1782.
Sworn: H. HUNTER, JNO ROBERTSON, LEWIS POPE, 23 Jan 1783 before BARY. POPE, J. P.
Bond: BRYANT RAELY, H. HUNTER BARY. POPE, 13 Oct 1782, Wit: JOHN ANDREWS, JESSE FORT.
Inventory 23 Jan 1783. Sale: ___ Jan 1783, Purchasers: BRYANT RYLEY(sic), HUGH MOUNTGOMERY, JOHN ROBERSON, DAVID MOUNTGOMERY, PETER CURREY, DUDLEY CURRY, BARY. POPE.

FREEMAN, FREDERICK Apt. 25 Pck.884
JOHN WILSON applied for admn. as nearest of kin, 1 Mar 1782.
Citation published in Twenty five mile Creek Meeting House, 3 Mar 1782, GABRIEL RAWLS.
Bond: JOHN WILSON; admr., JACOB LEWIS & JAMES LABON, sec., 25 Mar 1782. Wit: RACHEL HAMILTON.
Warrant of appraisement to JACOB LEWIS, JAMES LABON, ROBERT DUKES, WILLIAM SIMONS, & NIMROD MITCHELL. Appraisers sworn 25 Mar 1782: JACOB LEWIS, JAMES LABON, ROBERT DUKES. Inventory made 20 Apr 1782.

FULTON, JOHN Apt. 25 Pck. 885
EDWARD MOORHEAD applied for admn. as nearest of kin, his wife being the late wife of JOHN FULTON, decd., 11 May 1785.
Citation read in public 4 May 1785, by THOMAS H. McCAULE.
[N. B. EDWARD MOORHEAD died 4 Feb 1814, aged 70 years and is buried at old Beersheba Presbyterian Church, five miles west of York, S. C. JANE MOORHEAD died 21 Oct 1818, aged 54 years and is buried beside him.]

FULTON, PAUL Apt. 25 Pck. 886
JAMES McCULLOCH for himself, REBECKA FULTON & HUGH BENNET applied for admn. as next of kin & friends, 6 Feb 1782. Citation read by WM. FULLWOOD, 15 Feb 1782.
23 Dec 1782, JAMES McCOLLOUCH & REBECKAH FULTON made oath that PAUL FULTON left no will...ROGER WILSON, J. P.
Warrant of appraisement to JONATHAN SCARTH, JOHN OSGOOD, MATTHEW BENNET, CHARLES STORY & WILLIAM FULLWOOD, 5 Dec 1782.
Bond: JAMES McCULOUGH, REBECKA FULTON, HUGH BENNET, admr., JONATHAN SCARTH & MATHEW BENNET, Sec., 20 Nov 1782, Wit: WILLIAM BENNET, MARY McCOLLUGH.
Inventory 30 Dec 1782, by CHARLES STORY (O), JONATHAN SCARTH & JOHN OSGOOD. "Currency in Gorga, South Carolinah & Continental Bills."

FURMAN, BENJAMIN Apt. 25 Pck. 887
WILLIAM GUPHILL applied for admn. as greatest creditor, 24 Feb 1785.
Citation published in the Congregation of Camden after Divine Service on Sunday 13 Mar 1785, JOHN LOGUE.
Bond: WILLIAM GUPHILL; THOMAS GARNER, JOHN HUNTER, sec. 24 Mar 1785. Wit: JOHN HARBIRT, AND. ALISON.
Warrant of appraisement to THOMAS GARNER, JOSHUA ENGLISH, ROBERT HILL, JOHN BELTON, & THOMAS WATTS, 24 Mar 1784.
Swron 28 May 1784: THOMAS GARNER, JOSHUA ENGLISH, JOHN BELTON.
Inventory made 28 May 1785.

GALMAN, HENRY Apt. 85 Pck. 891
[N. B. see also estate of COLEMAN, HENRY]
Will of HENRY GALMAN of Camden District...money due me from THOMAS TAYLOR being ₤ 1600 lawfull money for a tract of land sold him, be given to my mother MARGARET FOUST & after her death divided among my Brothers and sisters born of my mother...step father JACOB FOUST, Exr...14 Aug 1780.
HENRICH GALLMAN[German signature], Wit: JOHN GEIGER, GASPER WARSHING (X), HENRY SMITH.
Proven by JOHN GEIGER, before H. HAMPTON, 5 May 1783.
Inventory 6 Sept 1783 by BENJ. GRUBB, STEPHEN CURRY, JOHN MAY.

GAMBLE, JOHN Apt. 25 Pck. 892
JANE GAMBLE and JAMES COCHRAN applied for admn. 13 July 1785.
Citation read in Waxhaw Congregation by ROBT FINDLY "Minister of that parish"

Bond: JANE GAMBRELL, JAMES COHERON, Admrs., JAMES MONTGOMERY & WILLIAM FARREL, sec., before I. ALEXANDER, 16 Aug 1785.
Warrant of appraisement to WILLIAM GAMBLE, JOHN CROCKET, JAMES MONTGOMERY, JOHN WHITE JR., & ROBERT DUNLAP, 13 Sept 1785. Sworn 8 Nov 1785: WILLIAM GAMBLE, JOHN CROCKET, ROBERT DUNLAP.
JEAN GAMBRELL swore to produce all goods & chattles of estate, 8 Nov 1785, before ROBT MONTGOMERY, J. P. Inventory made 9 Nov 1785.
Will of JOHN GAMBLE of Cravin Co....to wife JEAN, power over my movable estate & my son in law JAMES COCHRAN in giving my children their parts... to son ANDREW, all my lands, 28 Mar 1785. Wit: JAMES MONTGOMERY, JOHN LESLY, NINEN MOUNTGOMERY. "Will not confirmed".

GANTER, GEORGE   Apt. 25 Pck. 893
    SARAH GANTER widow of Camden applied for admn, 26 Sept 1786. "These may certify that the within citation was made publick as directed by Law. I ALEXANDER"
Bond: SARAH, widow of GEORGE GANTER, admx., ARCHIBALD WATSON & RICHARD STRATFORD of Wateree River, sec., 18 Sept 1786, Wit: JOSEPH BULKLEY.

GARDNER, JOHN   Apt. 25 Pck. 899
    Will of JOHN GARDNER of Bullocks Creek in New Acquisition, 2 Mar 1784, prov. 29 Mar 1784...Wife SARAH...daughters JEAN, HANNAH, MARTHA, MARY & REBECKAH (the latter "three young children" to be schooled) ...Exrs: friends THOMAS McAULEY & ROBERT KENNEDY, Wit: JAMES THOMPSON, JOHN SCOTT (X), DAVID DICKEY. Wife's concurrence witnessed by JOHN SIMONTON, WM. SCOTT, DAVID DICKEY.
Estate appraised by ALEXANDER BARRON, WILLIAM SCOTT, JOHN MARLEY, 2 Apr 1784.

GARDNER, WILLIAM   Apt. 25 Pck. 907
Bond: THOMAS GARDENER, admr., JOSEPH PLEDGER of Cheraw District & CHARLES McGINEY, sec., 1 Aug 1782, Wit: RACHEL HAMILTON.
Warrant of appraisement to DAVID NEILSON, JOHN MOORE, THOMAS LANOIR, MALACHIA MURPHY, & WILLIAM SAUNDERS, 1 Aug 1782. Sworn appraisers, 26 Sept 1782 before BURL BOYKIN, J. P.: DAVID NEILSON, JOHN MOORE, WILLIAM SAUNDERS. Inventory made 26 Sept 1782.
Buyers at sale, 26 Sept 1782: CHRS. McGINNEY, FRANCIS BOYKIN, DAVID NEILSON, WM SCRUGG, COLLN. HENRY HAMPTON, ROBT ELLIS, MOSES FERGUSON, JOSEPH PLEDGER, ABRAM COLE, THOS GARDNER, BURRILL BOYKIN.

GAULDEN, JOHN   Apt. 26 Pck. 926
    Will of JOHN GOLDING of South Carrolina...estate to remain together 8 years from this date & then wife SUSANNAH to have the part of two children & remainder divided among the children that are of age.... 15 Jan 1781...JOHN GAULDEN (SEAL),Wit: SAMUEL TYNES, JOHN BRUMFIELD, JAMES GOLDEN (X). Prov. by SUSANNA GAULDEN, 20 Jan 1782 before WOOD FURMAN.
Warrant of appraisement to JOHN JAMES SENR., WILLIAM DINKINS, & WILLIAM WRIGHT, 28 Jan 1782. Sworn, 18 Apr 1782.
Inventory made 19 Apr 1782, total £ 3277 11.0.

GAUNT, ZEBULON   Apt. 26 Pck. 927
    SAMUEL GAUNT applied for admn. of the estate of ZEBULON GAUNT, late of the Wateree, Mill Wright, 26 Feb 1787.
Citation published in the Congregation of Camden, 18 Mar 1787, JOHN LOGUR.
Bond: SAMUEL GANT, Admr., JOHN KERSHAW, & JOSEPH BREVARD, all of Lancaster County, sec., __ Mar 1787.
Warrant of appraisement, 20 Mar 1787 to MICHAEL GANTER, WILLIAM BOND, ARCHIBALD WATSON, JAMES SMITH & WILLIAM NETTLES.
Appraisers sworn, 14 Apr 1787, before I. ALEXANDER, J. P.: MICHAEL GANTER, WILLIAM BOND, ARCHIBALD WATSON,. & WILLIAM NETTLES.
Appraised, 24 July 1787. List of accounts: JOHN ADAMSON, ISAAC ALEXANDER, DAVID BUSH, JOHN BARRON, ISAAC DaCOSTA, THOMAS CHARLETON, BENJAMIN CARTER, JOHN HARKER, ALEXANDER IRVIN, JOSEPH KERSHAW, JOSEPH McCOY, JAMES PEIRSON, WILLIAM TATE, JAMES TATE, FIELDING WOODROOF, JAMES COOK, PAUL SMITH.

GAYLE, JOSIAH JR.   Apt. 26 Pck. 932
    REBECCA GALE applied for admn. as next of kin, 15 Aug 1782.
Citation read in publick meeting, 25 Aug 1782, SOLOMON THOMSON.
Bond: REBECCKAH GALE, amrx., JOSIAH GALE & JOHN HARNIN, sec. 16 Sept 1782,

Wit: JOSIAH FURMAN.
Appraisement, 2 Oct 1782, by ISHAM MOORE, REUBEN VASS, J. SINGLETON.

GEE, JOHN   Apt. 26 Pck. 933
Will dated 6 Dec 1780; proven 28 Dec 1784...to Rebecca TOMLINSON, her children BRIDGET GEE TOMLINSON & NAVIL GEE TOMLINSON...Executors: ETHEL HEATH[male], JAMES TAYLOR, Wit: HICKS CHAPPELL, JOHN PARTRIDGE. Appraisement by JOHN THREEWITS, LUDWELL EVANS, NOAH PHELPS (X), 29 Dec 1784, for L 743 4 0.

GINDRAT, ABRAHAM Apt. 26 Pck. 934
Will of ABRAHAM GINDRAT of Craven County, Provence of South Carolina...to son HENRY ABRAHAM GINDRAT, 10 negro Slaves (named), 2 Horses, etc. & if he died before he comes of age, to JENE FORGOSON, 2 negroes (named) and all the rest to my brother HENRY GINDRATS two sons...to CAPT JOHN COOKs son NATHAN COOK...WILLIAM LAMBRIGHT, HENRY GINDRAT & CAPT JOHN COOK, Exrs. 19 Feb 1785...ABRAHAM GINDRAT (SEAL), Wit: WM. HARDWICK, SARAH COOK.
Proved 31 May 1785 by WM HARDWICK.
Warrant of appraisement to ROBERT LYAL, JOHN MOORE, HICKS CHAPPEL, WILLIAM HERONS, THOMAS HUTCHESON & GREEN RIVES, 31 May 1785.
All sworn before TIMY. RIVES, Esqr., 28 July 1785.
17 June 1786, Memorandum of part of the Estate of Abraham Gindratt, a negro girl Penelopy, by HS. CHAPPELL, GREEN RIVES, JOHN MOORE.
The rest of estate appraised 28 July 1785.

GIBSON, MARY Apt. 26 Pck. 947
Will of MARY GIBSON of the Parish of St. Mark in Craven Co., S. C., widow...to son ROGER GIBSON, negros Dublin, Belinda, Silvia, Nanny...to grandson ROGER GIBSON, son of SAMUEL GIBSON decd., negroes (named); to daughter JANE SMITH, Negro (named) & her husband ALEXANDER SMITH...to the children of ISAAC ROSS SENR. decd., which he had by his wife MARY decd., my daughter, to ELIZABETH ROSS, JANE ROSS, ISAAC ROSS, EUPHEMY ROSS, negroes (named)...to MARY ROSS, daughter of ISAAC ROSS, an equal share...son ROGER to take care of Old Wench Tilly & son Roger, Exr; 28 Sept 1775...MARY GIBSON (SEAL), Wit: JNO MILHOUSE, ELIZA ADKISON, MARY KELLY (W). Proven by John Milhouse 6 July 1782 before BURL BOYKIN. Rec. in Book No. 1, fo. 44.

GIBSON, ROGER Apt. 26 Pck. 948.
[no will in package, see recorded copy in the South Carolina Magazine of Ancestral Research]
ALEXANDER SMITH applied for admn. as next of kin, 11 July 1782.
We do certify that this paper was Read publickly in an assembly of the people Coled Quakers this 21st of July 1782. Certifyed by ZIMRI, GAUNT, NEBO GAUNT, SAMUEL TOMLINSON, ZEBULON GAUNT, THOMAS ENGLISH.
Bond: ELEXANDER SMITH of the State of Virginia, & Wm WHITAKER JUNR & ISAAC ROSS of Camden Dist., 9 Aug 1782. Wit: RACHEL HAMILTON.

GILL, ROBERT Apt. 27 Pck. 953
JOHN GILL JUNR. and JOHN MILLS, Planters, applied for letters of admn. 2 Dec 1786. Citation read at Fishing Creek, 21 Jan 1787, by JOHN SIMPSON, V. D. M.
Estate appraised by ROBERT COOPER, HUGH WHITESIDE, HUGH WHITE & CHRISTOPHER STRIGHT, 8 Feb 1787.
JOHN GILL JUNR & JOHN MILLS bonded as admrs., 3 Feb 1787 with EDWD LACEY & ROBERT COOPER as securities.
[N. B. ELIZABETH GILL of Fishing Creek made affidavit that her deceased husband ROBERT GILL was a member of CAPT. ALEXANDER PAGAN'S Company; that he was employed as a blacksmith to make swords from scythes for the troop of horse; that he had made 12 swords and was on his way with them to Sumter's army when they and his horse were captured and he taken prisoner on Black River by a party of Tories; that he died 1786-- A. A. 2832]

"A Scedule of the book Accounts of Robert Gill Blacksmith Decd with the Bonds and Notes &C.

		L	S	d
ARMSTRONG, JAMES	By Book	18	18	7½
ARMSTRONG, WILLIAM	Do		13	3/4
BROWN, JOHN R	Do		3	8
BROWN, ISAAC R	Do			6

BROCKET, WILLIAM	Do			8
BOYD, DAVID	Do		1	2
BISHOP, WILLIAM R	Do		8	4
BROWN, ALEXDR.	Do		2	4
BROWN, SAML	Do		10	10
BISHOP, JAMES	Do		5	-
BROWN, SAML	Do	1	6	6
BROWN, JOHN	Do		3	-
BOYD, DAVID	Do		8	6
BLAYR, JAMES	Do		2	-
BLAYR, THOMAS	Do		2	-
COOK, DAINEL (sic)	Do		7	-
CRAGE, GEORGE	Do		6	3½
CARR, DAVID	Do		9	4½
CRAWFORD, JAMES	Do		13	-
DIKEY, GEORGE	Do		4	3
DOUDEL, ROBERT	Do		7	½
DAVISE, ELIJAH	Do	1	9	3/4
DOWNING, JOHN	Do	1	15	5
DUNN, JAMES	Do		1	3
DODS, HUGH	Do		11	-
DODS, JOHN	Do		11	9
DOWNING, ALEXDR.	Do		1	6
DASON, CORNELAS	Do			9
DAVIES, DAVED	Do		1	6
DIRK, CHARLES	Do		2	4
ELLIOT, ELIZBATH	Do			7
ELLIOT, ARCHD	Do	2	10	1
ELLIOT, BENJIMIN	Do		13	9
ELLIOT, WILLIAM D	Do		10	-
ELLIOT, WILLIAM	Do	1	5	8
FERREL, THOMAS	Do	7	-	4
FARGISON, PALL	Do	1	4	3
FERIS, WILLIAM	Do	1	3	-
FERIS, ALEXDR.	Do	9	17	9
FARGISON, JOHN	Do		8	1
GILL, THOMAS	Do		14	8
GILL, JOHN	Do	1	2	7
GILL, ROBERT SENR	Do		8	3
GRANT, JAMES R	Do		2	10
GASTON, JOSOPH	Do	1	13	14
GREEN, JOHN	Do			5
GEALLY, SAML R	Do		8	8
GILL, ARCHD	by Book	2	1	7
GILL, GEORGE SENR	Do	1	2	-
GASTON, ROBERT	Do		14	-
GILL, GEORGE JUNR	Do			9
HOGE, JAMES	Do		1	6
HOGE, MARY	Do		10	-
HARDGROVE, JEAN	Do		9	½
HUFFMAN, JACOB R	Do		1	8
HERIS, JOHN	Do	1	16	7
HAMBELTON, WILLIAM	Do		7	1¾
HAMBELTON, MARY	Do		2	-
HAMBELTON, SAMULL	Do	1	7	0
JAMESON, MARY	Do		2	10
JACK, JAMES	Do		10	4
JONSTONS, JAMES	Do		1	-
JONES JONATHAN	Do		13	3
KERSWELL, ANDREW	Do		2	
KELLSY, GEORGE	Do	3	12	10
KIRK, THOMAS R	Do			
KNOX, JAMES	Do	5	6	6
KULP, PETTER	Do		9	6
KELLSY, SAMULL JUNR	Do		6	5
KNOX, ROBERT R	Do			6
LEANEY, ISAAC	Do		10	½
LUSK, ROBERT	Do		2	1½
LATTA, JOHN JUNR	Do	1	10	10
LATTA, JOHN SENR	Do	2		7
LAMENT, MARTHA	Do		6	6

Name		Type	£	s	d
McGallyard, John	R	Do		6	6
Muldoon, James		Do			6
Morriss, John	R	Do		4	
Millen, John		Do		6	2
McCllen, Robert		Do		1	1½
McGerety, William		Do		3	4
Miller, Alexdr		do			11
Morrow, Joseph		Do	4	7	7½
McCants, Andw		Do	1	4	6¼
Millen, Robert		Do		19	6¾
Miller, John		Do		6	10
McElheney, William		Do		1	
McKenney, Samuel		Do		2	
Montgomery, James		Do		16	4
McCamon, James	R	Do		2	3
Morrow, David		Do		6	3
McFarling, John		By Book		16	9
McCants, Thomas		Do		14	11
Mills, John		Do		2	9
McGlamrey, John		Do		3	6
Miller, William		Do		6	6
McCluer, James		Do		1	9
McCants, David		Do		1	-
Neely, Mathew		Do		1	7
Neely, Hugh	R	Do			7½
Nelly, Robert		Do	1	13	7
Neely, Thomas		Do	2	2	10
Pearce, Hugh	R	Do		8	4½
Pagen, James		Do		1	2
Porter, John		Do		12	8
Porter, Josiah		Do		1	8½
Porter, David		Do		1	9
Robertson, Petter		Do		2	1½
Robeson, James		Do		6	4
Rosborough, Alaxander Senr		Do		7	7
Scot, John		Do		1	9
Strong, Jennet		Do		9	4
Smith, Samull	R	Do		9	3
Revt Simpson, John		Do		14	3
Strong, Cristopher		Do		7	3
Strong, James		Do		4	8
Townsend, Repentance	R	Do			10
Townsend, Samull	R	Do		1	1½
Townsend, Henery	R	Do		4	8
Townsend, Thomas	R	Do			4½
Tate, James		Do		2	
Wyile, William Junr		Do	4	10	2½
Wyile, William Do		Do		13	6
White, Hugh		Do	2	11	1½
Whiteside, Hugh		Do		14	9
Whiteside, William		Do	1	1	-
Wyile, Frances		Do		9	6
Wyile, William Senr		Do		2	4
Wyile, James		Do		16	
Weer, Samuel		Do		19	4
Walker, Robert		Do		2	6
Walker, Joseph		Do		6	4
John Gill and John Mills		Do	56	5	2 3/4
		Amount	127	16	6¼

P.S. The above Acounts marked this R the Debter is Removed so that We Count them Lost or dead Accts. Unot the Estate
Given under our Hands 31 March 1787   John Gill Junr, John Mills, Adm.

Bonds due from Hugh Knox, Jacob Sutton.

GLADDEN, RICHARD   Apt. 27 Pck. 956
          Bond: NANCY GLADEN (X) and JOHN HOLLIS (HOLLAN), 12 Dec 1783.
Warrant of appraisement to: JOHN DICKSON, JAMES PERRY, WILLIAM BROWN, JOHN LOWRY & SAMUEL SWELLY, 12 Dec 1783; NANCY GLADDEN, widow, Admx. of the estate of RICHARD GLADDEN.

Appraisers: JAMES PERRY, WILLIAM BROWN, JAS DISCSON, SAMUEL SUILEY, sworn, 18 Dec 1783, before JOHN LOWREY, JP.
Appraisement, 17 Dec 1783 by JAMES PERRY, WILLIAM BROWN, JOHN DICKSON.
Purchasers at sale (no date): ANN GLADDAN, REUBEN HARRISON, JEAMES BRIENT, JEAMES PERRY, WM. BROWN.

GLADEN, WM Apt. 27 Pck. 957
William Gladen applied for admn. on the estate of William Gladden, planter, decd., as next of kin, 21 May 1782. Citation read and certified by RALPH JONES, 26th Do(May 1782).
(No other papers in package).

GODFREY, JOHN Apt. 27 Pck. 963
ANNA MARGARET GODFREY applied for admn. on estate of JOHN GODFREY, late of Broad River, Wheel Wright, 26 July 1787.
Citation pub. by JACOB GIBSON SEN, Mg.
Dedimus to JOHN WINN ESQ. to admn. oath to ANNA MARGARET GODFRY, 17 Aug 1787. She took oath, 8 Oct 1787.
Appraisers sworn 8 Oct 1787 beofre JOHN WINN: JAMES EDERINGTON, CHRISTOPHER EDERINGTON, JOSEPH McDANIEL
Bond: ANNA MARGARET GODFREY, AROMANUS LILES & JOHN HILL(X), 8 Oct 1787, before JOHN WINN.
Warrant of appraisement to JAMES ETHERTON, CHRISTOPHER ETHERTON, JOSEPH McDANIEL, JOHN DIE & ELIJAH MEYERS(?), 17 Aug 1787
"Mizez Godfry Charge A Gainst the estate for rideing to Camdon for business done & expence at the burrough 9s 4d 3 days."
Appraisement. 10 Oct 1787.

GOOCH, CLABOURN Apt. 27 Pck 969
WILLIAM BOSTICK applied for admn. on the estate of Clayburn Gouge(sic) as nearest of kin (in right of his wife NANCY BOSTICK), 16 May 1783. Citation read 2 June 1783 in Bullocks Creek Church, by JOSEPH ALEXANDER, V. D. M.
Bond: WILLIAM BOSTICK, admr.; RICHD WINN, sec., before CHARLES BINNICKER, 15 Sept 1783.
Estate appraised 9 Oct 1783, L 188 15 5, by WM HENDLEY, JOHN REED & WM ROGERS, who were sworn by FRAME WOODS, J. P. 9 Oct 1783. WM. BOSTICK married the widow.

GOODALL, WILLIAM Apt. 27 Pck. 972
DANIEL McCLAREN was appointed admr. and bonded, 15 May 1783, sec.: ALEXANDER HENRY, MOSES KEMP. Wit: MINOR WINN.
Citation read 5 May 1783 by JOSEPH CAMP, M. G.
Estate appraised 2 July 1783, by JAMES COLLINS, WILLIAM COPELAND, SAMUEL COBB (C), JAMES BRIDGES, JNO BRIDGES.
Schedule of debts includes: JOHN LOGAN, WILLIAM COPELAND, THOMAS BROTHERS, MOSES KEMP, THOMAS CAMP. Claims: RICHARD WILSON, WIDOW WEAVOUR, ISAAC WRICE, WILLIAM FRAISHAIR, JOHN BRIDGES, JAMES COLLINS, JAMES BRIDGES, WILLIAM COPELAND, SAMUEL COBB, JOHN LOGAN, SAMUEL WRICE.

GOODWYN, FRANCIS Apt. 28 Pck 974
Will of Francis Goodwyn of Camden Destrict...to son JAMES, tract where I now live, to son JOHN WILLIAM, the High Lands upon Cedar Creek, that I Bought of WM HEATLY & the Land adjoining thereto...to two sons before mentioned, all rest of estate to be divided euqally when my Eldest son comes of age...friends Uriah Goodwyn, Andrew Heatly, & Thomas Hweol Exrs., 19 Jan 1785. FRANCIS GOODWYN SEN. Wit: WM HEATLY JUN., JOSEPH DULLES, JOS. McCORD.
Proved by JOSEPH DULLES & WM HEALTY, 21 Feb 1785.
Warrant of appraisement to: ROBERT LYLE, JOHN MOORE, WM GOODWYN, JOHN GOODWYN, JOEL McLEMORE., 6 Aug 1785.
Sworn before TIMY. RIVES, JP, 30 Sept 1785: WM GOODWYN, JOEL McLEMORE, & JOHN MOORE.
Appraised 27 Oct 1785; L 2432 10 5.

GOODWYN, HOWELL Apt. 28 Pck. 975
Will of Howell Goodwyn...estated divided between my two brothers WILLIAM GOODWYN & JOHN GOODWYN & my friend & relation Jesse Goodwyn... brother JOHN & friend JESSE, Exrs., 12 Apr 1785. HOWELL GOODWYN (+), Wit: WADE HAMPTON, MARY HOWARD, RICHD HAMPTON. Inventory made 5 Jan 1786, includes 42 slaves (named). Will proved by WADE HAMPTON, before WILLIAM

MEYER, JP, 21 June 1785.
Dedimus to WILLIAM MYERS or TIMOTHY RIVES to prove will 9 May 1785.
Warrant of appraisement to ROBERT LYALL, JOHN THREEWITS, THOMAS HOWELL,
ETHEL HEATH, LUDWEL EVANS & GREEN RIVES, 26 July 1785. Sworn: ROBERT
LYELL, ETHAL HEATH, LUD. EVANS.

GOODWYN, ROBERT   Apt. 28   Pck. 977
        Will of Robert Goodwyn of Camden District...plantation whereon I
now live to son WILLIAM GOODWYN & Boggy Gully Plantation, & horse Clinton
...the plantation whereon my father Lately lived incluuding the Brick
Chimney tract to son HOWELL GOODWYN & Green Hill plantation....parcels I
purchased of JAMES GILL, RICHARD STROTHER & JOHN MAY to son JOHN GOODWYN
...my Grist Mill on Mill Creek with all lands contingent to sons WILLIAM,
HOWELL, & JOHN...450 A granted to my brother FRANCIS GOODWYN, to him...
400 A on Cedar Creek to my Mother MARTHA GOODWYN...300 A adj. JOHN COOK
& BENJAMIN RAWLINSON to friend PHILIP PEARSON...my Wing Chair to niece
MARTHA-EPPS GOODWYN...L 500 to nephew JESSE GOODWYN...sons WILLIAM, HOWELL,
& JOHN not of age...Brother Francis and friend MALACHI HOWELL, JESSE
GOODWYN & PHILIP PEARSON, Exrs...8 Oct 1777. ROBERT GOODWYN (SEAL), Wit:
HARDY HAY, EPHRAIM REESE, CATY BLANCHARD.
Dedimus to WM MYERS to prove Will, 25 Mar 1785.
Warrant of appraisement to WILLIAM BISHOP, RICHARD EVANS, JOHN THREEWITS,
ROBERT LYAL & THOMAS HOWELL,27 Apr 1785.
Sworn appraisers: WM BISHOP, RICHARD EVINS & THOMAS HOWELL, 22 July 1785,
THOMAS TAYLOR, JP.
Inventory of the Estate of COL. ROBERT GOODWYN, 20 July 1785., L 8244 0 2.

GOODWYN, URIAH   Apt. 28 Pck. 978
        Will of Uriah Goodwyn...to two brothers FRANCIS & WILLIAM, tract
known as Frenchman's Bond, 200 A also all the pine land on the North side
Congaree River...to Brothers and Sisters: FRANCIS GOODWYN, WILLIAM GOODWYN,
KEZIA GOODWYN, AMY GOODWYN & ANGELINA HICKS, all estate (except L 100 to
MARY HAY)...FRANCIS & WILLIAM GOODWYN, Exrs., 30 Jan 1786. U. GOODWYN
(SEAL), Wit: J. MARTIN, JOHN MOORE, WILLIAM HOPKINS. Proved 12 Feb 1786
before WM MEYER, JP by JOHN MOORE & WM HOPKINS, who swore to JAMES MARTIN's
signature.
Dedimus to WM MYERS to adm. Exors oath, 25 Mar 1785.   Swron 3 Apr 1786.
Dedimus to WM MYERE to prove will, 3 Feb 1786.
Appraisers sworn 3 Apr 1786: GREEN RIVES, THOMAS HUTCHINSON & WM HOPKINS.
Appraisement 23 Apr 1786.

GOODWYN, WILLIAM   Apt. 28 Pck 979
        Will of William Goodwyn Senr. of Camden District...to wife MARY,
5 Negroes & to my three sons URIAH GOODWYN, FRANCIS GOODYWN JR. & WILLIAM
GOODWYN...to Eldest daughter ANGELINA HICKS, L 10...to daughter KEZIA
& AMY, 14 negroes...sons URIAH & FRANCIS, Exrs. 17 Oct 1783. Wit: JOSEPH
CULPAPPER, RICH PERDUE (X), MORRIS MOORE.   Proven by RICHARD PURDUE &
MORRIS MORE, 12 June 1784, before WM MEYER.
Dedimus to WM MYER to prove will, 15 May 1784.
Appraisement 9 Aug (no year given), by R. GOODWYN, FRANCIS GOODWYN SR.,
& ROBERT LYELL.

GOODWYN, WILLIAM   Apt. 28 Pck. 980
        JOHN GOODWYN SENR. applied for admn. on estate of WILLIAM GOOD-
WYN, planter, 11 June 1782.
Published in Camden District by me, June 16, 1782, CHRISTIAN THEUS, V. D.
Minister.
Will of William Goodwyn of Camden District...to nephew Jesse Goodwyn, son
of Thomas Goodwyn, negro Jack...to nephew Howell Goodwyn, son of Robert
Goodwyn, 132½ A, 6 negroes (named)...Brother Frances, Exr., 2 Jan 1781.
WILLIAM GOODWYN (SEAL), Wit: WM WILLSON, R. GOODWYN, JOHN GOODWYN JUNER,
DANIEL COLLSON. Prov. by ROBERT GOODWYN, 10 July 1782, before WOOD FURMAN.
Warrant of appraisement to: WILLIAM HOWEL, NATHAN CENTER, DAVID WAISTCOAT,
ROBT LYELL, JOHN BOYD & RICHARD EVANS, 10 July 1782.
Sworn: WILLIAM HOWELL, NATHAN CENTER, ROBERT LYELL, 31 July 1782, before
WM MEYER, Appraisement: 5 Sept 1782.

GORE, JAMES   Apt. 28 Pck. 981
        Will dated 3 Apr 1783, proved 29 Oct 1784...son JOHN ASHFORD GORE,
son JOSHUA FORE, son ELEAZER GORE, two grandsons MICHAEL DOWDEN & DAVIS
GORE. Extx: wife ELIZABETH, Exr. son JAMES...to son in law (not named)...

Wit: GEORGE THOMAS, ELISHA GORE, MICHAEL GORE. Dedimus to JOHN HITCHCOCK.
Estate appraised 9 Dec 1784 by JOHN PRATT, PETER SEALEY, JOHN COLVIN.
Purchasers at sale, 9 Dec 1785: JAMES FORE, JOHN GORE, JOHN TAYLOR, ELIZA-
BETH GORE, JOSHUA FORE, ELEAZER GORE, WILLIAM WATTS.

GOYEN, AMOS   Apt. 28 Pck. 984
    JOHN BYRNS & MARY BYRNS his wife applied for admn, 28 Nov 1786.
Citation published 3 Dec 1786, by RALPH JONES.
Bond: JOHN BRYNES, MARY BRYNES, JOHN TURNER & JAMES JOHNSTON, all of
Fairfield County, 20 Dec 1786.
Letter from JOHN TURNER (not dated) states that he will be security.
Warrant of appraisement to ANDREW WALKER, ROBERT ADAMS, JOHN WAUGH, JOHN
BYRNS, & HENRY RUGELEY, 19 Dec 1786.
Sworn 22 Jan 1787, before JOHN TURNER, JP.: ROBERT ADAMS, JOHN WAUGH,
ANDREW WALKER.

GRAVES, JOHN   Apt. 28 Pck. 999
    Will of John Graves of Craven County...to wife ANN GRAVES, bay
mare, Phenix...to son JAMES GRAVES, land on S side Duchmans Creek...to son
WILLIAM GRAVES, all remaining part of the land where I now live, but ½ to
wife...to son WM, horse worth £ 70, when he becomes 14 years of age...the
negro oweing from RICHD WINN & THOS BAKER...£ 60 in JAMES HARRISONS hands
...to JOHN FORGUSON, sl sterling...to son JOHN GRAVES, sl sterling...to
JOHN SMITH, sl sterling...to daughter LUCEY, sl sterling...RALPH JONES,
WM CASSON & WM GRAVES, Exrs...7 Apr 1780...JOHN GRAVES (SEAL), Wit: RALPH
JONES, JAMES PORTER, WM RODEN. Prov 1 Mar 1784 by RALPH JONES.
Bond: JAMES GRAVES & WM GRAVES, 20 Feb 1784, Wit: JNO HARBIRT.

GRAVES, JOHN JUNR   Apt. 28 Pck. 1000
    Dedimus from WM BURROWS, Ordy of SC to RICHD WYN & BARNABY POPE
to prove will of JOHN GRAVES, 24 Nov 1779. Proved by JAMES GRAVES SR. &
JOHN WITHERSPOON, 4 Jan 1780. RICHARD WINN.
Will of John Graves Junr. of Camden Destrict...to wife ELIZABETH GRAVES,
a third part of my stock and house hold furniture, one negro wench Venice
and land that I now live...to daughter ELIZABETH GRAVES, a tract of
land on the Dutch mans Creek Below where I now live, 100 A and Negro gal
Silvey, 1/3 of stock...to son JOHN GRAVES, negro Taff and 125 A & 1/3 of
stock.-.JOHN WITHERSPOON, JOHN GRAVES SENR & JOHN ARMSTRONG, Exrs...8
Sept 1779. JOHN GRAVES (SEAL), Wit: CANNON CASON, WILLIAM CASON, JOHN
GRAVES SENR.
Warrant of appraisement to RALPH JONES, WILLIAM CASON, HENRY PAGE, MOSES
SMITH & CANNON CASON, 24 Aug 1782. Appraisement: Oct 1782, by RALPH JONES,
WILLIAM CASON & HENRY LAGE (CAGE?).

GRAY, JOHN   Apt. 28 Pck. 997
    FRED. KIMBALL applied for admn. on Estate of JOHN GRAY, 16 June 1783.
20 Aug 1783, Read in a Publick Congregation by me, THOS MIERS, A. M.
Bond: FREDK. KIMBALL & JAMES TOLAN, 5 Sept 1783. Wit: RICHARD WINN.
Fredk. Kimball swears that it is out of his power to find moveable property
belonging to JOHN GRAY, Decd., 9 Dec 1783, before WILLIAM WELSH, JP.

GREER, WM.   Apt. 28 Pck. 1004
    MARY GREER, widow, of WILLIAM GREER of York County, applied ford
letters of admn, 11 Nov 1786. Citation read in Bullocks Creek Church, 26
Nov 1786 by JOSEPH ALEXANDER V. D. M.
Bond: MARY GREER, 4 Jan 1787, sec.: ROBERT McCURDY, WILLIAM CARR, before
JOHN CROW FOSTER, JOHN THOMPSON.
Estate appraise 4 Jan 1787 by WILLIAM CARR, JOHN THOMPSON, & ARTHUR DUDNEY.
Claims against the estate made by ELIZABETH MILLER, Spartanburg County;
JOHN HOPE, WILLIAM SMITH, JAMES GILHAM, REV. JOSEPH ALEXANDER for stipend,
CHARLES WALKER, HUMPHRY BARNETT.

GRIFFEN, JONAS   Apt. 28 Pck. 1008
    Will of Jonas Griffen of Lancaster County, Camden District....
to son BENJAMIN, one negro girl Tener and feather bed and Bolster, 2 sheets
...to son MAJOR, one negro boy Sam and feather bed, bolster, and two sheets
...to son JONAS, all my Land and three Negroes (named)...to grandson
ROBIN GRIFFEN, one Negro girl Winne and bed and two sheets & bolster...to
daughter JENNET BREWTON, negro girl Rose...son JONAS to take care of grandson ROBIN untill he is of age...13 Feb 1786...JONAS GRIFFIN (I) (SEAL),
Wit: THOMAS MIERS, FERGUSON HAILS, SUSANNA HAILE, BENJAMIN HAILE.

Will prved by FERGUSON HAILE, before ISAAC ALEXANDER, JP for Lancaster Co., 15 Mar 1786.
Dedimus to JOHN MARSHALL or prove will, 15 Mar 1786.
Warrant of appraisement not filled out.
Inventory 18 Mar 1786 by Francis Bettes, John Baker (+), & John Rennington (+).

HADDEN, WILLIAM Apt. 29 Pck. 1016
    MARY HADDEN (Widow) applied for admn, 16 Nov 1784.
Nov. 21, 1784. Citation read at Waxhaw Congregation by Robt Finley.
Letters of admn. dated 8 Dec 1784.
Bond: Mary Hadden, James Hadden, John & Robt Lockhart, 8 Dec 1784.
Wit: Joseph Owens.
Warrant of Appraisement: to GEO. DAVISON, ROBERT McCUNE(McKOWN), JNO KENNEDY, JAMES STRAIN, & JAMES CLAIR, 8 Dec 1784.
Appraisers sworn before ANDREW FOSTER, JP, 6 Jan 1785: ROBERT McKOWN, JAS BLAIR, GEORGE DAVISON.
Appraisement 22 Jan 1785, at Ł 72 0 4.

HALL, JOHN Apt. 29 Pck. 1039
    Will of John Hall, 21 March 1783 of Campdon (sic) District...wife and children to live on my plantation until my son Major Temple Hall arrives to the age of 14 years...wife to sell negro Tom if he does not behave himself...daughter Jennet Faris, one heifer...children Margaret, John, William, James, Alexander, Brown, Josiah, Prudence & Major Temple... John Hall (Seal), Prudence Hall (Seal). Wit: John Patteson, James Faries, William Faries. Proven by JOHN PATTESON, 15 July 1784, before JOHN HARBIRT, JP.
Warrant of appraisement to: JAMES SIMRIL, ALEXANDER McWHORTER, WILLIAM BERRY, JOHN EAKIN & JOHN McMICHAEL.
Sworn: JOHN McMIKEL, JAMES SIMEREL & JOHN EAKIN 5 Aug 1784, WILLIAM HILL, JP.
Appraisement, 5 Aug 1784
Buyers at sale 7 Oct 1784: ROBT THOMPSON, GEORGE CUNINGHAM, JOHN PATTESON, JOHN BROWN, JOHN McWHORTER, JOHN McMICHAEL, PRUDENCE HALL, JNO ROBINSON, JAMES BLARE, ALEXANDER FARIS, ABRAHAM McCORKILL, JOHN EAKINS.

HALL, THOMAS Apt. 29 Pck. 1047
    CIBILA HALL applied for admn. on estate of THOMAS HALL, Planter, 13 Nov 1782. Nov. 1-, 1782. Citation published by Ralph Jones.
Bond: CYBILLA HALL, MOSES HOLLIS & JESSE GLADIN, 30 Dec 1782. Wit: RACHEL FURMAN.

HANCOCK, GEORGE Apt. 30 Pck. 1071
    Will of George Hancock Senr of South Carolina...to son Edward Hancock, 1/14 part of my estate...remainder divided between wife Rachel Hancock, son George, and my daughters MARY RAIFORD, JUDITH & ELIZABETH Hancock...son George, Exr. & wife and daughter Mary, Extxs., 22 Dec 1780. Geo: Hancock (Seal0, Wit: THOMAS SANT, MARY SIMMONS (+), JANE SMITH (0). Proven by all three wit., 14 Dec 1781, before BARNY POPE. Proved by Thomas Sant, before Richd Winn, JP, 7 Nov 1782.
Dedimus to Richard & John Wyn to prove will 31 Oct 1782.
[at bottom]: Dr Sir--Inclosed is my fathers Will. it has been provd before Barny Pope but as there was no Didimus from the Ordinary, the probate is invalid...2 Novr 1782 Geo. Hancock.

HAMILTON, WILLIAM Apt. 30 Pck. 1058
    MARY HAMILTON applied for admn, 2 Feb 1784. Citation read at Fishing Creek by Jno. Simpson.
Bond: MARY HAMILTON, admx., JOHN McGLAMERY (X), Sec., 19 Feb 1784 before WILLIAM ANDREWS.
SAMUEL GALEY, WILLIAM McCAMON (X), and JAMES McCAMON sworn as appraisers 27 Feb 1784. Warrant issued to them and DAVID HUNTER.
Estate appraised for Ł 640 9 6, 3 Mar 1784.
Purchasers at sale, 9 Mar 1784: WILLIAM McCAMON, MARY HAMILTON, SAMUEL GALEY, JAMES McCAMON, DANIEL COOK, JEAN HAMILTON, JOHN McGLAMERY.

HARBISON, WILLIAM Apt. 30 Pck. 1072
    ANN HARBISON applied for admn, 9 March 1784. Citation read by Rev. THOS SIMSON.

Bond: ANN HARBISON, Extx, DAVID McCREIGHT, sec., 24 Mar 1784. Wit:
J. HARBIRT, EPHM CULLY.
PHILIP WALKER qualified ANN HARBISON as Extx., 24 May 1784.
Estate appraised by JOSEPH TELFORD, ROBERT JAMIESON & PATRICK HAMILTON,
3 June 1784 at Rocky Creek. Appraisement includes notes by HUGH WHITE,
JAMES CRAFFORD, SAMUEL WILLIAMSON, JOHN CARSON.

HARDEN, HENRY   Apt. 30 Pck. 1073
    ELIZABETH HARDEN applied for admn. 15 July 1783. Citation read
Sunday, 20 July 1783 to a Considerable Audience, Pr. James Fowler,
Camden District. Sandy Run.
Ltrs. of admn, dated 15 Sept 1783.
Warrant of appraisement to JOHN TERRELL, BEN. CARTER, ESWAR HENDERSON,
JAMES GOORE & JOHN SEALEY, 15 Sept 1783.
Sworn 12 Dec 1783 before JOHN HICKCOCK, JP: JOHN SEALY, BENJAMIN CARTER,
& JOHN TERRY.
Appraisement 12 Dec 1783.

HARPER, ROBERT   Apt. 30 Pck. 1075
    JOSEPH LEE, in right of his wife AGNESS as nearest of kin, applied
for admr., 15 May 1783. Citation read at Waxhaws, 7 July 1783, by JOHN
SIMPSON, V. D. M.
Bond: ROBERT HARPER, admr., Nathaniel COUSART, ROBT DUNLAP, sec., 4 Nov
1783, Wit: ROBERT OWENS (X).
Estate appraised by SAMUEL McCLELAN, ALEXR THOMSON, JOHN DUNLAP, 22 Nov
1783, for L 120 11 3.

HARRIS, JAMES MORTIMER Apt. 30 Pck. 1078
    Will of James Mortimer Harris of St. Marks Parish in Camden Dist.,
Planter...all my land in Toccaw Swamp in the following tracts, of JAMES
HIGGS, 150 acres, of JOSEPH BEE, 450 acres, of JAMES HARTIMER HARRIS &
CHARLES HARRIS, 250 acres, of THOMAS EUSTACE, 200 acres, about 1400 acres
with all my Negroes, cattle, etc...debts of Messrs, HYETT & BARCLAY of
Charter House Squre, Merchants in London, L 6000...to WILLIAM CROSLEY of
Bishopgate St., Linnen Draper in London, L 2000...to Capt. WILLIAM COOMBES
SENR. of Rotherith in London, L 1500...to Capt. WILLIAM COOMBES JUNR. in
London, L 2500...to Mr. FRANCIS FAWSON in London, L 1800...to widow
POUPAREL of Smock Alley, Bishopgate St., London, L 600...to ROBERT STORER
of Clarkenwell in London, Watchmaker, L 500...to PHILIP MOORE, Merchant in
Savannah, Ga., L 50...to WILLIAM CLAY of Piccadilly in London, Pencil
maker, L 35...to WILLIAM HASLEWOOD of Philadelphia, coombmaker, L 10...all
sums in SC money...to brother in law THOMAS ROWE, silver Table & Tea
spoons & Tongs & books (named)...to friend Dr. GEORGE CARTER, L 50...to
friend MR. HENRY BEMBRIDGE, L 50...to friend MR. JOHN DAVID MILLER, L 50,
all three in Charles Town...to brother in law THOMAS ROWE of Islington
in London, L 100...to Mr. JOHN GEORGE HARRIS, receiver on the Island
of Guernsey L 7000 SC currency...brother CHARLES HARRIS of Charles Town,
SC...friend SAMUEL LITTLE, Esqr., planter...29 Sept 1780...JAMES MORTIMER
HARRIS (SEAL), Wit: HENRY RICHBOURG, JAMES RICHBOURGH, JOHN RICHBOURGH.
Warrant of appraisement to RICHARD GOWER DENNIS, WILLIAM RANSOM DAVIS,
JAMES DAVIS, JAMES HARPER, JOHN GARNET & JOHN FRIERSON, 16 Feb 1782.
Sworn 28 Mar 1782: WILLIAM RANSOM DAVIS, JAMES DAVIS, JOHN FRIERSON,
before WM HANLIN(?), JP.
Appraisement: 28 Mar 1782.
Notes: on JNO GIBSON, WM MARTIN, JAMES GIBSON, DAVID GARRETT.

HARRISON, EPHRAIM   Apt 30   Pck. 1082
    FREDERICK BELL applied for admn. as greatest Creditor, 13 Dec
1783. Citation read in the Congregation at Camden, Sun., 15 Feb 1784, by
JOHN LOGUE.
Warrant of Appraisement to JAMES GALBREATH, SAMUEL MATHEWS, GEORGE BROWN,
JAMES CANTEY & Z. CANTY & ROBERT REED.   Sworn: SAMUEL MATHIS, ZECK. CANTEY,
& ROBERT REED, 15 May 1784 before J. GALBRAITH, JP.
Warrant prolonged three months from 17 Mar 1784.
Advertisement that sale of estate of EPHRAIM HARRISON & ISAAC HIGGS to be
held at FREDK. BELL, 2 Oct 1784.
Buyers at sale: FREDERICK BELL, THOS NEWMAN & JONATHAN NEWMAN(?), 2 Aug
1784.   Inventory 15 Mar 1784 includes two negroes (named).

HART, JACOB   Apt. 30 Pck. 1084
    WILLIAM MILLER applied for admn. 26 Nov 1784. Citation read at
Fishing Creek, 5 Dec 1784 be JNO SIMPSON.
Bond: WILLIAM MILLER, admr., JOHN ADAMS sec., 16 Dec 1784, before THOS
    BAKER.
SAMUEL HAMILTON, CAPT. JOHN MILLS & DAVID PORTER sworn as appraisers by
PHILIP WALKER, Esqr. Estate appraised 17 Dec 1784 by them, for ₤ 105 4 8.

HAWTHORN, JOHN SENR   Apt. 30 Pck. 1086
    Will of John Hawthorn Senr of South Carolina in Craven County,
11th Sept 1786...to wife ELIZABETH, house & plantation I now live on
during her life & one cow to my grandson JOHN HAWTHORN at her death...
to my daughter MARGRET JOHNSTON, ₤ 2 SC money...to son ADAM HAWTHORN, ₤ 2
SC money...to son JAMES HAWTHORN, ₤ 2 SC money...to son JOHN HAWTHORN,
₤ 2 SC money...to daughter MARY FORBES, ₤ 2 SC money...to sons JOSEPH &
BENJAMIN HAWTHORN, 300 A...to daughter ELIZABETH HAWTHORN, 100 A of land
bought from JAMES OGILVIE...3 sons JAMES, JOHN & ROBERT HAWTHORNE..[not
dated and not wit.]...Prov. by ROBERT BRYNAN & wit. were JOSHUA EDWARDS,
PAUL GARRISON & MARGARET GARRISON., 16 Mar 1784.
Dedimus to JOHN BUCHANAN Esq. to admr. Exr's oath, 10 Apr 1784.
Dedimus to PHILIP PEARSON, to prove will, 16 Mar 1784.
Inventory made 30 Apr 1784.
Also "An Accompt of Receipts for the British" & 1 guinea pd. to ADAM
HAWTHORN.
Will proved by JOSHUA EDWARDS SENR & MARGARET HART, 29 Mar 1784.
Warrant of appraisement to: JOHN CAMERON, THOMAS CAMERON, WM CRAIG,
JAMES CAMERON & JOHN LONG JUNR., 10 Apr 1784. Sworn 24 Apr 1784: JNO
CAMERON, THOMAS CAMERON, & WM CRAIG.

HAY, ELIZABETH   Apt. 30 Pck. 1087
    WILLIAM DORTCH applied for letters of admn. as nearest of kin, 7
April 1783. Citation read 11 Apr 1783, pr RALPH JONES.
Bond: GILBERT GIBSON, WM DORTCH, & ROBERT GOODWYN, 15 May 1783, before
JOHN MARSHEL.
Warrant of appraisement to ROBERT GOODWYN, ROBERT LOYAL, JOHN BOYD, LUD.
EVANS, RICHARD EVANS, 15 May 1783. Sworn 21 May 1783 before WILLIAM
MEYER: ROBT GOODWYN, ROBT LYELL, & LUD EVANS.
Appraisement including 19 negroes (named), 20 May 1783.

HAY, WILLIAM   Apt. 30 Pck. 1088
    Will of WILLIAM HAY of the Congaree in Craven Co., planter, 7 Oct
1782...to son DORTCH HAY, negro Robin...to son HARDY HAY, Negros Carolina,
Rose, Kate & Jude & dwelling house & 20 A I purchased of the late RICHARD
JACKSON decd., on Mill Creek of the Congaree & where I now dwell; to
grandson DAVID HAY, son of DORTCH HAY, Negroe Sal & Colt mare...to grand
son WILLIAM HOWELL HAY, son of HARDY HAY, Negroes (named)...to grandson
JAMES HAY, son of HOWELL HAY, negro (named)...to SARAH BOWERS, widow of
the late HENRY BOWERS decd...sons DORTCH & HARDY, Exrs...WM HAY (SEAL),
Wit: ROBERT LYELL, TAYLOR HOLLOWAY, THOMAS RICKARD
    Inventory & appraisement 31 July 1784. Includes acct. against the
estate of WILLIAM RIVES, Estate of NATHAN CENTER, Estate of HOWELL HAY.
[Another will in the same package slightly different in content]:
to URIAH GOODWYN, 3 negroes (named), dated 12 Apr 1784...WM HAY (SEAL),
Wit: R GOODWYN, FRANCIS GOODWYN SENR., JOHN MOORE. Prov. 7 May 1784
by FRANCIS GOODWYN & JOHN MOORE.
Long statement in questions and answer form about the probate of the will

HAYS, DAVID   Apt. 30 Pck. 1089
    MATHEW TALBERT of the State of North Carolina applied for admn. as
nearest of kin in right of his wife, 17 May 1783. Citation published
25 May, by RALPH JONES.
Letters of admn. dated 26 May 1783.
Warrant of appraisement to JAMES CRAGE, WM KIRKLAND, WM BOYD & WM DORTCH
& JACOB BETHANY, 26 May 1783.
Sworn 16 June 1783 before JAMES CRAIG, J. P.: JACOB BETHANY, WILL DORTCH,
JAMES CRAIG.
Bond: MATHEW TOLBERT, admr., ROLF JONES, MINOR WINN, sec., Wit: NATHL
MARTIN.
Appraisement, 16 June 1783. Sale not dated, no purchasers listed; a
balance due for JOHN ERRIK.

HAY, HOWELL   Apt. 30 Pck. 1090
      LUCY HAY(S) & ROBERT GOODWYN applied for admn. as near[est] of kin, 17 June 1782. Citation published 28 June 1782. CHRISTIAN THEUS, V. D. Minister.
Bond: LUCY HAY(S), ROBERT GOODWYN, Admrs.,FRANCIS GOODWYN & JAMES TAYLOR,
    sec., 10 July 1782, Wit: MARY THRWITS [sic].

HAYS, HOWELL   Apt. 30 Pck 1901
      JESSE GOODWYN applied for admn, 28 Apr 1785. Citation read 1 May 1785 by JOSEPH REES.
Estate appraise 30 July 1785, for ₺ 114 7 2, by RICHARD EVANS, WOOD TUCKER, LUDWELL EVANS.
GILBERT GIBSON and JESSE GOODWYN bonded 9 May 1785 with JACOB BETHANY as security, in presence of MARY OWENS (X).

HEATH (HEETH), THOMAS Apt. 31 Pck. 1097
      ELIZABETH HEATH & FREDERICK HEATH applied for admn. 14 Feb 1784. No citation.
Bond: ELIZABETH HEATH, FREDERICK HEATH admrs., 23 Feb 1784, HICKS CHAP-
    PELL, sec., Wit: LABAN CHAPPELL, ROBERT CHAPPELL.
Dedimus to ROBT GOODWYN 25 Feb 1784, Estate appraise by LABAN CHAPPELL, RICHARD PARDUE (X), RICHARD EVERIT, 23 Mar 1783.
Purchasers at sale, 23 Mar 1784: LABAN CHAPPELL, CONROD MYERS, ROBERT CHAPPELL, HICKS CHAPPELL, PETER DESACHAR, THOMAS JEFFRYS, JOHN EZEL, WILLIAM BREEDLOVE, HENRY RIVES, FREDERICK HEATH.

HENDERSON, NATHANIEL Apt. 31, Pck. 1101
      Dedimus to FRED. KIMBALL to admn. oath to ELISABETH MARLOW, 29 July 1784.
Warrant of appraisement 9 Feb 1784 to: NATHL ROSE(?), JESSE TILMAN, WM HICKLIN, WM MARLOW & JOHN HICKLIN. Swron 6 Jan 1785: WM HICKLIN, WM MARLOW & JOHN HICKLIN.
Appraisement 25 Jan 1785. Sale 25 Jan 1785, no purchasers listed.
Will of NATHANIEL HENDERSON of Craven Co., & Parish of St. Martains, Province of South Carolina...to wife, land where I now dwell...s 1 to be put to my son RICHARD, NATHANIEL, EDWARD JOHN, ANNE, WILSON, TYRE, WILLIAM, PATIANE, ARCHABEL, JAMES being eleven in number,..to my daughter ELIZABETH and son SHEROD, all estate at the decease of my wife...dau. ELIZABETH and son SHEROD Exrs., 15 July 1776. NATHENAL HENDERSON (SEAL), Wit: RICHD BURNETT, BENJ. BURNET, A. BURNETT. Proven by RICH BURNET before WILLIAM WELDON, JP 10 Oct 1782, and again before FREDERICK KIM-
BALL JP 4 Oct 1784.

HERMON, ANDREW Apt. 31 Pck. 1104
      Dedimus to Philip Walker to admn. oath 22 Sept 1784. Oath admrd. 29 Sept 1784.
Will of Andrew Hermon of Rouckie (sic) Creek, 10 Aug 1784...to old[er] son Steven hearmon, half of land, goods and chattels, and to my younger son Robert, the other half...James Peden & Buckner Hegood, sole Exrs...
Andrew Hermon (X), Wit: James Peden, George Stanford, David Ceareal(O).
Prov. 23 Sept by George Stanford.
Warrant of appraisement to Thomas Stanford, James Herbison, John Bayley, Hugh Park, and Andrew Hemphill, 22 Oct 1784.
Purchasers at sale (no date): Alexr Walker, Jas Cloud, Elisalth Carreal, William Stroud, Jas Oyns, Wm Martin, Wm Sandiford, Tho. Stroud, Isbeal Kenge, John Konneld, Thomas Day, Isbel King, John Morries, Jenneat Garton, David Cerall, Edmund Strang, Eillean Willie, Margret Gaston, Bukner Hewood, Mrs. Street, Thomas Gerrot, Phillip Walker, John Carson, Steven Hermon, William Forgison, Thomas McCalla, Ketris Blear, Cristy Strong, Ben Morise, Willem Reves, Willem Sibely, Elisebith Heighs, John Stuert, Robert Mertin, John Ceall, John Bellie, Willem Hakins, John Knox, John Gaston, Peatrick McGerity, John Steel, Thomas McGerity, Thomas Gerreat, Willem Rossel, Frances hennerson, Josof Cinkart, James Harbison, John Coll, John Hikes, John Rondls, George Moris, Thomas Day.

HERON, WILLIAM Apt. 31 Pck 1111
      Mary Heron & Burrel Cook applied for admn, 16 July 1785. Citation read 31 July 1784(sic).
Bond: Mary Heron, Burrel Cook, admrs., John Harbirt, sec., 5 Aug 1785, Wit: William Kirkland. Estate appraised by John Hopkins, Joel McLemore, Thos Jeffrys, for ₺ 354 19 5.

HIGGS, ISAAC Apt. 31 Pck. 1098
    Frederick Bell applied for admn, 17 Mar 1784. Published sitation (sic) in the fork of Lynches Creek, Tuesday ye 6 of April 1784. Joshua Permon, Minister of the Gospel.
Bond: Frederick Bell, admr., Jno Jinnings & John Belton, sec. 13 Apr 1784. Wit: John Gaston.
Warrant of appraisement: to Andrew Debusk, William R. Bell, Umphrey Higgs, Joseph Commander, Peter Debusk, & James Parnel, 13 Apr 1784.
Qualified 21 June 1784: William R. Bell, Humphrey Higgs, James Parnel, by J. Galbraith, JP.
Appraisement 21 June 1784 by W. Rasor Bell, Humpy Higgs, & James Parnal.

HINSON, PHILIP Apt. 31 Pck. 1112
    Dedimus to William Pegues Esqr. of Cheraw District, to qualify Exr. 10 Nov 1784. Qualified John Henson, 20 Nov 1784.
Will of Phillip Hinson of Saint David Parish...to wife Mary, my Manor Plantation, 2 negroes Harry & Judith; at her deceased to be divided among my six sons Benjamin, Bartlett, John, Isham, Obidiah, and Charles Hinson; to my eldest son, Benjamin, negro Patience; to son John, negro Delila; to son Isham, 300 L So. currency; to son Charles, negro Charity; to daughter Kenianna(?), negro boy Jemmey, which she now has; to son Obidiah, all lands including the plantation he now lived on; to grandson William Hinson, s 30; sons Benjamin and John, Exrs., 21 Jan 1777. Phillip Hinson (P); Wit: Thomas Dickson, Stephen Tomkins, Francis Tomkins. Proved in Cheraw Dist., by Thomas Dickson, before Wm Pegues, 20 Nov 1784.
Warrant of Appraisement, 26 Nov 1784 to John King, John Wats, Thomas Gaven, Charles Johnston & John Hollis.
Sworn 10 Dec 1784: John King, John Woods, and Thomas Gaven, before Chas. Pickett, JP.
Appraisement, 10 Dec 1784.
Purchasers at sale, 20 Dec 1784: John Henson, Obadiah Henson, Bartlet Henson, Thomas Gaven, John Hollis Junr., Isaac Gibson, Charles Graham, Nathan Sanders, Henry Sanders, Charles Pickett, John Lewis. Balance due from Jeremiah Jagars, John Chasnut.

HOLLEY, JOHN Apt. 32 Pck. 1138
    Thomas Parrott Senior of Fairfield County, applied for admn. 26 Apr 1787. Citation read Sunday, 5 May 1787, Jacob Gibson, M. G.
Bond: Thomas Parrot, Sr., admr., Jno Gregg, Thos Parrot, Jr., sec., 18 May 1787.
Warrant of appraisement: 18 May 1787 to John Ogilvie, James Davis, Samuel Proctor, William Nelson, Charnal Durham.
Appraisement 27 July 1787 by James Davis, Saml Proctor, Wm Nelson. Prov. 7 Aug 1787 before J. Pearson, JP. Sale 27 July (no buyers listed).

HOLLIDAY, DANIEL Apt 31 Pck. 1120
    (only one document in package)
Account of Sales of the Estate of Daniel Holladay, deceas'd of St. Mark's Parish, Craven Co., 6 Jan 1785. Purchasers: Isaac Brunson, Charles Brunson, Elliott Holladay, Daniel Holladay, John Polladay, Will: Holladay, Benjn. Holladay, Peter Brunson, Miss Letty Holladay, Capt. Hill, John Barden, Robt. Lewis, Willm Brasey, Thomas Gibs. Total L 1399 5 3½.

HOLLIS, NOTTLEY Apt 32 Pck. 1144
    John Hollis applied for admn, 19 Mar 1782.
Citation pub. 24 March by Ralph Jones.
Bond: John Hollis, admr; Moses Hollis, Daniel Going, sec., 7 May 1782.
Warrant of appraisement to: Moses Knighton, Charles Lewis, John King, Charles Picket and Thomas Stone, 7 May 1782. Sworn 17 May 1782, before Charles Pickett, JP: Moses Knighton, Charles Lewis, John King. Appraisement made 17 May 1782.
Purchasers at sale (no date): Moses Hollis, Stasey Hollis, John Hollis, Worner Lewis, John Havis, Charles Picket, John Glading, Wm Lewis, Isaac Grimes, Michl Gibbins, John Watts, Luke Bissip, Charles Johnson, James Grimes, James Hollis Jr., Daniel Goyen, Richd Glading.

HOPE, JOHN Apt. 32 Pck 1153
    Charles McGinney, planter, in right of his wife Ann McGinney, widow of John Hope, decd., planter, applied for admn, 21 Dec 1781. Citation read at John Moore's Mill, 13 Jan 1782, by Joshua Palmer.

Appraisers sworn 20 Apr 1783: John Wheeler, John Moore & David Nelson. Appraised estate for ₤ 3184.
Bond: Charles McGinney, admr. William Wright, James McCormick, sec., 12 Feb 1782.

HOPKINS, DAVID   Apt. 32 Pck. 1152
John Hopkins, planter, of Congaree River, applied for admn. as nearest of kin, 28 Oct 1786. Citation read by Joseph Rees, 1 Nov 1786. Roling Williamson entered a caveat against granting letters of admn. to John Hopkins, 16 Nov 1786. Rolling Williamson and wife Alcey applied for admn, 1 June 1784. Bond: Roling and Alcey Williamson, admrs., 10 June 1784, Robert Goodwyn, sec. Test: WM Meyer, JP
Uriah Goodwyn, Robert Lyell & Wood Tucker appraised estate 2 Aug 1784, for ₤ 54 10 0.
Articles of agreement between Roling and Alcey Williamson and Henry Hampton, ordy. 15 June 1784, to promote the interest of the intestate's sons's in his father's estate, and that Col. Thomas Taylor, Major Robert Lyell and Col. Robert Goodwyn be appointed to judge whether this is done. Test: Jno Harbirt.

HOWARD, SARAH   Apt 33 Pck 1185
Thomas Wright and John Wright applied for admn, 12 Dec 1785, citation published by Lewis Collins, 1 Jan 1786.
On 23 Jan 1786, William Wright, Asberry Sylvester, and William Dinkins swore that Sarah Howard made no will, before Wm Murrell, JP.
Bond: Thomas Wright, William Wright, Heli Howard, Asbury Silvester, William Dinkins, & John Wright, 2 Jan 1786.
Warrant of appraisement, 2 Jan 1786, to William Barden, Leonard Powell, John Millet, Archibald Henson & John Denny. Sworn before Wm Murrel, 23 Jan 1786; William Barden, Leonard Powell, John Denny. Inventory made 24 Jan 1786.
Sale, 15 Feb 1786, purchasers: Heli Howard, Wm Wright, A. Sylvester, Wm Dinkins, John Wright, Wm Murrell, James Howard, Thomas Bradford, A. Henson, Alexr Smart, Robert Lewis, A. Gibhart, David Gilbert, Leond. Powell.

HOWELL, MALACHI   Apt. 33 Pck. 1186
Martha Epps Howell, widow, applied for admn. as next of kin, 5 Apr 1782. Read citation in my congregation, 13 Apr 1782. Joshua Palmer. Bond: Martha Epps Howel & Thomas Howell, 2 May 1782.
Inventory of Malachi Howell, late of the Congarees, by Robert Goodwyn, William Howell & William Boykin, 20 July 1782. ₤ 14904 2 -.
Sale by Wade Hampton, in right of his wife, Martha Epps, 7 & 8 Jan 1783: Wade Hampton bought entire estate, (negroes in estate sale named).

HOWELL, WILLIAM   Apt. 33 Pck 1188
Will dated 20 June 1776, proved by John Boyd (no date)...names wife Lucy; eldest son Thomas, 150 A on which my mother lived known as Fwell's Ferry; daughter Grace Howell; sons Thomas,William, Malachi, James. Exor: Friends Grace Russell, John Taylor, James Taylor, James Taylor, Malachi Howell, Thomas Taylor, Nathan Center & sons Thomas Howell & William Howell. Wit: John Boyd, Henry Smith, James Leviston (X).
N. B. "as I have not time to now draw my will and had a son born since named Robert..." Wit: Joseph Tatum, James Leviston. Estate appraised by Thos Hutchinson, Richard Evans, Wm Bishop, 26 Feb 1784 at ₤ 9033 15 4½.
Dedimus to qualify James Taylor, admr. 13 Jan 1784.

HUDSON, LODWICK   Apt. 33 Pck. 1192
James Hudson applied for admn as nearest of kin, 14 Aug 1783. Citation read by Lewis Collins, 24 Aug 1783.
Dedimus to Isaac Alexander to admn. oath to James Hudson, 8 June 1783. Oath adm. 4 July 1786.
Bond: James Hudson, Nathl Pace & David Neilson, 8 June 1786.
Charles McGinney, Nathl Miller, Douglas Stark, sworn appraisers 4 July 1786.
James Hudson applied for admn. again 7 Apr 1786. Citation published 22 Apr 1786 by Lewis Collins.
Samuel Hudson applied for admn. 1 May 1783. Citation published 10 May 1786 by Ralph Jones.
Bond: Samuel Hudson & Jos. Kimball, 10 May 1784. Warrant of appraisement

to Charles McGinney, Douglass Stark, Nathl Miller, Israel Mathis, & George Pee, 8 June 1786.
Appraisement 2 Aug 1786, including negroes named. ↳ 66 1 0.

HUEY, HERCULES Apt. 33 Pck. 1193
Dedimus to Robert Montgomery to prove will. Proved 5 Aug 1785.
Will of Arculeas Hughey...to wife Cattren Hughey and my six Childer(sic) Alexander, John, James, and Arculeas, Mary and Eleasebth(sic), all my Real and Personal Estates Shear and Shear a Like Except one Cow to my son and Daughter Abrham(sic) and Margret Adams...my wife to live on the plantation together that I now live upon on Cain Creek until they come of age and if Eleasebth should die before they come of age their Peart of the land is to go to the Rest...and if my son Alexander Comes from Inland and what money he Brings with him or Goods of my Property he is to Deliver them up to the Executors or he is to have no Peart of my Estate...wife Cattren Hughes Sol Executor and John Crage to Joyn her and see Justise Dun...26 Sept 1775...Hercules Hughey (Seal) Wit: John Walkr, David Morray, Andrew Walker.
Appraisers sworn 1 Sept 1785: John Coffey, Abraham Adams and John Huey. Appraisement not dated.

HUGHES, JOSIAH Apt 33 Pck 1198
Elizabeth Hughes, widow of decd., applied for admn as next of kin (no date). Citation read 19 May 1782 at Fishing Creek by John Simpson. Bond: Elizabeth Hughes, admx. Francis Henderson (X), Patrick McGarrity (X), sec., 4 June 1782. Philip Walker, JP, Wit.
Appraisers sworn 5 June 1782: John Adams, John Kell and John Wear (Wier) by Philip Walker, JP. Estate appraised at Francis Henderson's of Rocky Creek in Craven County, St. Marks Parish & Camden District, July ye 23d 1782, for ↳ 285 13 0. Sale at Elizabeth Hughes 17 July 1782 and 27 Dec 1782. (purchasers not listed).

HUNT, JOSEPH Apt 34 Pck. 1213
Samuel Simmons applied for admn, 24 Feb 1784. Citation published by Jacob Gibson, M. G. 7 Mar 1784. Bond: Samuel Simmons, John Harbirt, 15 Mar Warrant of appraisement: to Barnaby Pope, John Brent, Thomas Harbirt, James Beard, George Ashford.
Sworn: John Brent, Thomas Harbirt, James Beard, 22 May 1784, before John Harbirt, JP. Inventory made 12 June 1784.

HUNTER, HENRY Apt. 34 Pck. 1215
Will of Henry Hunter, 19 Mar 1783...wife Fanney, plantation where I now live & negroes (named)...to my two sons Henry and Henry Starke Hunter residue of estate when my eldest son becomes 21, they paying to my mother Sarah Hunter, ↳ 8 sterling pr year...if they die, to be divided among my 4 sisters children...plantation on N side of Roaneoak(sic) River in North Carolina, to be sold and divided among my four nephews: Henry Hunter, son of my sister Elizabeth Thomas; Caffield, son of my sister Mary; Henry Hunter, son of my Brother Thomas Hunter, and Henry Turner, son of my sister Sarah Hunter, except 20 guineas to buy my nephew Archibald Hunter a horse...friend John Chesnut & sons Henry & Henry Starke Hunter, Exrs...
H Hunter. Wit: Robert Weston, John Starke, Elizabeth Peay(+), John Belton. No proving date.
Inventory 4 June 1785: (includes negroes named), by Douglas Starke, John Belton, Josiah Scott.

HUSTON, WILLIAM Apt. 34 Pck. 1217
Eleanor Huston, widow, applied for admn 15 Nov 1784. Citation read at Sharon Meeting House on Fishing Creek, 15 Nov 784 by Wm Martin, minister.
Bond: Eleanor Huston (X), admx., and William Ferguson, and Abraham Ferguson, admrs, 1 Dec 1784, Wit: Wm Wiley, Andrew Stephenson.
Estate appraised by William Wylie, Andrew Stephenson, John Ferguson, 11 Jan 1785, for ↳ 14 2 9. Sale bill for ↳ 13 9 3.

JACKSON, AMBROSE Apt. 35 Pck. 1231
Robert Howell applied for admn, on estate of Ambrose Jackson, late of the Congarees, as a principal creditor, 8 Apr 1786. Citation read "at the meeting of my congregation in the forks" by John Logue, 9 Apr 1786. Endorsed "Read at Camden."

Bond: Robert Howell, Admr., Arthur Howell, Green Rives, sec., 15 July 1786, Wit: Mary Pearson, Allbright Everit.
Green Rives, Arthur Howell, John Bryson, Isaac Raiford, and John Hamilton, appointed Appraisers; Estate appraised by Green Rives, Arthur Howell and John Bryson, Ł 33 17 2.

JENKINS, RICHARD   Apt. 35   Pck. 1252
John Mobberly applied for admn. on estate of Richard Jenkins(it is said adm. was granted to Catherine, the widow, who intermarried wtih James Matthews and died) as near[est] of kin, 14 Aug 1782.
Citation was "Read on 25 August to a considerable Congregation on Sandy [River]" by Jas. Fowler, V. D. M. Citation was read on Aug. 17th by Jacob Gibson also.
Bond: John Mobberly, admr., William Mobberly and Henry Rogers, sec., 10 Sept 1782, before Josiah Furman.
Estate appraised 4 Nov 1782, for Ł 1347 8 0, by Jeremiah Davis, Ambrose Nix and Peter Sealey, who were sworn by David Hopkin, JP.

JENKINS, THOMAS WILLIAM   Apt. 35   Pck. 1253
Will of Thomas William Jenkins of St. Mark's Parish, son of William Jenkins, Malster and Storekeeper of the Town of Usk in the County of Monmouth, South Wales, and nephew to Walter Jenkins, Esqr., High Sheriff for the City of Bristol in England, 6 Aug 1786...daughter Susannah,wife of James Corbett...good friend Richard Richardson; children: Mary Jenkins, now in London; Anne Jenkins, Elizabeth Jenkins, Sarah Jenkins, Caroline Jenkins...Exor: Friend Richard Richardson and daughter Elizabeth Jenkins; Wit: Richd Newman, Beny Corbett, Thomas Richard Davis. Proved in Lancaster County by Thomas Richard Davis, before Isaac Alexander (no date).
Articles of agreement made in Clarendon County, 22 Nov 1786 (unsigned) by Ann, Elizabeth, Sarah and Carolina Jenkins to include their sister Susannah Corbett for an equal share.
Dedimus issue 24 Oct 1786 to qualify the wit. Elizabeth Jenkins qualified as Extx, 16 Mar 1787.
Estate appraised 23 Apr 1782 for Ł 1196 2 10½, by Patrick Brock, Thomas Maples, and Wm Little, who were sworn 8 Mar 1782.

JOHNSTON, JOHN   Apt. 35   Pck. 1271
Archibald Steel and William Davison applied for admn, 15 Nov 1784; Citation was read by John Murphy"in the Congregation where the within mentioned John Johnston, deceased Lived" 22 Nov 1784, per W. Bratton, JP.
Bond: Archibald Steel, William Davis, admr., John Anderson, James Greer, sec., 22 Nov 1784. Test: W. Bratton, JP.
Estate appraised by Robt Patton, John Anderson and James Greer, 10 Dec 1784 for Ł 143 1 7.

JOHNSON, NEAL   Apt. 35   Pck. 1265
Henry Peebles applied for admn. as a particular friend, 11 Oct 1785. Citation was read 25 Oct 1785, at Flat Creek by Joseph Ferguson. Thomas Frizzel (X) entered caveat against granting letters of admn. to Henry Peeples, 21 Oct 1785. Blank undated admrs. bond singed by Thomas Frizzel (X), Sarah Deeson, Fredk Kimbrall, Francis Bettis. The widow married _____ Deeson. Neal Johnson died 22 Mar 1781.
Return shows payment to Benjamin Deason, Susannah and Lawed Johnson and three children (not named).
Appraisers sworn: John Baker, John Kennington, Gace Frizzle Senr., Benjamin Ladd, Senr. Value Ł 1227 13 6 or Ł 175 7 7½ sterling.
Purchasers at sale, 13 Feb 1786: Gaal Frizzle Senr, Benjamin Deason, Frederick Kimball, Benj. Ladd Senr, Benj. Burnett, Ben Haile.

JONES, JOHN   Apt. 36   Pck. 1291
Will dated 21 Jan 1779, prov. 5 Aug 1782...daughter Judy Jones (under 18). Exor: friends Capt. Robt Lyell and Lieut. Malachi Howell. Wit: Winney Meyer & Wm Meyer. John Jones was a carpenter. Estate appraised 13 Sept 1782 by Robert Goodwyn, William Howell, and Richard Evans.
Warrant of appraisement was issue to the three appraised and Richard Evans, John Boyd and Wood Tucker.

KELL, MATTHEW   Apt. 37   Pck. 1319
Bond: James Kell, admr. John McClenahan, Sec., 4 May 1784.
Schedule of debts due the deceased from James Bigham, William Rea, John McCullaam, Archibald Kell, James Kell, and debts owed by deceased to

Andrew Stevenson, John Rogers, John Delap, John Bell, and William Rea.
Estate appraised 3 Aug 1784, by John Kell, Thomas Garret, and Thomas Morton.
John Hunter and Robert Rainey appraised a horse lost while in the service
of the state under Genl. Sumter, before Jas. Knox, JP, 3 June 1783.

KELLEY, JAMES   Apt. 37 Pck. 1323
    Will of James Kelley dated 30 Jan.1779; prov 9 Apr 1785...daughter
Arabella Cantey, two sons James Junr and Samuel; wife Arabella...Wit:
David Thorn, Sophia Thorn (X), Elizabeth Skipper (X).
Bond: Samuel Kelley, admr. 16 Dec 1783, John Boykin, William Harrison, sec.,
Wit: William Whitaker, Junr. & Ralph Jones.
Estate appraised 2 Apr 1784 for L 511 5 8 by Francis Boykin, James Cantey,
Arthur B. Ross.

KELLY, JOHN Apt. 37 Pck. 1325
    Jane Kelley and James Kelley applied for admn, 23 Jan 1784. Citation read by James Fowler, V D M, 25 Jan 1784.
Bond: Jane Kelley and James Kelly, 30 Jan 1784, admrs.
Joseph Brown qualified Jane and James Kelly, 3 Feb 1784.
Estate appraised 6 Feb 1784 by James Fowler, Andrew Lathem and John McKnight.
Warrant of appraisement issued to appraisers above and Thomas Clendennum
and George King.
Estate appraised at L 245 14 6.
Purchasers at sale, Jan 1784: Jane Kelley, William Kelly, Rebecca Kelly,
James Kelly, Mary Kelly, Andrew Leathem, Elijah Kelly, John Walker,
Godfrey Adams, James Brown, James Mitchell.

KENNEDY, JAMES   Apt. 37 Pck. 1338
    Will dated 29 June 1779; prov: 1 Nov 1782...wife Ann, daughter
Margaret Kennedy, son William; brother Gilbert. Ex: father Felix Kennedy,
wife Ann, and brothers John Kennedy and John Davies. Wit: Andw Boyd,
Hugh Rogers, Jas. McCullock.
Dedimus to Robert Patton, JP to qualify wit. and exrs. 4 Sept 1782.
Estate appraised by John Arnel Pender, James Blair, and Robert Patton, 2
Nov 1782, for L 757 12 6. John Forster and Robert Thomspon were also
listed on warrant of appraisement.

KENNEY, JOHN   Apt. 37 Pck. 1345
    (only one document in package)
    William Gouyen applied for admn, 7 July 1787. Citation read at
the place of worship on Swift Creek, 10 July 1787. Richard Furman.

KERSHAW, WILLIAM   Apt. 37 Pck. 1363
    Samuel Mathis applied for admn, 18 Apr 1786. Citation read to a
publick Congregation in Camden, 23 Apr 1786. Beverly Allen.
Bond: Samuel Mathis and John Adamson, 22 June 1786.
Book Accounts of William Kershaw deceased: Joseph Legare, Sarah Kershaw,
John Wyly, Robert Reid, Samuel Breed, Duncan McRa, Kershaw, McRa & Co.,
Duncan McRa & Co., John Jones, John Woodward, Ann Cusack, Richard Cole,
Moses Murphy, Daniel O Quin, James Crocker, Guthridge Lions, John Smith
Junr., Brick Johnston, Mr. Simms, William Rea & Co., John Speed, Samuel
Gaunt, William Ellerby, Ethelred Clary, Christopher Gewin, William Hatcher,
James Duncan, Zebulon Gaunt, Michael Crawford, John Cook, William Riddell,
Henry Rugelly, Frederick Brigs, Moses & Mines, Ann Windsor, John Furman,
McKinnie's Plantation, Robert White, Ely Kershaw's Estate, William LeConte,
Thomas Wade, Elizabeth Dupree, William Boykin, William Tomlinson, Ebenezer
Bagnall, Philip Platt, Morton Brailsford, James Brown, John Adamson, Capt.
_____ Booker, Robert Morris, Arthur B. Ross, David Rush, Austin & Moore,
Kershaw & Riddell, Heylegar & Benners, Negro Leah, John Marshall, Samuel
Midwood, Mrs. Bartlam, George Melcom McGregory, Edward Clark, Jolly
Batchelor, Joseph Willingham, William Mason, James Sinclair, Isham Moore,
Joshua Hargreaves, Daniel Huger, Alexander & Brownfield, John McCord,
Richard Winn, Doty Brown & Brisbane, George Brown, John Thompson, Daniel
Lundey, Richard Farr, William Cammeron, James Scott & Co., Samuel Doty,
Negroe Digo, James Allison, Hane & Birk, George Wade, James Bohannan,
Conrod Shum, King Street Store, Boat Ranger, Francis Bremar, Alexander
Porter, Thomas Stewart, John McCambridge, Charles Cogdell, Isaac Doty,
John Lahaffe, John Belton Junr., Boat Batchelor in Co., Samuel Mathias &
Co., John Milhouse, Taylors & Rea, Mackie & Potts, John C: Martin, Thomas
Aikins, Daniel Bourdeaux, Mrs. E. Davis, Arthur Honeywood, Junk Foskey,

Richard Whitaker, Robert Mylis, John Compty, James Cook, John Burton, William Gilbert.
I do hereby certify that the above is a true list of Debts & credits taken from the Books of William Kershaw deceased. Saml Mathis administrator. Camden 31st March 1787.
Appraisement 31 Mar 1787 includes ½ of right of Boat Jolly Batchelor, other ½ belongs to George Wade.
  at Ranger.
Returns for 1789, 1790, and 1791 in package.
Sale 1786 & 1787, purchasers: Christr. Williams, John Smith, Saml Mathis, Richard King, Francis Wolf, John Harker, Thomas Brown.

KIMBALL, BENJAMIN   Apt. 38 Pck. 1366
    Will of Benjamin Kimball Senor...son Charles to have negro Peter; to son John, plantation he now lives on; to son Fredk Kimball, negroes (named); to Daughter Mary Roberson, boy Essex; to daughter Lucy Burnet; girl Beck; to daughter Elizabeth O'Bannon, ₤ 250 SC money; to daughter Fanny Robe.son, negro George; for son Benja. Kimball's five youngest children, negroes (named) and the plantation he lately from (sic)...Fredk Kimball and William McDonald, Exrs., 18 Apr 1781, Benj. Kimball (H) (Seal) Wit: Jas Kennedy, Thos Thomson, Proved by Maj. Thomas Thomson 28 Sept 1782, before Robt Patton.
Letter from Charles Cotesworth Pinckney, 30 Apr 1785, taking the oath of Maj. Thomas Thomson.
Sworn before John Marshal, JP for Lancaster County, 4 Feb 1786.
Fredk Kimball sworn 8 May 1786.
Warrant of appraisement, 15 Apr 1786, to William Welch, Jacob Gray, Sherrod Gray, Edward Narramore, and William Jones.

KING, FRANCIS   Apt. 38 Pck. 1367
    Thomas King, "living at a place called Bullocks Creek", applied for admn, 10 Nov 1781. Citation read 20 Nov 1781 at Bullock Creek by Jos. Alexander, V. D. M.
Bond: Thomas King, admr., Abraham Smith and John Smith, sec., 25 Jan 1782; Wit: Richard Furman.
Accounts current: Richard Foster, William Car, William Byers, Joseph Camp, Newbury Stockton, Abraham Barron, John Ross, Henry Smith.
Estate appraised by Abraham Smith, John Smith and Samuel Denton, 11 Feb 1782, for ₤ 2657 4 6.
Purchasers at sale, 22 Feb 1782: William Smith, Henry Neal, Henry Smith, Joseph Brown, Abraham Smith, John Smith, Thomas Gilham, John Burd, Gabriel Pickens, James Dervin [Darwin], James Brown, William Steen, Jas. Powel, Thomas King, John Patrick, Peter Akins, Hannah King, Judah King, Samuel Denton, Abraham Smith.

KING, JOHN   Apt. 38 Pck. 1368
    Will of John King of the Town of Camden, 8 Aug 1779 (No prov. date); wife Priscilla; children Elizabeth, John, Joseph, George, Ann, and Sarah King. Exor: Joseph Kershaw Esqr & wife Priscilla. Wit: Thomas Jones, Jams. Brown, Reason Nelson.
Dedimus to John Galbraith, JP 17 Dec 1783 to qualify Joseph Kershaw as Exr

KING, MICHAEL   Apt 38   Pck. 1369
    Will of Michael King of North Carolina in Bertie County...wife Isbell King, five Negroes (named) and horses, cattle, etc; to Each of my children 3 sows and pigs, when they come of age; to wife one gold ring and to my son Michael after her death; to son Michael, negroes (named), and land I bought of Richard Byrd; to son Henry King, 2 negroes (named), 225 A, my manor plantation; to daughter Catherine King, negro (named); to daughter Esbelle King, negro (named); to daughter Penelope King, negro (named); to daughter Mary King, negroe (named); wife and Coll. Robert West and his son Robt West, exrs., 20 May 1741. Michael King (Seal), Test: Roger Snell, Jno Hill, J. Hollbrook.   Oct 29, 1741. John Hill proved will before J. Montgomery, JP;Copy sent.J Glasgow, Secretary.
Proved in Fairfield County, SC before John Turner, JP by John King Jr., 2 Apr 1787.

KING, NATHANIEL   Apt 38 Pck. 1370
    Will dated 8 May 1785; prov. 5 Dec 1785. Thomas Flowers, Lucia Flowers, brother and sister in Great Britain and Petter Guerrey Senrs. children which he had by Hannah King, late his wife of S. C.; friend

David Tateman of S. C., Exor: Daniel Tateman, Petter Guerrey Senr & Legrand Guerrey. Wit: Jacob Geiger, Lewis Speikerman, Ann Tateman.

KING, ROBERT   Apt. 38 Pck. 1371
       Henry King applied for admn as next of kin, 24 April 1782.
Citation read at Fishing Creek, 12 May 1782 by John Simpson, V. D. M.
Bond: Henry King, admr., Frederick Kimball, William Robinson, sec, 24 July 1782.
Warrant of appraisement to George Wade, Middleton McDaniel, William Beard, Jesse Tillman, Rolley Cornelius, and William Marlow. Sworn 28 Sept 1782 before Robert Patton: George Wade, Rolly Cornelius. Estate appraised 17 Oct 1782 by George Wade, Roley Cornelius and William Baird, for ₤ 241 10 0.

KINSLER, HERMAN   Apt. 38 Pck. 1373
       Christian Kinsler applied for admn as nearest of kin, 9 Apr 1783.
Citation published by Ralph Jones. Bond: Christian Kinsler, admr. Timothy Kerving(?), Rd. Goodwin, sec.
Warrant of appraisement to John Gegar, John Reamer, Michael Church, Jacob Buckman, 15 May 1783.
Appraisers sworn 5 June 1783: Michael Church, John Ramer, and John Giger. Inventory not dated.
Purchasers at sale: Mecal Church, William Kerthland, James Ogelve, John Hemiter, Elizabeth Kinsler, Felix Turnipsead, Briant Riley, Jacob Gradock, Harman Kinsler, John Turnipsead, Jacob Cradock, Mary Kinsler, Christian Kinsler, William Bel, Peter McGrew, Solomon Lee, Thomas Hunter, Godfrey Cromer, John Murph, Benjamin Evant, James Beard, James Nipper, James Merphy, Barny. Pope. (no date).

KIRKPATRICK, JAMES   Apt. 38 Pck. 1393
       Will of James Kirkpatrick of York County, 10 Mar 1786, prov. 14 Nov 1786, before Joseph Brown; son Robert, 200 A on which I live with reversion to Robert's wife Rebecca; son Francis; daughter Ann; son Samuel; son William's four youngest children; son Thomas's four youngest sons; daughter Agness' two youngest children; son James's four youngest children; son John's four youngest children; daughter Jane's four youngest children; ₤ 5 11 0 due from John Watsons estate; son Robert's children; daughter Agnes; son Francis; grandson Robert Kirkpatrick. Son Francis and son Robert, Exrs., Wit: Jas. Love, Rebekah Kirkpatrick, Esther Gaston(X).
Appraisers appoint 23 Nov 1786: William Gaston, Alexander Tomb, Charles Gilmore, George Dickey, and James Hillhouse. Estate appraised 28 Dec 1786 for ₤ 123 7 8 by Wm Gaston, Alexr Tomb, Charles Gillmore.

KIRKPATRICK, THOMAS   Apt. 38 Pck. 1394
       John Kirkpatrick and Margaret Kirkpatrick applied for admn 27 Feb 1782. Citation read at Bullocks Creek Church, 4 Mar 1782, by Joseph Alexander, V. D. M.
James Love, William Gaston, and Joseph Feemster sworn as appraisers 25 Nov 1782, by Joseph Brison, JP and estate appraised 25 Mar 1782 at ₤ 1140 15 0. Estate sold 26 Mar 1782, for ₤ 1857 0 6.

KITCHEN, CHARLES   Apt. 38 Pck. 1396
       Letters testamentary to Jane Kitchen, 5 Oct 1771 " Rec. Book G, page 489" (Charleston Records).
Copy of will sent from Secretary's office: (recorded in Charleston Records). Will of Charles Kitchen of the County of Craven...to wife Jane Kitchen, 100 A to include the Plantation whereon I now Live, to begin at the lower corner of my land and to lie on the South side of Rockey Creek, and Negro man Bass, woman Judy; in case of her death or marriage, to descend to my son Ely Kitchen; to William Kitchen (Alias William Summerford My Son by Jane Summerford), 200 A, part of the tract where I now live, on N side Rocky Creek, and Negro man Sharper and one Rifle gun; to son Zachariah Kitchen, 150 A at the upper end of the tract I now live on, and negro man Arch and one Smooth bor'd Gun inlaid with Brass...to daughter Priscilla Kitchen, negro Girl Beck...to son John Kitchen, Negro Boy Harry; to son James Kitchen, negro Girl Rose; to daughter Ann Kitchen, negro Girl Grace; to son Charles Kitchen, negro Phillis; & in case my wife shall be now with Child, to sd. Child Negro Lucy; if not, sd. Lucy to my daughter Mary Mackey; to my dau. Mary Mackey, ₤ 200 and 1000 lbs. weight of Hemp...wife Jane Kitchen and Friend John Winn Esquire, Extx & Exor, 14 May 1771...Charles Kitchen (Seal), Wit: Thomas Garret (T), Hannah Garrot, William McKinney (N).

Received _____ 1784 ot Thomas Gather Exr. (in right of his wife Jane Gather), the Legacys of Charles Kitchings and Ely Kitchings as guardian... John Ratton (R). Wit: Jno Harbirt.

KITCHEN, JAMES Apt. 38 Pck. 1397
(only one document in package)
Before John Harbirt, appeared Sarah Dye who swore that in the year 1779 John Kitchen and James Kitchens (a short time before the said Kitchens's were going on a tower (sic) of Militia Duty) that she heard James Kitchens say that if he should die while in Camp that his Brother John should have all his Estate in possession of Thomas Gather...Sarah Dye (+). Sworn 11 Oct 1784.

KNIGHT, WILLIAM Apt. 38 Pck. 1398
Letters of admn to William Collins, 23 Oct 1783.
Bond: William Collins (W), and Samuel Lindsey, 23 Oct 1783, Wit: James Winn.
A Brown Ross, David Jones and Zach Collins, sworn appraisers 16 Dec 1783. Appraisement 15 Jan 1784.

KNOX, JAMES Apt. 38 Pck. 1401
Janet Knox bonded as admx. 21 Feb 1785, Robert Miller, sec. Citation read at Fishing Creek, 13 Feb 1784, by John Simpson. Estate appraised 22 Feb 1785 by John Porter, Peter Eoff, Robert Knox, for ₤ 33 14 4.

LADENHAM, WM Apt. 39 Pck. 1404
Bond: William Smiley (Smyley), 3 Jan 1785, admr., Sameul Bell and William Addison,sec., before J. Harbirt.

LAND, JAMES Apt. 39 Pck. 1427
John Kitchen for him and wife applied for admn, 26 Apr 1782. Citation read at Rocky Creek 14 May 1782, by John Simpson, V D M. Bond: John Kitchen admr, William Gladen (X), John Dye (X), sec., 25 May 1782.
Warrant of appraisement to William Gladden, John Dye, Richard Gather, James Machie and Edmund Stange, 21 May 1782. Estate appraised for ₤ 169 15 0, by Edmund Strange, Richard Gather, Wm Gladdin.

LAND, JOHN Apt. 39 Pck. 1405
James Owens applied for admn, as nearest of kin in right of his wife, 24 Feb 1784,; Citation read March 14, 1784 by Ralph Jones.
Purchasers at sale: Littleton Isbell, Thos. Stroud, James Owens, Marv Land, Thomas Garret, James Peden, Elliner Land, Thomas Morris, Benjamin Owens, Daniel Green, Edmund Strange, Andrew Hemphill, Thomas Land, Thomas Dye.

LeCONTE, William Apt. 39 Pck. 1429
Francis Boykin was granted letters of admn on the estate of William LeConte, late of Claremont County, 10 Dec 1788. (No other papers in file.)
[N. B. William LeConte, evidently son of above, left Camden District owing about ₤ 120, and moved to Georgia. His sons John and Joseph, noted scientists and founders of the University of California, were born in Liberty County, Ga.]

LEE, JOHN Apt. 39 Pck. 1436
Will of John Lee, farmer of Little River, Fairfield County, 16 Nov 1786; prov. 20 Apr 1787. Wife Mary; son Stephen; daughter Elizabeth, wife of William Marchel; daughter Sarah; daughter Agness; son John; daughter Rachel; son Francis; daughter Rosana; daughter Rebecca. Ex. son John Lee and son in law Alexander Gordon, Wit: Stafford Curry, James Turner, Benjamin Halsell. Dedimus to John Turner, JP 7 Apr 1787 to qualify wit.

LITTLEJOHN, SAMUEL Apt. 40 Pck. 1455
Thomas May and Mrs. Jemima Pope made oath 28 June 1787 that they signed as wit. the will of Samuel Littlejohn about 27 or 28 March 1787, before James Craig, JP of Fairfield County. No will in file. Dedimus to James Craig 17 May 1787 to qualify wit.
Warrant of appraisement 28 May 1787 (not filled out completely)...John Robertson, Exor of Samuel Littlejohn. No appraisement in file.

LIVINGSTON, JAMES Apt. 40 Pck. 1457
        Will of James Livingston, 10 Dec 1784, prov. 7 Jan 1786.
Brother Duncan Livingston; friend William Scott; natural daughter of my
deceased sister Elizabeth Livingston by the name of Lucy (under age);
James Livingston (X), Wit: Abiah Croft, T. Hutchinson.
Dedimus to Isaac Alexander, JP to qualify wit. 6 Jan 1786.
Warrant of appraisement 7 Jan 1786 to Thomas Williams, Daniel Ford, Abiah
Croft, Joel Adams and Reuben House. Dedimus 7 Jan 1786 to qualify Duncan
Livingston and William Scott as Exors and Daniel Ford, Abiah Croft and
Reuben House as appraisers; all qualified 21 Jan 1786.
Appraisement by Daniel Ford, Abiah Croft and Reuben House, L 746 14 9.

LOVE, ROBERT Apt 41 Pck. 1475
        Mary Love applied for admn, and citation was read at Bullocks Creek
9 June 1784, by Joseph Alexander, V. D. M., but he lost her application.
Bond: Mary Love, admx, Clayton Rogers, sec., 4 June 1784, Wit: Richard
Sadler and Mathew Rogers (X).
Inventory by Clayton Rogers, Thomas Robbins and Stewart Brown, 10 Aug 1784.
Book accounts: Robert Tindall, James Hamilton, Andrew Woods, John Anderson,

LOVE, ROBERT Apt. 41 Pck. 1476
        Will of·Robert Love of Craven County, Camden District...to son in
law Robert Barnet, stone horse & gelding; to grandson Robert Barnet, 100 A
on Moris Creek adj. Ruben Harrison; to daughter Maglen Love, 100 A I now
live on; to Mary Love, daughter of Jacob Love, one heifer; friend John
Witherspoon and Isaac Love, Exrs; 19 Jan 1779...Robert Love (LS), Wit:
John Burns, Dennis Burns (?), John Aldridg (,). Prov. by John Burns, 10
Oct 1779 before Joseph Mickle, JP.
Appraisers sworn 10 Nov 1779: Nicholas Peay, James Harrison, Wm Harrison.
Warrant of appraisement dated 22 Jan 1779.
Inventory 19 Nov 1779, L 36520 00 00.

McCALLUM, HENRY Apt. 47 Pck. 1663
        Will of Henry McCallum, planter, 17 Feb 1778, prov. 23 Nov 1782;
eldest son John; son Henry; daughter Jean Watson; daughter Sarah Mobly;
wife Ann, tract where he lived during her natural life; son James, home
tract at my wife's decease; Ex: Wife Ann and son James; Henry McCollom (X)
(Seal); Wit: Joseph Attaway, John Allen Tharp, Jesse Tharp (X).

McCLENDON, DENNIS Apt 48 Pck. 1684
        John Stone, in right of his wife Martha Stone, applied for admn
18 Mar 1784. Citation pub. 17 Apr 1784 by Lewis Collins.
Warrant of appraisement to William Spivey, David Robinson, Charles Price,
John cook and William Dampio. Sworn 16 July 1784, before Roger Wilson,
JP; William Spivey, David Robinson, Charles Price.
Bond: John Stone (X), admr., Burl. Boykin, sec., Wit: Jno Harbirt.
Estate inv. 16 July 1784, for L 300 1 0.

McCLURE, JOHN Apt. 48 Pck. 1689
        James and Hugh McClure applied for admn, 31 July 1785. Citation
read 7 Aug 1785 at Indian Land Meeting House by Jno Simpson.
Bond: James and Hugh McClure, admr., Edwd Martin sec, 11 Aug 1785.
Estate appraised by James Wylie, Hugh Gaston, Edwd Martin, James McClure,
for L 100 0 0.
Property in hands of Mary McClure, Senr, Mary McClure Junr., Hugh Gaston,
Margaret McClure, Hugh McClure, 22 Apr 1786.
[N. B. Capt. John McClure died of wounds received at the battle of
 Hanging Rock, 6 Aug 1780]

McCorkle, WILLIAM Apt. 48 Pck. 1697
        Will of William McCorkle of Bever Creek on North east side of
Wateree River, 12 July 1779; prov. 1 Jan 1785; "to be buried at the
Meeting House." sons James, William, Robert (all minors), wife (not named);
daughters Jean and Elizabeth; Exor: Brother Andrew McCorkle and brother in
law John Willson...William McCorkle (Seal), Wit: Jas. Bredin, D. S.,
William Nutt, Alexander Archer.
Robert Hood applied for letters of admn, 24 July 1787. Citation read 5 Aug
1787 in Waxhaw Congregation, Lancaster County, SC by Robert Findly.

McCOY, SAMUEL   Apt. 48 Pck. 1705
          Citation was issued out of Ordinary's Office, 3 Dec 1785 at the
instance of Frederick Bell for admn, and citation was never returned.
Jesse McCoy applied for admn, 24 June 1786, as nearest of kin.
Citaiton read 2 July 1786 by Thos Reese in his Church.
Bond: John Armstrong, admr, Robert Reid, Benjamin Carter, sec., 14 July
1786, before Henry Rugeley and James Elliott.

McCRARY, ADAM   Apt. 48 Pck. 1707
          Bond: Simeon Cameron (X), admr., James Cameron, Joseph Cameron,
sec., 13 Sept 1783, before Francis Pringle.
Purchasers at sale, 10 Nov 1783: Thomas Sant, Alexr Robinson Junr., James
Cameron, John Doyle, Alexr Roseborough, John Gray, Benjamin Caves, Margaret Robinson, Andrew Cameron, Hugh Milling, Total sale L 29 14 2.

McCURDY, JOHN   Apt. 48 Pck. 1709
          Bond: Robert McCurdy admn, William Maccadoo (McDow)(McAdou), sec.,
26 Jan 1782 and John Gardner, sec., before Richard Furman.

McDILL, NATHANIEL   Apt. 48 Pck. 1710
          Will of Nathaniel McDill of Wateree Creek, 24 Sept 1783, prov.
16 Apr 1785. Wife Mearey(sic), and seven children (not named)...Ex:
William Boyd and James Pedin, and overseers Thomas McDill and James Mane...
Nathal McDillill(sic) (Seal), Wit: David Carns, Hugh Smith, Wm. Boyd.

McDONALD, JAMES   Apt. 49 Pck. 1717
          Dedimus to John Dickey to prov. will & admn oath, 10 Feb 1787.
Prov. 15 Feb 1787 by Dr. Alexander Pruvis.
Will of James Mcdonald...to three sons John, Daniel and James, two tracts
of High land, 500 A and two tracts of River Swamp, 600 A; to wife Rachel
negores (named) and grey horse I purchased of John Lawson; my seven children: John, Daniel, James, Binkey, Sarah, Mary Dorathy, and Rachel and in
case my wife be pregnant, an equal share to the child...brother Archibald
McDonald and friend Hezekiah Maham, Philip Williams, Exrs., 12 Jan 1780.
James McDonald (Seal), Wit: Alexr Purvis, Wm Buford, John McDonald (?).
proved before Jno Dickey, JP for Geo. Town District, 15 Feb 1787.
Rachel McDonald, James Davis and Frederick Lessesne applied for admn with
the will annexed 10 Feb 1787. Citation published at Santee Meeting house
18 Feb 1787 by John Hudleson, M.
Sworn appraisers 18 Feb 1787: Saml Bennet, William Montgomery, and Jno
Gambell.
Bond: Rachel McDonald, Frederick Lesesne, James Daivs, admrs., and Archd.
McDonald, and John Gambell, sec, 18 Apr 1787.
Appraisement, St. Mark's Parish, Camden Dist., 18 Apr 1787, L 2549 13 9.

McGOWAN, JOSEPH   Apt. 49 Pck. 1740
          Dedimus Post. to John Cantey Esqr to qualify Lydia McGowen, John
Andrew and William McGowen, admrs. on est. of Joseph McGowen, 17 March
1784. Sworn 30 Mar 1784.

McGOWAN, MARY   Apt. 49 Pck. 1741
          William McGowen, Lydia McGowen and John Andrews applied for admn,
27 Feb 1784; citation read 1 Mar 1784 by Ralph Jones.
Dedimus to John Cantey to qualify them, 16 Mar 1784.
Bond: Wm McGowen, Lydia McGowen, admrs., 30 Mar 1784, (no sec.)
Warrant of appraisement to Samuel Little, William Little, James Davis,
John Frierston, Alexr Cokely and James McCauley, 16 Mar 1784.
Estate appriased by Alexdr. Colclough, Capt. J. Davis, and James McCauley,
30 Mar 1784, for L 283 17 0.

McGRAW, EDWARD   Apt. 49 Pck. 1742
          Will of Edward McGraw, 10 Jan 1781, prov. 3 Feb 1784... all my
former children viz. James McGraw, William McGraw, Edward McGraw, Arthur
and Enoch McGraw, decd., Sarah Sharpton and Mary Wrandor have formerly recd
their Legacies; son John McGraw, Elizabeth McGraw, Obedience Lucy Martha
Patience McGraw; Jacob McGraw, son Reuben McGraw; son Benjamin McGraw;
my children Priscilla, Janet, Dorcas, and Solomon McGraw, wife Ainay
McGraw...Edwd M'Graw (x) (Seal), Wit: Jacob Gibson, Jesse Fort.

McGREW, ALEXANDER Apt. 49 Pck. 1744
        Margaret McGrew, widow of Alexr McGrew late of Congarees, planter,
applied for admn, 5 Mar 1787. Citation read 11 March 1787 by Joseph Rees.
Bond: Margaret McGrew (X), admx., William M'Grew, Benjamin Everit, sec.,
4 Apr 1787, before Rich. Hampton.
Estate appraised at Congarees, 12 Apr 1787 by David Westcott, William
Taylor, Benjamin Everit, for ₤ 294 1 2.

McGrew, MARGARET Apt. 49 Pck. 1745
        Alexander McGrew applied for admn of Margaret McGrew, late of
Camden District, widow, 12 Feb 1786.
Alexander McGrew made oath that the citation was published in two different
assemblies of people, 2 Feb 1786, before I. Alexander, JP.
Dedimus to Thomas Taylor to admn administrators oath, 2 Feb 1786. Sworn
12 Feb 1786.
Bond: Alexander McGrew, John Surginal, and Mathew Howell, all of Congaree
River, planters, 2 Feb 1786.
Warrant of appraisement: 2 Feb 1786, to David Wescote, John Surginal,
Mathew Howell, Wm McGrew, Benjamin Evrit.
Inventory 16 Feb 1786 by David Westcott, John Surginer, Matthew Howell.

McLENNAN, ANDREW Apt. 50 Pck. 1771
        William Makee (McKee) and Charles Barber applied for letters of
admn, 24 Nov 1781. Citation published by Joshua Palmer, 21 Dec 1781.
Bond: William MacKee, Wm McGill, 9 May 1782, Wit: Samuel Timmons (?).
Warrant of appraisement to: Patrick Muckfadyen, Thomas Craton, Walter
Thopshire, Hugh Beard, Peter Torley, William Twaddle. Appraisement 6
June 1782, by all five appraisers.

McMEEN, THOMAS Apt. 50 Pck. 1787
        Elizabeth McMaan applied for admn as next of kin, 13 Dec 1782.
Citation read in Fishing Creek Congregation 27 Dec 1782, by Robt. Mc-
Clintock.
Bond: Elizabeth McMaan(X), admx., James Thomson, Robert Dunlap, sec., be-
fore James Simpson, JP.
Appraisement 11 Feb [1783] by Joseph McMeen, Robt Dunlap, James Thomson,
for ₤ 646 8 0.

McNEESE, JOHN Apt. 51 Pck. 1799
        Will of John McNees of Creven County...to wife Mary, ___ in gold;
to my daughter Marget Rogers, one geney & also to my daughter Jean Mertin
one geney, to my daughter _____ Waldrop, one geney, and to my daughter
____ Armstrong one geney, to son James McNise, one giney, to Mary Young,
wife of Hugh Young, one giney; to my daughter Mary McLaclen, one geny,
also my daughter Ann Rogers; friends Adam McCool Exr, 27 Nov 1779, John
McNees (Seal), Wit: James Johnston, Adam McCool,Jean McCool.
South Carolina, Ninety Six District: Proven by all three wit, 1 March
1780 before Thos Brandon JP, Wm Kaneday (Kennedy) JP.
Inventory ₤ 2987 19 0. Produced a Deed for 300 acres of Land in
Charlotte County, Va., ____ said John McNease by Francis Forguson, then
Governor, dated 1767. 1 March 1780, John Love, Richd Brandon, Hezekiah
Love.

MARION, JOHN Apt. 43 Pck. 1504
        Samuel Ervin applied for letters of admn with the will annexed, 1
May 1785. Citation read by Th. McCaule, V. D. M., 15 May 1785.
[For additional information, see my Probate Records of South Carolina, Vol
II--Letters of Admn, Vol. K]
Will of John Marion of Craven County, ST. Mark's Parish, to son John, my
Gun & Couterments (sic), one case of Razors, Shoe & Knee Buckles...to son
Nathaniel Wickam Marion, gold rin, Buckles; to son John and Nathaniel
Wickham Marion, household and kitchen furniture; to daughter Martha Wickam
Marion, 7 negroes (named) and teaspoons, etc; to Miss Jane Logue, a Riding
Horse; ₤ 17,000 due me by Wade Hampton; my oldest daughter Mary Roberts
and her two children; friend Mauris Simons, and son John, Exrs...John
Marion (Seal), Wit: Saml Logue, Maruice Simons made oath to the signature
of John Marion & Saml Logue is now also dead, 26 Mar 1784.

MARKEL, JOHN Apt. 43 Pck. 1505
        Paul Smith applied for admn, 6 Sept 1784; citation read 26 Sept
1784 in Congregation in Camden, by John Logue, D. M. V.(sic).

Bond: Paul Schmidt, admr, Hugh McDowell, Joseph Buckley, William Wyly, sec., 1 Oct 1784, Wit: Jno Harbirt, J. Galbraith.

MARTIN, JAMES   Apt. 43 Pck. 1530
Will of James Martin of Wattaree...to son William and John 400 A upon Little River; the plantation which I now occupy, divided among my sons James and Andrew; to daughter Jane, negro Dolley...wife and four sons... Capt. Hugh Smith, Thos Johnston, and David Carnes, Exrs., 19 Sept 1781... James Martin (Seal), Wit: Joseph Milligan, Robert Leavender, Saml McKee. Codicil made 29 Sept 1782...see to John Milling, two negroes and pay Mr. Robert Holt Levinder a Resonable price for his expenses, Wit: W M Bell, Robert Leavender.
Proven in Abbeville County, 9 Jan 1786, by Joseph Milligan before Pat Calhoun, JP
Dedimus to John Winn Esq. or James Craig, Esq. to prove codicil, 20 Dec 1785.
6 Mar 1785, took oath of Wm Bell saying that James Martin was not of sound mind when he made the codicil, James Craig, JP Fairfield County.

MARTIN, NICHOLAS   Apt. 43 Pck. 1532
John Jones of Peedee applied for admn, 22 Nov 1785. "This sitation has bin properly published by me in the Desrick of Camden. February 15, 1786 Hartwell Hull"

MARTIN, WILLIAM   Apt. 43 Pck. 1537
Rebecca Martin, Isaac Bagnal and Samuel Montgomery applied as friends for admn, 23 Dec 1785,; citation published in the Church of Williamsburg, 25 Dec, by S. Kennedy, V. D. M.
Bond: Rebecca Martin, Isaac Bagnal, and Samuel Montgomery, admrs., Ebenezer Bagnal, sec., 13 Jan 1786.
Estate appraised by Jno. Gambell, Arthur White, and Ebenezer Bagnall, 21 Jan 1786, for ₤ 481 14 10.

MARTIN, BENJAMIN Apt. 43 Pck. 1527
Francis Bottace applied for admn, 5 Mar 1784. Citation read by Rev. Thos Simson.
Bond: Francis Bettis, Lewis Faile, and Jacob Grös(?) (German signature), 24 Mar 1784.

MILES, THOMAS   Apt. 44 Pck. 1570
Isaac Knighton applied for admn, 21 June 1782.
Published by Ralph Jones, June ye 30th.
Bond: Isaac Knighton; admx, Moses Knighton and John King, sec., 18 July 1782.
Appraisement 1 Aug 1782 by Moses Knighten, John King, John Byrd. Purchasers at sale (no date),: Isaac Knighten, Thomas Knighten, Michael Gibbins, Michal Byrd, Charles Lewis, Sarah Knighten, Micajah Pickett, Charles Pickett, Leah Tidwell, William Miller, James Hollis, Alex. Knighten, Charles Johnson, Moses Knighten, John Byrd.

MILLER, SAMUEL   Apt. 45 Pck. 1577
Will of Samuel Miller [which begins abruptly]...100 head of breeding cattle, 2 Negroes, 4 horses, to son Morris Miller, to be taken care of by Luke Mann, Josiah & James Powell, till he is 21, the income to be spent in schooling...to Miller White Morris, daughter of my friend Thomas Morris, negro, cattle...residue of my estate to wife Mary and three children Mary, Ann and Morris; land and grants as may be run in Georgia, jointly to my wife and children...wife Mary, Lyman Hall, Josiah Powel, Samuel Burnley, and Thomas Morris, Exrs...Peter Manleys three sons to be schooled ...Capt. Morris, Stroud, ₤ 100...Samuel Miller, 26 Nov 1781, Wit: Samuel Boykin, William Brummett, John Boykin. Prov. 12 Jan 1782 by Wm Brummett.

MILLWEE, WILLIAM   Apt. 45 Pck. 1581
Will of William Millwee, 26 Sept 1784; prov. 28 Nov 1784..."to be decently buried at Deep Creek" by my Brother and "the man that makes my coffin to have a guineay for his trouble" and also to John Brown, ₤ 5 as a debt...to John McMullin, Sarah McMullin, and Agness McMullin, ₤ 225 and lands equally divided amongst them; 2 years after my death John Millwee, James Millwee and William Milwee may have ₤ 10 each; to Mary Ridgell, ₤ 30...to Robert Ridgell, saddle and wearing aperill; to Elizabeth Gamble,

Ł 30 and my chest; to Jean Gamble, Ł 1 s 7; to Robert Gamble Junr, Ł 10...
if anything is left out of my Publick Indents, William Ridgill,Junr may
have it; to John Rafeilds sons Ł 14; to Elizabeth Gamble Senr, Ł 7...to
Jean Rafeild Senr, Bible and spectacles; to Jean Rafeidl Junr, bed and
bedclothes...John, Sarah and Agness shall prove themselves to be children
of James McMullin and Mary Ervin before they can enjoy their portions...
John Ridgill and Elizabeth Gamble Junr, Exrs., 26 Sept 1784...William
Millwee (Seal), Wit: Richard Ridgill, Mary Ridgill (X), John Ridgill.
Prov. by Richard Ridgill 20 Nov 1784.
Dedimus to William Martin JP to admn oath, 16 Nov 1784.
Warrant of appraisement 13 Nov 1784 to Robert Crawford, John Rafeidl,
Saml Reily, William Richburg, John Gibson.
Appraisement 1 Dec 1784: Robt Crawford, John Rafeild, Saml Reily.

MIXON, WILLIAM   Apt. 45 Pck. 1592
    Will of William Mixon of St. Marks Parish, ___ Jan 1778 (1773?)...
to my son George the Plantation and tract of Land whereon I now live...to
my daughter Prudence, a cow and calf; to daughter Elizabeth a Feather Bed
a Chest, a Dish or bason and a Plat, a Box Iron and one Cow and Calf; to
my daughter Frances, a Linnen wheel; to daughter Sabra a Bed and Bedstead,
a pewter Dish or Bason and a Plat, one Large looking Glass and the newest
of the Linnen wheels, and cow and calf...to grandson Elijah Dixon, the
dee plates, one Feather Bed, Cow and calf and bay mare...William Mixson
(W) (Seal), Wit: Denis McLendon, Samul Ratcliff, William McClendon.
Prov. 13 Jany 1783 by Jesse Barber who swore that he was well acquainted
with Denis McLendon (who is now deceased) and William McClendon (who is
now supposed to be gone with the British) and their handwriting and that
the other Witness Samuel Ratcliff is Defunct.

MOODY, HUMPHREY   Apt. 45 Pck. 1602
    Louisa Moody applied for admn as next of kin 5 Nov 1782. Citation
was published in Congregation, 10 Nov 1782. Timothy Dargan.
Bond: Louisa Moody (X), Admx, Hampton Sullavent and Elias Dubose, Senr,
sec., 13 Nov 1782. Wit: Eliaz Dubose Junr, Margaret Dubose.
Warrant of appraisement: to John Huggins, Samuel Chandler, Thos Chandler,
Jonathan Newman, John Hixon, 20 Jan 1783.
Sworn by Roger Wilson JP: John Huggins, Samuel Chandler, Thomas Chandler.
Appraisement 18 Mar 1783, Ł 382 12 6.

Moody, Slomon   Apt. 45 Pck. 1605
    Will of Slo(w)mon Mooday of the county and parish of St. Marks...
to Mary Moody, one Inglish shilling and likewise to Burril Moody; to son
Slomon, one horse coult, and to wife, remainder...20 July 1781...Slomon
Moode Senr (+), Slomon Moody Junr ()X, Heli Howard. Prov. by Heli
Howard 17 May 1782.

MOORE, ISRAEL   Apt. 45 Pck. 1611
    Will of Israel Moore Senr of Singleton's Creek, on the North east
side of Watree River in Camden District, 10 Apr 1780...to son Samuel Moor,
100 A he now lives on, part of my 300 A on Singletons Creek; to son Israel
Moore, s 10; to the heirs of my late Daughter Elizabeth Kimbal; to my
daughter Jane McCullough, to daughter Christian(sic) Marshall; to my daughter Agnes Beard; to my daughter Elinor Moor, the sorrel mare with cattle
and sheep; to wife, two Milch cows, etc; to son John Moor, remainder of
200 A; heirs of my son Saml Moor; Israel Moore (Seal), Wit: Jas Breedin,
Mary Bredin Sen (X), Mary Bredin. Prov. 17 Aug 1782 by James Breedin.

MOORE, JAMES   Apt. 45 Pck. 1612
    Thomas Moore bonded as admr, 16 Aug 1786 with Francis Watson,
Robert Watson sec. Test: David Hopkins, William Allen Burton, Thomas
Jenkins.

MOORE, JOHN   Apt. 45 Pck. 1613
    Will of John Moore 9 July 1781, prov. 23 Aug 1781...Brother Sam
Moore, all real and personal estate...John Moore (Seal), Wit: David Leech,
Isaac Ball. "This will not in proper form"
Samuel Moore applied for admn, 22 July 1782. Citation read 28 July 1782
by John Simpson, V. D. M.
Bond: Samuel Moore, admr, Isaac Ball, James Mitchel, sec., 20 Aug 1782,
before Saml Rainey and Adam Williamson. James Mitchel, James Moore, and
William Adair sworn as appraisers 20 Aug 1782 by William Bratton, JP.

MOORE, LAZARUS Apt. 46 Pck. 1616
    Sarah Moore applied for admn as nearest of kin, 7 May 1783.
Citation pub. 25 May by Ralph Jones.
Bond: Sarah Moore, Henry Wimpey, 14 May 1783.

MORRIS, ROBERT Apt. 46 Pck. 1622
    John Arnold Bender [Pender] applied for admn on estate of Robert Morris, late of Fishing Creek, 6 June 1786. Citation read in Waxhaw Congregation, 11 June 1786. Robert Findly.

MOTHERSHEAD, PETER Apt. 46 Pck. 1632
    John Jet Mothershead applied for admn, 15 Aug 1782. Citation read in "Wax-Haw Congregation" on 2 Sept 1782 by Fras. Cummins, Preacher.
Bond: John Jet Mothershead, Francis Mothershead and William McGarragh, 10 Sept 1782. Wit: Sherd James Jr(?).
Warrant of appraisement to Wm McGarragh, Henry Mucklevein, Thos Glaze, Aaron Prescot, and Henry King, 10 Sept 1782. Sworn 9 Nov 1782, Thos Glaze, Aaton Prescot, and Henry King.
Inventory 9 Nov 1782, including one negro boy (not named).

MOTTE, DAVID Apt 46 Pck. 1639
    Agnes Motte applied for admn as nearst of kin, 8 Sept 1785.
Citation read in Winnsborough Congregation 9 Oct 1785. Robt McClintock.
Bond: agnes Motte (X), James Brown, 11 Oct 1785. Wit: J. Harbirt.

MYERS, CHRISTOPHER Apt. 46 Pck. 1650
    John Marshall applied for admn as greatest creditor, 18 Apr 1783.
Citation was read in publick Congregation, 23 Apr 1783. A. Marshall, V D M.
Bond: John Marshall, admr., Geo: Dunlap and William Deason, sec., 15 May 1783, Wit: Richd Winn.
Warrant of appraisement to William Welch, Josiah Cantee and Col. Kimball & James Kelly, 15 May 1783.
Appraisement 5 June 1783, in cludes two negroes (named), ₤ 100, by Josiah. Cantey, Col. Kimball and James Kelly, sworn before Wm Welch, JP

NANCE, PETER Apt. 52 Pck. 1819
    Will of Peter Nance, 13 Feb 1780; prov. 16 May 1783. Sons William and John, 400 A on Rock y Creek to be equally divided; wife Elizaebth, my temporal estate; daus.Eliz.Mary Ann Nance, Pattie Tims, Sally Cloyd Nance, Johannah Nance and Ellinor Nance; sons Peter and Richard, s 5 sterling.
Exors Brother in law Philip Sanders and son William. Wit: Amos Tims, Joseph Tims, Thomas Humphries. Inventory by John Terry, Benjamin Carter, James Gore.
Bond: Elizabeth Nance, admx, 15 May 1783, Joseph Tims, Eleazar Gore, sec.
Wit: Noah Martin.
Schedule of accounts includes: Daniel McDaniel, Hester Sanders, John Stokes, Robert Henderson, Hollis Tims.
In file is an order from the Court of Common Pleas, Chester Dist., Augt. term 1822, case of James Martin vs Hugh Simpson, for Ordinary of Camden Dist. to deliver the original will of Peter Nance to Hugh Simpson on his giving sufficient security. Bond signed by Francis S. Lee, 2 Oct 1822.

NEELY, WILLIAM Apt. 52 Pck. 1822
    Will of William Neely, 10 Oct 1778, Wife Mary; son Samuel, son William; daughters Elizabeth, Mary and Catharine; John Miller of Ninety Six District to make deed to my brother-in-law John Anderson of 200 acres where he now lives, Ex: wife Mary and James Miller, Wit: William Smith, John Scott, and Samuel Neely.
Mary Neely and James Miller applied for admn, 16 Nov 1779. Citation read at Fishing Creek, 16 Jan 1780 by John Simpson, V. D. M.

NEELY, WILLIAM Apt. 52 Pck. 1823
    Jane Walker applied for admn as nearest of kin, 11 Apr 1783. Citation read at Fishing Creek, 13 Apr 1783 by John Simpson, V. D. M.
Bond: Jane Walker (X), admx, Philip Walker, John Walker sec, 15 May 1783, Wit: William Elliott.

NEWTON, JANE Apt. 52 Pck. 1846
    Will of Jeane Newton; to daughter Mary Colclough, negroes (named); to grandson John Bosher, mulatto Bob; grandson Thomas Bosher; four grandchildren (not named); to Mary Bosher, To Sarah Bosher; Exrs: John Bosher,

Alexr Colcough, John Cantey, 30 Jan 1783, Jean Newton (X) Wit: Peter Nephew, James Harper, Salley Winsley.
Dedimus to William Martin to admn oath, 9 Nov 1784. James Harper proved will 12 Dec 1784.
Warrant of appraisement 12 Dec 1784: to Robert Dingle, James Harper, James Printer.
Appraisement 6 Jan 1785.

OWEN, THOMAS Apt. 54 Pck. 1885
    Will of Thomas Owen of Craven County...37 A in Peters Township, Cumberland County, Pennsylvania, for the use of the Baptist Society; 250 A I now live on to wife Abigail Owen; son Samuel Owen; Children (not named); 3 Oct 1781...Thos Owen (Seal), Wit: Jonathan Lewelling, James Hawthorn (X), Phil. Pearson.
Dedimus to John Pearson to admn oath 30 Apr 1787. Prov. by Philip Pearson, in Fairfield County 10 May 1787.

PEARY (PERRY), BENJAMIN Apt. 56 Pck. 1958
        (Two wills in package)
Will of Benjamin Perry of South Carolina; wife Mary, negroes (named) & then to my two youngest daughters Wineford and Elizabeth,; son Zadock Peary, negro (named); sons Zadock and Rigdon, 300 A; son Benjamin Peary, negro Robert & 300 A; three grandchildren Peary Hodes, Alcey Rodes, and Henry Rodes, negro Venue when he becomes 21 years old; to daughter Sarah Peary, negro (named); each of my girls Mary Peary, Sarah Peary, Wineford Peary, and Elizabeth Peary, each at the age of 15 to have a horse; 23 Mar 1779...Wit: Jeremiah Burge, John Rains Burge, George Peay.

Will of Benjamin Perry of South Carolina; to wife Sarah, negro Peter, and then to son Zadock, all that tract he lives on up the river as far as lick Creek that I bought of William Simpson; to son Benjamin Perry, remainder of tract I bought of William Simpson and three negroes (named); to daughter Mary Cotes, two negroes (named); to daughter Sarah Perry, three negroes (named); for Alse Roades, my granddaughter,; to son Zadock and Benjamin my new survey...8 Oct 1789, Benjamin Perry (Seal), Wit: James Perry, Elizabeth Benson, Esther Duke.
A true copy, certified by Elir. Alexander, Clerk of Lancaster County Court, (No prov. date for either will).

PEGAN (PAGAN), ALEXANDER Apt. 56 Pck. 1943
        Will of Alexander Pegan of Fishing Creek, planter, 1 June 1778, prov. 20 Oct 1783; wife Janet, now pregnant, daughter Agness, brothers James and Archibald; Exors uncle Robert Gill and uncle John Mills, Wit: John Latta, Robert Cooper, John Linn, Citation on estate of Alexander Pagan read at Fishing Creek, 27 July 1783 by John Simpson, V. D. M.
Estate of Capt. Alexr Pagan appraised 18 Nov 1783 by Hugh Whiteside, John Walter (T), and Samuel Kelsey, at ₤ 261 8 6.

PERKINS, LEWIS Apt. 56 Pck. 1954
    Lydia Perkins applied for admn, as next of kin, 9 Nov 1782.
Citation "Published in a Congration(sic) at Mr. Hortons on Hanging Rock, Sunday November ye 24, 1782" by Joshua Palmer.
Bond: Lydia Perkins, Richard Middleton, and William Williams, 13 Dec 1782.
Warrant of appraisement to: John Marshall, David Perkins, John Watts, Thos Watts, James Marshall, and Lovel Rochel, 13 Dec 1782.
Sworn 12 Feb 1783: James Marshall, David Perkins, and John Wats, before Andrew Baskin Esq.
Inventory 12 Feb 1783, includes negroes (named), ₤ 1757 8 9.
Sale 6 Mar 1783 (no purchasers listed).

PERRY, JACOB Apt. 56 Pck. 1961
    Will of Jacob Perry of Craven County; my Lawfull married wife Judith Perry, plantation where I now live; at her death to youngest son Lewis Perry, to daughter Patience Perry; to daughter Ruth Watts; to daughter Mary Wilson; to grandchild Sarah Watts; to son Jesse Perry; Robert Duke and Lamuel Perry, my son, Exrs...Jacob Perry (Seal), Wit: George Watts, Henry Neal (E). Prvo. 5 June 1784 by Geo: Watts.

PERRY, SILAS Apt. 56 Pck. 1973
    Esther Perry, widow applied for admn as next of kin, 14 Aug 1782.
Certified read 17 Aug 1782, Robert Courtney.

Bond: Esther Perry (X), Joseph Perry and Joshua Draun, 10 Sept 1782.
Wit: Rachel Hamilton. Securities signed Job Perry, J. Draughon.

PETERS, SOLOMON   Apt. 56 Pck. 1975
   Will of Soloman Peters, Sunday January 14, 1787...wife Sarah Peters, all real and personal property; two brothers Jesse and Elijah Peters; wife Sarah and Thomas Taylor and James Taylor, Exrs....Solomon Peters (E) Wit: Benj. Allen Cooper, Gab. Parker, Jean Cooper. Prov. 9 May 1787 by Gabriel Parker.
Dedimus to William Meyer, JP 25 Mar 1787 and 30 Apr 1787.
Warrant of appraisement to: John Patridge, Thomas Green, Gilbert Gibson, Dotch Hay, Jos: Gibson, 25 May 1787.
Appraisement 4 June 1787 by Jno. Partridge, Josyah Gibson, Gilbert Gibson

PETTY, LUKE   Apt. 56 Pck. 1979
   Will of Luke Pettey of a Lo state of health...to my beloved wife one third of the free hole Land I now posess remainder to be equally divided amongst my Children (not named)...30 Sept 1780...Luke Petty (Seal), Wit: John Graham, Walter Shropshire, Monnaca Duven (X).
Bond: John Hood, John Taylor, and Benedict Best, 28 Apr 1785. Wit: Jesse Goodwyn.
Appraisement 15 May 1785, by Walter Shropshire, Abraham Wimberly, John Lake.

PICKENS, THOMAS   Apt. 56 Pck. 1983
   Bond: _____ 1784, Lewis Perry, George Watts, Wit: Jno Harbirt.
(no other documents in package).

PICKETT, JAMES   Apt. 56 Pck. 1984
   Will of James Pickett of Camdon District, all estate divided between Susannay Pickett my wife and All my children Namely: John Pickett, Frankey Pickett, Ruben Pickett, Elisabeth Pickett, when my oldest child comes of age; Brother Micajah Pickett, and friend Frederick Briggs and wife Susanny, Exrs., 2 June 1783...James Pickett (Seal), Wit: Nezerus Whitted, John Lewis, Ann Whitted (A).
Warrant of appraisement to: Moses Knighton, Nazerous Whitehead, Charles Lewis, Peter Matthews, John Key, 27 Sept 1783.
Sworn 31 Oct 1783 before Chas. Pickett, JP.
Inventory 5 Nov 1783 by Moses Knighton, Nazerous Whitted, John Key.

PIERCE, JAMES   Apt. 55 Pck. 1923
   Naomi Pierce, widow of James Pierce, Edward Dudley and William Scott, applied for admn, 18 Nov 1785. Citation published by Jos. Rees, 20 Nov 1785.
Dedimus to Wm Meyer to adm oath 7 Jan 1786. Sowrn 14 Jan 1786.
Warrant of appraisement to Thomas Williams, Daniel Ford, Abiah Croft, Joel Adams and Reuben House.
Inventory 14 Jan 1786, ₤ 717 7 6, by Daniel Ford, Thomas Williams, and Abiah Croft.

PLATT, HEZEKIAH   Apt. 57 Pck. 1992
   John Platt applied for admn as next of kin, 22 Nov 1782. "I have published the citation several Sunday, 23 Dec 1782, Wm Hux"
Bond: John Platt, John Boykin, 24 Dec 1782, Wit: Richard Furman.

PORTER, NATHANIEL   Apt. 57 Pck 2000
   Will of Nathaniel Porter, 7 Apr 1784; prov. 29 Apr 1784 by David Byers; Eldest brother Matthew Porter, sister Agness, Brother David, brother James, sister Violet, sister Rebeckah, sister Ruth, sister Ann, Mother [Sarah]; Exor: Mother and William Byers; Wit: Edward Byers, Adam Meek. James Meek, Joseph Scott, David Dickey, John McNabb were appointed to appraise est. 29 Apr 1784, produced by Sarah Porter, and William Byers Exrs.
Inventory of Nathaniel Porter, Bullock's Creek appraised 21 June 1784 by Joseph Scott, John McNabb, James Meek.

POWELL, WILLIAM   Apt. 57 Pck. 2007
   Barnaby Pope applied for admn, 27 Aug 1784. Citation pub. 29 Aug 1784 by Jacob Gibson, Minr. of Gosp.
Bond: Barnaby Pope, Thomas Parrot, _____ 1784, Wit: Samuel Proctor.
Warrant of appraisement 9 Sept 1784 to Thomas Parrot Sen, Samuel Proctor,

James Ogilvie, William Cato, Thomas Parrot Jun.
Sworn 30 Oct 1784 before Phil Pearson, JP; Thomas Parrot Senr, Samuel Proctor, James Ogilvie.
Accounts Current (1785-1790) with John Ogilvie: Barnaby Pope, John McKaime, Hiney Crumpton, John Pearson, Elizabeth Powell, Ann Powell, Thomas Parrot Jr. "Raising the Children" "Raising the Least child named Penelope"
Inventory 30 Oct 1784.
Sale returned by John Ogilvie, gdn.
Purchasers 7 Sept 1789: Thomas Parrot Sr, John Miles, Thomas Parrot Jr., Major Yarborrough, Thomas May, Wm Cato, Wm Watson, Philip Pearson, Daniel Wooten, Wm Rabb, Rev(?) Pope, Colon Haile, Thos Watts, Jacob Gibson Jr, John Wooten, James Nelson, C D Bradford, Samuel Proctor, John Young.

PRITCHARD, DAVID Apt. 57 Pck. 2015
    Ann Pritchard applied for admn, 10 July 1782. Citation read 21 July 1782 by John Logue.
Bond: Ann Pritchard, Roling Williamson, Wood Tucker, Wit; Henry Clark.
Warrant of appraisement: to Nathan Center, Robert Loyal, Jas. Taylor, Thos Taylor, Stephen Curry, Rolling Williamson, and Wood Tucker, 5 Aug 1782.
Appraisement: Congarees, 11 Sept 1782 includes Negroes (named), by Thomas Taylor, Colo., N. Canter, Wood Tucker Sr.

RATCLIFF, JAMES Apt. 58 Pck. 2032
    Joseph Warren applied for admn, 11 Feb 1782 as nearest of kin.
Citation was read in the Congregation of Mr. Solomon Thompson, he not being in place this 24 day of February 1782. Isaac Jackson, Clark.
Bond: Joseph Warren, admr., Robert Lewis, John Warren Senr (X), sec., 5 Mar 1782, before John Warren Junr.
12 Nov 1782, Prudence Ratcliff, Widow, complained that Joseph Warren obtained letters of admn. surrepticiously, and John Cassels cited Warren to appear at the House of Wood Furman 29 Nov 1782 and answer her complaint.
Inventory 8 Feb 1783 by Robert Lewis, John Warren Senr, John Warren Junr.
Purchasers at sale 10 Feb 1783 Prudence Ratcliff, Joseph Warren.

RATCLIFF, SAMUEL Apt. 58 Pck. 2033
    John King applied for admn, 18 June 1782. Citation read in the Congregation of Salem, 30 June 1782, by Thos. Reese.
Bond: John King, admr, Thomas Goodwin (X), Samuel Ratcliff, sec., 18 July 1782 before Josiah Furman.
Warrant of appraisement to: Moses Knighton, Isaac Knighton, Charles Lewis.
Sworn 18 July 1782: Moses Knighton, Isaac Knighton, Charles Lewis.
Estate appraised by them (no date). Purchasers at sale (no date): John King, Charles Pickett, Rachel Butler, Peter Ridwell, John Watts, Moses Knighton, Zilpah Tucker, Amos Windham, Robert Roberts, Absolam Galloway, John Turner, Charles Kimbrell, Frederick Bell, Addison Scarborough, Susanna Ratcliff.

REES, EDWIN Apt. 59 Pck. 2051
    Will of Edwin Rees of St. Marks Parish, Planter, 22 Feb 1782; prov. 29 July 1782. Wife Mary, daughters Sally and Elizabeth, Ex: Brothers Hugh Ree and Isham Rees...Edwin Rees (Seal), Wit: Philip Pettypool, Sarah Rees, Thos Andrews.
Inventory by Isham Moore, Huberd Rees, Abijah Rembert, 17 Aug 1782; mentions Philip Pool, Matthew Gayle, Adam F. Brisbane, Samuel Hatfield, Robt Dearington, Thomas Andrew, Doctr. Wright, Capt. Josiah Furman, Peter Brunson, Henry Whelar, Mr. Hardis, George Spain, David Neal, Col. Nathl Moore, Wm Moore, Wm Rees, James Habersham, Wm Dinkins, Flemin Tynes, Mr. Grimes, Henry Clark, Caleb Gayle, Wm Barden, Greenberry Caper, Isaac Knighton, Edward Lane, Willis Ramsey, Charles Leflour, Alexander Campbell, James Borough, Benjamin Holloway, Lenard Powell, Capt. Lewis, Matthew Peterson, Mr. Skiner, Robt Moses, Ephraim P. Pool(Pettypool), Gilbert Croswell, Archablad Henson, John Denny, Philip P. Pool (Pettypool), John Hamilton.

REES, JOHN Apt. 59 Pck. 2052
    Inventory and appraisement of estate by Isham Moore, Asbury Silvester, and John James, 1 March 1782, as shown them by Huberd Rees, Admr. total ₤ 2886 12 6. (No other papers in package).

REILY, ROBERT Apt. 59 Pck 2054
    Samuel Reily and John Vertu applied for admn 1 Nov 1784, as nearest of kin. Citation was read in a public congregation 7 Nov 1784 by Solomon Thomson, Minister of the Gospel.
Bond: Samuel Reily, John Vertu, admrs., James Gibson, sec., 16 Nov 1784, before Wm Martin.
Warrant of appraisement to John Gambell, John Rafield, Ebenezer Bagnall, John Bagnall, and Arthur White. Sworn before Wm Martin, 23 Nov 1784: John Gambell, John Rafield, Ebenezer Bagnall. Estate appraised 23 Nov 1784.

RICHARDSON, ARTHUR Apt. 59 Pck. 2067
    Hannah Richardson and Reuben Jackson applied for admn, 4 Oct 1782. Citation read in a public meeting 6 Oct 1782.
Bond: Hannah Richardson (X), Reuben Jackson, admrs., Isaac Jackson Junr, Thomas Jackson, sec, 30 Oct 1782. Wit: Rachel Furman.
Estate appraised 30 Dec 1782 by Isaac Gidens (X), Thomas Jackson, Daniel Norton, for L 637 10 2.

RICHARDSON, RICHARD Apt. 59 Pck. 2069
    Will of Gen. Richard Richardson, 2 Sept 1780; prov. 22 Mar 1782; wife Dorothy; nine children Susannah, James Burchell [Gov. of SC 1802-04], John, Peter, Charles, Thomas, Richard, Edward; grandson Richardson. Ex: wife Dorothy, Richard Richardson and Peter Sinkler, Esqr., Wit: Thos Wm Jenkins, Joseph Terry, James Mason.
Estate appraised by William Canty Senr, Thomas William Jenkins, and Joseph Terry, 16 Apr 1782, for L 48,645 10 0.

RICHARDSON, THOMAS Apt. 59 Pck. 2070
    Will of Thomas Richardson Senior of Craven County, SC, 18 Mar 1783...Wife Margaret, her third part of my 200 A of land that I now live upon at Little River during her life; son William, son Thomas Junr, daughter Jennett Kennedy, daughter Mary Richardson, son Samuel; daughter Margaret Richardson, 100 A of my 300 A of my land at Packlet; son Robert, Ex: wife Margaret and son Thomas Junr...(remainder of will missing)...
James Rabb and Hannah his wife appeared before John Winn Esqr. a Justice of Fairfield Co., and swore that they wit. the will, and that it was wit. and written by Robert Branham, now dead, and the will delivered into the care of his mother, was lost but lately found in its mutilated condition.
Thomas Cameron appeared before John Buchanan JP of Camden Dist. 31 Mar 1786 and swore that he heard Thomas Richardson Senr of Fairfield Co., say two days before his death that he had formerly made a will but it had been so long ago that he wished Cameron would destroy it which he says he did and then made a non cupative will in which he devised his moveable property be equally divided between his widow and four children who lived with him viz: Samuel, Robert, Mary, and Margaret Richardson. This was corroborated by oaths of Susannah Cameron and Mary Richardson (daughter of the decd).
Margaret Richardson, widow of Thomas, planter, applied for admn, 25 Aug 1786, citation not returned.
Estate appraised 18 Oct 1787 by John Hawthorn, John Elliot and Thomas Richardson. They were qualified 18 May 1787.

RIDDLE, JOHN Apt. 59 Pck. 2074
    Will of John Riddle of Camden District, 27 Sept 1780; no prov. date; Wife Mary, sons James, John, Patrick and George. Ex: friend John Fields, Patrick McFadden, and William Twadell...John Riddle (X) (Seal), Wit: Patrick McFaden (X), William Twadell, John Fields.
Dedimus 19 Jan 1786 to Isaac Alexander Esqr. to qualify wit.
Warrant of appraisement to Alexander Archer, John Brown, William Anderson, William Twadell and Francis Adams. Sworn 20 Jan 1786 by Samuel Dunlap, JP of Lancaster Co., SC: Alexander Archer, John Brown, William Anderson.

RIVES, WILLIAM Apt. 59 Pck. 2077
    Will of William Rives Esqr of Camden Dist, 26 Aug 1783...to wife Lucy Rives, plantation where I now live and negro Jemmey; to son Henry Rives, 1/2 the value of the River plantation; sons Green Rives and William Rives, plantaion on the River; negroes to my children under age, to remain on plantation untill William becomes 21 years old; to son Silas Rives, plantation where I now live; 500 A in Ninety Six District, and land on

Mars Bluff to son John Rives; remainder divided among my sons Henry, Green, William Silas, John and daughter Rebecca Hutchitson and wife Lucy; friend Col. Thomas Taylor, Brother Timothy Rives, Exrs., with sons Henry and Green Rives...Wm Rives (Seal), Wit: James Baird, Priscilla Rives (X), Elizabeth Rives (X).
Inventory by John Hirons, Joel Adams, Joel McLemore, L 2597 19 7.

ROBERSON, JOHN Apt. 59 Pck. 2086
    William Miller applied for admn as creditor, 23 Aug 1784.
Citation pub. 27 Aug 1784 by Ralph Jones.
(No other documents in package).

ROBERTS, WILLIAM Apt. 59 Pck. 2083
    Susannah Roberts applied for admn as next of kin, 20 May 1782.
Citation published in the church of Salem, Thos Reese (no date).
Bond: Susannah Roberts, Robert Roberts, admrs., Robert Lewis and John Westbury, sec., 10 June 1782.
Warrant of appraisement 10 Aug 1782 to Henry Cassels Jr., Moses Gordon, Elias Dubose and James Carter.
Inventory 27 July 1782 by Henry Cassel Jr., Moses Gordon, James Armstrong, L 3532 17 -.

ROBERTSON, WILLIAM Apt. 59 Pck. 2087
    Hugh Bennet and Christian Robeson applied for admn as next of kin, 13 Sept 1785. Citation read 25 Sept by Robert Courtney.
Bond: Hugh Bennet, Christian Robeson; admrs., James McCollugh and Wm McCollugh, 15 Oct 1785.
Dedimus to John Dickey to qualify admn, 10 Oct 1785. Sworn 15 Oct.
Inventory 29 Oct 1785, L 66 10 3, by William Burnson Jr., Agusteen Swetman (+) and Thomas Belcher.

ROBINSON, ALEXANDER Apt. 59 Pck. 2088
    Will of Alexander Robinson; estate to wife Sarah and children (not named); Exors Brother William Robinson, wife Sarah and son John; 18 Oct 1783. Alexr Robinson, Wit: Willm Wheeler (X), Michl Birch, Prov. by Michael Birch 9 Aug 1784.
Inventory made 30 Sept 1785, sworn 2 Nov 1784, L 83 6 00 sterling, including negroes (named) by James McCauley, Wm Robertson, James Frierson, before John Cantey, JP.

RODGERS, JOHN Apt. 59 Pck. 2104
    Elizabeth Rogers applied for admn of her late Husband, 16 Nov 1781. Citation read 18 Nov 1781 by Solomon Thomson.
Bond: Elizabeth Singleton and Thomas Jones, Mathew Singleton, 15 Dec 1781.
Wit: Isham Moore, Peter Mellet.
Inventory 14 Feb 1782 by Isham Moore, John James, Peter Mellet. Sale 15 Mar 1782, L 3131 18 -.

ROGERS, WILLIAM Apt. 60 Pck. 2111
    Will of William Rogers of Camden District; to Ralph Rogers, L 214 sterling; to sister Edith Woods, L 35 s 10 sterling; to sister Margaret Rogers, L 35 s10 sterling; to brother Ralph Rogers, L 35 s 10 over and above the L 214; to sister Rachel McMan, L 35 s 10 sterling; remainder to brother Clayten and Ralph Rogers for supporting Margary Rogers, 24 Feb 1784...Wm Rogers (Seal), Wit: William Bostick, Floyd Bostick. Prov. by William Bostick 15 Mar 1784.
Dedimus to Frame Woods Esqr to prove will of William Rogers 12 Mar 1784.
Warrant of appraisement to William Nelson, James Hamilton, William Bostick, John Foster and George McWhorter, 12 Mar 1784. Sworn appraisers 15 Mar 1784: James Hambelton and Wm Bostick before Frame Woods. Appraisement 15 Mar 1784.
A schedule of accounts and obligations due the Estate of William Rogers. a Bond of James Lindsay in Va. currency. Note, John Mongomery in Va. currency.
Certification from the Commissioner of Publick accounts against: Edward Moorhead, Robert Good, Harrison Bell, John Foster, James Lindsay, Ralph Rogers, William Bostick, James Derven, John Bird.

ROSS, HUGH Apt. 60 Pck. 2119
    Elizabeth Ross applied for admn 10 Mar 1784; citation read at Rocky Creek, 17 Mar 1784. Estate appraised by John Turner, John Flemming, and

William White, 11 May 1784, for ₤ 31 7 9.
Warrant of appraisement to above appraisers and Hugh Smith & Robert Ewing.
Bond: Elizabeth Ross (X), admx., 17 Apr 1783, John Sarvis (X), Robert
Ewing, Hugh Smith, sec., Test: Jno Harbirt.

RUSH or RISH, FREDERICK Apt. 60 Pck. 2127
Will of Frederick Rush, late of the province of SC, but now of St. Augustine, province of East Florida; to wife Mary, 1/3 of 200 A on Otter's Creek, near Lynches Creek, SC; children Jacob Rush, Abarilla Rush, remaining 2/3 of land...wife Mary and John Scott, son of the late Jonathan Scott, of SC, Exrs. 2 Feb 1784; Fredrich Rish (LS), Wit: WM McEnery, John Harrison William Johnson, John Mills, Notary public.
Prov. by J. Harrison and William Johnson before Patrick Tonym, Gov. of East Florida, 3 Apr 1782.
H. Beaumont swore to Signature of David Yeats, secry, 3 Nov 1785, Adam Brisbane, JP
Letters testamentary from East Florida, 3 Apr 1784.
Bond: Mary Rish, widow of Frederick 9 Nov 1785.
Warrant of appraisement (not filled out).
John Bibbe, Jacob Baker, John Getsinger, appraised a horse 5 Feb 1787, before John Craig, JP.

RUSSELL, JOHN Apt. 60 Pck. 2135
Bond: Wm Thomson, William Myddleton, Wm Heatly Jr., 4 Nov 1785.
Wit: Malcom(sic) Clarke. Estate of John Russell late of Congaree River.
Dedimus to Malcolm Clark, 1 Nov 1785.
Appraisement of Capt. John Russel, 14 Nov 1785, by Arth. Ferguson, Wm Myddleton, Moses Leviston.

RUSSELL, SAMUEL Apt. 60 Pck. 2137
Will of Samuel Russell of Camden District, Blacksmith, 2 Nov 1782; prov. 20 Nov 1782; son Samuel, my plantation on Wateree River 150 A, when he arrives at the age of 21 years, daughters Elizabeth, Hannah, Ann and Olive (all under age), wife Rosannah...Ex. & Gdn wife Rosannah and friend Samuel Pearson, Senr of Bush River, and John Milhous of Wateree River...Samel Russel (Seal), Wit: Isaac Pidgeon, Samuel Pidgeon.
Inventory 30 Nov 1782 by John Wyly, William Lang, Wm Wyly, for ₤ 854 16 3.

SADLER, JOHN Apt. 61 Pck. 2144
Will of John Sadler, dated 7 July 1782; prov. 4 Oct 1784 before Frame Woods, JP...Wife Mary, son Richard, son George, daughter Easter Lacey and her husband, daughter Deborah Bell and her husband, three grandsons John, Samuel and George Conn. Ex: sons George Sadler and William Bell [son in law]...Wit: James Hetherington, James Bell, Harrison Bell.
Codicil: James Hetherington of Turkey Creek and Richard Sadler of Fishing Creek to settle affairs; Wit: Same as will.
Inventory by Zachariah Bell, James Bell, and Harrison Bell, 2 Jan 1784, for ₤ 1421 9 4.
Warrant of appraisement to above and Ezekiel Gilham and Isaac Gilham.
Inventory lists bonds on David Patterson, David Stevenson, William Miles, William Brown, Samuel Carson, Gdofrey Adams, John McConnel, Robert McCleave, Thomas Reany, James Gibson, Hugh Neely, James McNeal, David Leech, Samuel Glen, William Burrace, John Carson, George Sadler, William Ross, William Bell, George Sadler, John Wallace, Reuben Lacey.

SANDERS, WILLIAM Apt. 61 Pck. 2161
Ester Saunders and Joseph Tims applied for admn, 3 May 1783; Citation published 11 & 13 May 1783 by Thomas Duke.
Bond: Easter (X) Sanders, Joseph Timms, admx & admr, Eleazar Gore and John Ashford Gore, sec., 15 May 1783.
Estate appraised by John Terry, John Colvin, John Pratt.

SCHEURER, ELIZABETH Apt. 61 Pck. 2168
Will of Elizabeth Scheure of Broad River in Craven County, Widow...two children Jesias and Barbara Scheurer...to son Jesais, 150 A on N side Broad River granted to me 19 June 1772, on the condition that he give to my daughter Barbara, 100 A granted to John Martin Scheurer, 6 Oct 1752...friend Daniel Gartman and Casper Pierly [Bierly], Exrs...
5 Oct 1773...Elizabeth Schuere (Seal), Wit: Peter Oster, Maria Ostrin, Conrad Zuber. A copy from the Secretary's Office, [Charleston], Letters testamentary dated 29 Oct 1773 to Gartman and Pierly, Rec. Book H, p. 210

SCOLDFIELD, PHILIP   Apt. 61 Pck. 2172
            Will of Phillip Scoldfield of the County of "fare field", 7
Aug 1786...daughters Elizabeth More(?), Nancy Webb and Nelly Elkins,
one silver dollar each; to daughter Hannah Scolfield, 100 A I now live on;
to grandson William Scofield; freind Zachariah Nettles and Robert Martin;
Philip Scoldfield (Seal), Wit: Isaac Love, Ann Martan (X), James More.
Proven by Ann Martin and James More, (no date).
Dedimus to Isaac Alexander 4 Oct 1786 to prove will, and Zachariah Nettles
and Robert Martin qualified as Exors.
Inventory, 10 Nov 1786, for L 71 0 7, by Gardner Ford, John McKiney,
William Cloud.

SCURRY, GIDEON   Apt. 61 Pck. 2181
            Thomas Scurry applied for admn as nearest of kin, 24 Mar 1785.
Published in the audience of a Congregation, 10 Apr, Robert Courtney.
Bond: Thomas Scurry, James Clark, Isham Clark, 27 Apr 1785, Wit: Joseph
McCay.
Inventory by Richard Bradford, Isham Clark and James Clark at Mr. Thomas
Scurrys, 25 May 1785. L 10 14 8.

SHELTON, GEORGE   Apt. 62 Pck. 2207
            Priscilla Latta applied for admn 23 Oct 1784. Citation read at
Congregation at Sharon Meeting House on Fishing Creek, 20 Oct 1784.
Rocky Creek. Wm Martin, Min.
Bond: Priscilla Latta, John Kitchen, 15 Nov 1784.
Warrant of appriasement 15 Nov 1784 to John Allen, Thomas Geather, John
Dye, and Buckner Hegood.
John Dye and Jno Allen sworn 12 Feb 1784(sic) before Phil. Walker, JP

SHEPPARD, GEORGE   Apt. 62 Pck. 2209
            James Corbett and wife Susannah aplied for admn of George
Sheppard, late of High Hills of Santee, Carpenter, 30 July 1787.
Published at the Meeting on the 4 Aug 1787, Solomon Thomson, Minister of
the Gospel.

SIMMERLY, PHILIP   Apt. 63 Pck. 2229
            Camden District, Will of John Philip Simerly, for Love Goodwill
and affection to my wife Christiana Simmerly, 50 A in Craven County, on
N side Congaree opposite to Saxagotha Township, adj. Alexander Dayley,
Mary King, widow, and Stephen Curry, Nicholas Grubb...13 Oct 1784, Wit:
Nicholas Grubb, Gasper Bush, Elizabeth Bush (X). Proven by Nicholas
Grubb and Gasper Bush, 27 Jan 1785.
Inventory of what I have given to my wife Christiana Simmerly, 13 Oct 1784
by Philip Simerly, Wit: Nicholas Grubb, Gasper Bush.

SIMPSON, WILLIAM   Apt. 63 Pck. 2232
            Will of William Simpson of Camden District, 20 June 1783, prov.
21 Dec 1784...wife Mary, granddaughter Sarah Simpson, daughter of William
Simpson, when she becomes 18 years of age; son James, the plantation on
which I now live daughters Mary, Jane, Elizabeth, and granddaughter
Martha Adams, daughter of Thomas Adams; grandson John Simpson; grandson
William Simpson, son of James Simpson, 200 A on Rocky Creek on E side of
Catawba River...Ex: Son James Simpson...William Simpson (X) (Seal), Wit:
Joseph Lee, James Fleming, John Foster. Dedimus to Robert Montgomery, JP
to qualify James Simpson as Exor. Qualified 21 Dec 1784.
Warrant of appraisement to Joseph Lee, William Baird, William Simpson,
Alexander Thomson, Andrew McIlwain and Robert Bartley, 17 Dec 1784.
Joseph Lee, William Baird, William Simpson, appraised est. ___ Dec 1784.

SPRADLIN, CHARLES   Apt. 65 Pck. 2294
            Will of Charles Spradling of Craven County, 1780, 7 June...to
wife Martha, negroes (named); to son Charles, land where I now live, 200
A; to daughter Agnis, feather Bed and furniture; to grandson David Sprad-
ling, negro (named)...to daughter Ann, s5 sterling; Henry Wimpey, Exr;
Charles Spradling (CP) Wit: John Wilson,William Strowd (W), Hamton Stroud
(X).
Daniel Aires of sd. District hath a claim to this estate and suspects that
Charles Spradlin Jr. is about to convey away the whole estate...sd. Charles
to appear in court in August...31 Aug 1784.
Dedimus to Charles Pickett JP to examin Wm Strowd and Hampton Strowd, 30
Dec 1783. Warrant to Henry Wimpey, Constable, for appearance of William

Strowd as he has refused to attend to the will, 3 Jan 1784.
Warrant of appraisement 8 Mar 1784 to William Simmons, James Lohon, Nimrod Mitchell, John Wilson, and Jesse Wilson.
Inventory 6 Apr 1784 by John Wilson, Jas. Laughon, Nimrod Mitchell.

STARKE, THOMAS   Apt. 65 Pck. 2300
    Keziah Starks applied for admn as next of kin, 13 Sept 1782.
Citation published in a Congregation at David Clentons Mill on Singletons Creek, 6 Oct   Joshua Palmer.
Duglass Stark applied for admn, 13 Apr 1784. Citation published 2 May 1784 by Lewis Collins.
Bond: Douglass Stark, Reuben Stark, 26 May 1784.
Dedimus to Burwell Boykin to admn. oath to Duglass Stark, 26 May 1784.
Inventory 14 Aug 1784 and 6 Sept 1784, including 9 negroes (named), by Jno Milhous, James Scott, Thos Vaughan.

STALLINGS (STALLIONS), JOHN JUNR.   Apt. 65 Pck. 2297
    Will of John Stallings 12 Aug 1783; (no prov. date)...wife Mary; son James, 82 A, being part of the land I bought of Peter Kuykendall, 6 June 1768, at the Road opposit my House on Milican's branch; to son in law Demcey Winborn, land on W side Fishing Creek adj. Wm Barrows; to son Silas his manor plantation and all remaining land; granddaughter Levinah Cook; grandson Benjamin Cook; daughter Winney Winborn. Exors: James Stallings, Demsey Winborn and Daniel Green...John Stallings (X). Wit: H. Hunter, David Andrews, Wm Andrews.
Inventory of estate of John Stallings Junr by Jas Love, Jos. Boggs, Benjn Cook, sworn before W. Bratton JP, 14 May 1784.
Bond: James Stallings admrs, 23 Feb 1784, Demcy Winborn sec., Wit: Susannan Hampton.
Purchasers at sale, 27 Feb 1784: William Love, James Cunningham, William Byers, James Douglass, David Byers, Demcy Winborne, John McMichael, Silas Stallings, John Glass, James Hanna Senr, Mary Stallings, James Stallings, Jesse Winborne, William Hanna, John Henderson, James McCaw, Elijah Fleming, Edward Hill, George Cunningham, James Clinton, Henry Bonner, Benjamin Cook, Capt. ___ Hanna, John Young, Edward Andrews, George Scott, David Andrews, Wm Willingham, John Aulston, James Andrews Junr., Mrs. Woodward.

STOGNER, BENJAMIN   Apt. 65 Pck. 2311
    William Johnson of Lynches Creek, planter, applied 28 Nov 1785 for admn, on estate of Benjamin Stoggler, late of Lynches Creek, as greatest Creditor. Citation was read at Flat Creek Meeting 19 Mar 1786, by John Cato, Minister of the Gospel
Bond: Glass Caston, admr., 18 Apr 1786, Henry Horton, Jesse Haves, sec., before Geo: Brown.

STONE, JOSHUA   Apt. 65 Pck. 2319
    Mary Stone applied for admn, 24 Feb 1784. Citation read at Bethel by Solomon Thomson, min. 29 Feb 1784.
Bond: Mary Stone, William Dukes, 15 Mar 1784.
Warrant of appraisement 15 May 1784 to John James, William McConnico, William Canty, Edward Broton and Thomas William Jenkings.
Inventory 3 June 1784 by Wm McConnico, Wm Cantey, Thos Wm Jenkins, for Ŀ 520 12 0.

STRANGE, CHARLES   Apt. 65 Pck. 2330
    Comfort Strange, widow, applied for admn 15 Mar 1782. Citation read by Joseph Cook, 15 Apr 1782 at Half Way Swamp Meeting House.
Bond: Comfort Strange (X), admx, John Hilton, Gabriel Gerrald, sec., 26 Mar 1782.
Estate sold 25 June 1782 for Ŀ 1056 3 0. Purchasers: Andrew Hilton, Thomas Sumter, William Cantey, John Davis,, Nancy Strange, Abraham Felder, Ezekiel White, Lucretia Davis, William Ridgell, Gabriel Gerrald, Joseph Smith, William Ragon.

STRONG, CHARLES   Apt. 65 Pck 2331
    Will of Charles Strong 20 July 1781, prov. 13 Jan 1783, before Philip Walker, JP...wife Jennet, 1/4 part of Ŀ 1000 currency due me from Jonathan Jones' notes and 1/4 part of $740 on book due from Robert Cooper; daughter Littija; daughter Margaret; son Christopher; son in law Richard Gladney, Ex: wife, John Gaston Esqr., aond son Christopher. Wit: Robt Cooper, John Belley [Bailey], Robert Strong.

Estate appraised by John Mills SEnr, John Downing and John Mills, for
Ł 161 3 0.

STEWART, ROBERT   Apt. 65 Pck. 2335
    Will of Robert Stewart, freeholder of Camden District, 17 Oct
1784; prov. (no date given); wife Elizabeth; Littleton Esbell's two daughters, Elizabeth Isbell and Kinhappuck Isbell, both under 21, 300 A bought
of Peter Pirkins (Colo.), on Caskain Creek in Pitsilvania County in Virginia; bonds of William Randels; to Littleton Isbell, my saddle and silver
watch; wife and Andrew Hemphill Exrs...Robt Stewart (Seal , Wit: Daniel
Green, William Stinson, James Hemphill.
Elizabeth Stuart applied for admn of her decd husband, 7 Nov 1785. Citation
read at Rocky Creek, 20 Nov 1785 by William Martin, Minister.
Elizabeth Stewart sworn as Extx by Andrew Hemphill, JP, 31 Dec 1785.

STROTHER, WILLIAM   Apt. 65 Pck. 2333
    Will of William Strother of Camden District; to wife Catharine,
all stock of cattle and use of plantation I now live on; _____ me from
Gabriel Gerrald; to son John Dargan Strother; 300 A granted to Henry Middleton, 400 A granted to Davdi Hay, 200 A on Trukey Creek granted in my
name; to son William Strother, 350 A on Crane Creek granted to Joseph ___
...3-- A granted to Richard Strother; to daughter Catharine, negro girl___
Dulcena, mare and colt; land purchased by Richard Strother and myself from
Jacob Swechart, to son Kemp Talaferro Strother; all negroes to be sold...
friend ____ Taylor and son Kemp T. Strother, Exrs., 16 May 1779...Wm
Strother (Seal), Wit: Drury Andrew, Christian _____ and Richard _____.
(will in poor condition). Proved by Richard Gradick who swore to the sig-
natures of Christian Kinsler and Drury Andrew, 9 Jan 1783.
Warrant of appraisement to Timothy Rives, Richard Strother, Christian Kin-
sler, John Dieger and Wm Kirkland, directed by Kemp Talaferro Strother
and Thomas Taylor, Exrs., 9 Jan 1783.
Inventory 14 May 1783 by Timothy Rives, Wm Kirkland and Thos Baker.
Buyers at sale, 28 Feb 1784: Kemp T. Strother, Willm Strother, Benjamin
Harrison, James Hart, Thos Scent, Mrs. Strother.

STUART, JOHN   Apt. 65 Pck 2334
    (only document in package)
Bond: Richard Gladden (X), admr., Moses Hollis, Daniel Going (O), sec.
Wit: Rachel Hamilton, 7 May 1782.

STUART, WILLIAM   Apt. 65 Pck 2336
    Will of William Stuart of Craven County; to daughter Mary, daughter
Ede, daughter Ann, daughter Stacy, daughter Esther, son William, daughter
Sarah, one shilling sterling each; to son Isaac 150 A on S side Dry Creek
and Two cows; to wife Sarah remainder of Estate and at her death to son
Isaac...18 Sept 1782...William Stewart (Seal), Wit: Bailey Fleming, Micajah
Crenshaw, William McGarrow (|).
Proved in Lancaster County by William McGarrow, 30 Dec 1786 before Saml
Dunlap, JP.   Proved by Bailey Fleming 25 Apr 1787
Warrant of appraisement 26 Apr 1787 to Bailey Flemming, Macajah Grenshaw,
William McGarrow, William Stevens, and William Bailey.
Sworn 17 May 1787 before Saml Dunlap: M. Crenshaw, Bailey Fleming, Wm
McGarry.
Inventory 19 May 1787, Ł 16 6 6.

Apparently another William Stewart's estate is contained in this package:

John Bostick of the Congarees applied for admn as greatest creditor, 28
July 1785. Citation published by Joseph Rees, last day of July 1785.
Inventory 15 Sept 1785 includes one negro in possession of Capt. Jas
McCauley; one Race horse in possession of Fielden Woodroughf (sic); horse
in possession of James Gibson, and James Petegrew.
Notes on Nathaniel Newsmith, Richard Gowen Dennis, Godart Debruell; one
on Joseph McGowen payable to Wm Lewton. Rect fro Col. Wade Hamton to Fiel-
den Woodroof
Letter headed Congarees 4th Augt, W. Goodwyn agrees to be security for
John Bostick.

SUMMERVILLE, GEORGE Apt. 65 Pck. 2339
    Martha Summerville, James Miller and Hugh Summerville applied

for admn, 1 Nov 1785.
Citation read in Waxhaw Congregation, 6 Nov 1785 by Robt Findly.
Bond: Martha Summerville, Hugh Summerville, Jas Mciller, admrs., John McKee, sec., 30 Nov 1785.
Administrators'oath admrd. by Andrew Baskins, 30 Nov 1785.
Inventory 3 Dec 1785 by Adam Thomson, William Thomson, George Miller.
Sale 13 Dec 1785, purchasers: William Farell, William McGill, Thomas Balard, Hugh Somervell, John Marshall, John Colvin, James Miller, David Russell, James Simpson, Robert Lee, Robert Marshall, John Davison, Elisabeth Twadel, William Brown, Richard Scoofel, James Duglas, William Crage, Matthew Somervell. Certified 27 Apr 1786.

SUMMERVILLE, HUGH   Apt. 65 Pck. 2340
    Rachel Summerlin, widow & Relict of Hugh Summerlin, late of Cedar Creek, James THompson and Thomas Thompson, applied for admn. 16 Sept 1786.
Citation published 28 Sept 1786, Lancaster County, Waxhaw Settlement, by Robert Findly.
Bond: Rachel Summerville, James Thompson, Thomas Thompson, admrs; David Russell, James Simpson, sec.,   1786.
Dedimus to Samuel Dunlap 5 Oct 1786 to qualify admrs.
Warrant of appraisement to James Simpson, John Fletcher, David Russell, Edward Rogers, and John Maxwell, 25 Oct 1786.
Inventory of Hugh Summervell (no date) by James Simpson, David Russel (+), John Fletcher.

SWAN, ADAM   Apt. 65 Pck. 2344
    Dr. Thomas Brown applied for admn on the estate of Adam Swan, late of Camden, Carpenter, 28 Sept 1786. Citation published in the Congregation at Camden, 1 Oct 1786. John Logue.
Bond: Thomas Brown, admr; William Lang, John Harker, sec., 25 Nov 1786.

TANNER, LODOWICK   Apt 66 Pck 2347
    James THomson applied for admn on the estate of Lodowick Tanner, late of Georgia, decd, 1 Dec 1786.
Camden, 3 Dec 1786, Citation read by John Logue.
Bond: James Thomson, admr; Robert Carter, Benjamin Carter, sec., 1 Dec 1786.

TAPPLEY, JOHN   Apt. 66 Pck 2348
    Letters of admn. granted 8 Nov 1786 to Mrs. Mary Ta ey, on estate of John Tappley, planter.
Warrant of appraisement to Simon Woodward, Frederick Atkinson, Isaac Lenoir, John Woodward, and John Malone. Estate appraised 28 Nov 1786 by John Malone, Isaac Lenoir, and John Woodard.
Bond: Mary Tapley, admx; Barnaby Baxter (X), William Going (M), sec., 8 Nov 1786. Wit: N. Robinson.

TATE, ROBERT   Apt. 66 Pck. 2353
    Bond: Elizabeth Tate (X), Moses Kemp (W), admrs., Thomas Camp, Wm Green, sec., 20 May 1785. Wit: Dad. McCreight.

TATE, THOMAS   Apt 66 Pck. 2356
    James Tate & Jno McDaniel applied 23 Feb 1785 for letters of admn on estate of Thomas Tate, as nearest of kin. Citation read "in sundry meetings" by Joseph Rogers, minister.
Bond: James Tate (X), John McDonal, admrs., Jer. McDanal, Thomas Willingham (X), sec., 25 Mar 1785, Wit: Jno Harbirt.

TATE, THOMAS JR.   Apt. 66 Pck 2355
    Fanny Tate applied for admn as nearest of kin 13 Oct 1783. Citation read 23 Oct 1783 by Jos. Camp, Mr.
Letters from Fanny Tate to Ordinary 24 May 1785 requesting that Joseph Camp be admr. in her place.
Letters of admn. to Fanny Tate and Joseph Camp, 28 May 1784.
Estate appraised 27 June 1785 by Thomas Camp, Peter Quinn & Jno Baron.
Bill of sale 27 June 1785 by Fanney Tate, widow, and Jos. Camp admr. (No names of purchasers listed.) Return on estate made 27 June 1785 by Fanny Tate of York County, wife of Thomas Tate, decd., before Jas. Wilson, JP.

TATE, THOMAS SR.   Apt. 66 Pck. 2354
    Elizabeth Tate and Moses Kemp granted letters of admn, 6 June 1785.

Estate appraised by Thos Camp, Peter Quin & John Baron.
Bill of sale 27 June 1785 by Moses Camp, Elizabeth Tate, admrs. shows purchases made by Elizabeth Tate, the widow, John Bradley, Joseph Camp, Sarah Wood, Peter Quinn, Isaack Green, Richard Wilson, James Bridges, William Green, Moses Camp, Thomas Wilson, James Wilson, John Fondren. L 122 0 11.
Receipts for legacies signed before Michael Hogan 27 June 1785: Sarah woods (X), Jos. Camp, Suky Bradly (X), Solomon Kemp, Frances Tate (0), Betty Thomason (X).

TATUM, JOSEPH Apt. 66 Pck. 2359
  Wood Tucker Jr. and Martha Tucker applied for admn as next of kin. Citation read 14 July 1782 in Camden by Christian Theus, Minister.
Bond: Wood Tucker Junr, admr; Ann Pritchard (X), Roling Williamson sec., 5 Aug 1782, Wit: Henry Clarke.
Estate appraised 13 Sept 1782 by Robert Lyell, Richard Evans and Ludwell Evans. Warrant of appraisement to aforesaid appraisers and John Boid, Nathan Center, and Wm Howell.

TAYLOR, JACOB Apt. 66 Pck 2363
  William Taylor applied 6 Oct 1784 for letters of admn as next of kin. Citation read in Waxhaw Congregation 14 Oct 1784 by Robt Findly.
Bond: William Taylor, admr, Archibald Davie, Jno Crockett, sec., 29 Nov 1784.
Warrant of appraisement to Robert Montgomery, Archibald Davie, John Crockett, Henry Foster, Solomon Hopkins. Estate appraised 6 Jan 1785, for L 556 0 5, by Jno Crockett, Soln Hopkins, and Archibald Davie.

TAYLOR, JAMES Apt. 66 Pck 2364
  John Taylor applied for admn as next of kin, 13 Sept 1782. Citation read by Christian Theus, 29 Sept 1782.
Bond: John Taylor, Francis Goodwyn Senr, Frans. Goodwyn Jr., Wit: Robert Smith, 10 Oct 1782.

TAYLOR, JOHN Apt. 66 Pck. 2365
  Will of John Taylor in Craven County, planter...wife Sarah, 1/3 of two plantations on Wateree bought of James and William Harrison, 4 Negroes (named), and cattle & horses; to beloved son John Taylor, 200 A bought of James Harrison; to son Simeon Taylor, 200 A on Wateree bought of Wm Harrison; to son William Taylor, two tracts on twenty five mile Creek, 500 A; to daughter Mary Taylor, 300 A in the fork of Wateree & Cedar Creek given to me by my brother Thomas Taylor; wife and Brother, Sarah Taylor and James Taylor, Exrs., 16 Mar 1781...John Taylor (Seal), Wit: John Hirons, Jane Curry, Hanah Grubb (   ). Proved 2 Nov 1782, by John Hirons.
Warrant of appraisement to John Hirons, Drury Wyche, Joel Mcnamore, Joel Adams, and Wm Rives, 2 Nov 1782.
Inventory by Wm Rives, Drury Wyche, Joel McLemore, includes Negroes (named), 14 Nov 1782, L 8150 14 0.

TAYLOR, WILLIAM Apt. 66 Pck 2368
  Mary Taylor applied for admn, 11 June 1783. Citation read by Jno Simpson, V. D. M. Fishg. C:k June 15, 83.
Bond: Mary Taylor, admx, Binjamin Culp (X), Andrew Lockhart, sec., 21 June 1783, Wit: Richd. Winn.
Sworn appraisers 18 July 1783, Jacob Cooper, Mc McDaniel and Alexr Crawford, before Jas. Knox, JP
Estate appraised 18 June 1783, for L 1446 12 6, by Jacob Cooper, William McDonald, Alexd. Crafford.

TERRY, STEPHEN Apt. 66 Pck. 2376
  Samuel Boykin bonded as admn, 11 May 1782, Douglas Starke and John Chesnut, sec.
Appraisers sworn, 8 July 1782: Malachi Murphy, John Boykin, James Wren, by Burl. Boykin, JP.

THOMAS, RICHARD Apt. 66 Pck 2383
  Will of Richard Thomas of Battourt (sic) County in the State of Virginia...to mother Mildred Thomas, negro Hanner and after her death to my sister Sarah Thomas; to my brothers James and George Thomas, 1400 A in Jefferson County, Va; remainder to my sister Sarah Thomas; friends

Patrick Lockheart and John Todd, Exrs., 15 Aug 1782...R. Thomas (Seal),
Wit: Isham Moore, Huberd Rees, Benjamin Wallis. Proved by all three wit.
16 Oct 1782.

THOMPSON, BENJAMIN   Apt. 67 Pck. 2400
            John Thompson applied for admn, 7 Apr 1783. Citation published
by Ralph Jones (no date).
Bond: John Thomson, admr., William Deason, Jno Marchasl, sec., Wit: R.
Winn, 15 May 1783.
Warrant of appraisement to Saml McCleland, Henry Foster, John Dunlap,
Robt Dunlap, 15 June 1783.
Inventory 5 July 1783, Ł 1568 7 6, includes Negroes (not named).
Paper in estate file " The entries in the ordinary's book after 5th
Feby 1783 are wanting apparently cut out"

THOMPSON, MOSES   Apt. 66 Pck 2395
            Mary Thompson applied for admn as next of kin, 10 July 1782.
Citation published by Christian Theus, 14 July 1782 in Camden Dist.
Bond: Mary Thompson, admx., Francis Goodwyn, sec., Wit: John Hamilton.
Warrant of appraisement to Francis Goodwyn, Joseph Lloyd, Jacob Fitzpatrick,
Edmund Carryll, and John Joiner, 13 Aug 1782. All sworn 15 Sept 1782.
Inventory by all 5 appraisers, 16 Sept 1782, Ł 566 7 6.

THOMSON, ELEANOR   Apt. 67 Pck. 2401
            Guardianship Bond: George Dunlap & Thomas Dunlap gdns; Samuel
Dunlap and David Carns, sec., 3 June 1783...Eleanor Thomson, minor daughter of Benjamin Thompson, decd, Wit: Richard Winn, Henry Foster.

THREEWITS, JOEL   Apt. 67 Pck. 2421
            Bond: Mary Threewits, admx., Robert Goodwyn, James Taylor, sec.,
10 July 1782, Wit: Josiah Furman.
Warrant of appraisement to William Howel, Nathan Center, Robert Loyal,
Rowland Williamson, Francis Goodwyn, John Boyd, 10 July 1782.
Inventory of Capt. Joell Threewits, by Robert Lyell, William Howell, and
Nathan Center, includes Negroes (named), 5 Sept 1782.

TILLMAN, WILLIAM   Apt. 68 Pck. 2438
            Jesse Tilman applied for admn for him and Elizabeth Tilman, 6
June 1782. Citation published at Ephraim Pools, 31 June 1782 by Joshua
Palmer.
Bond: Jesse Tilman, admr., William Tilman, sec., Wit: Rachel Hamilton, 4
July 1782.
Inventory includes Negroes (named) by Middleton McDonald, Glass Caston,
and George Wade, 13 Aug 1782, for Ł 4888 11 6.
Sale 13 Aug 1782, Buyers: Elizth Tillman Senr, Jessy Tillman, Zedick Perry,
Wm Tillman, Robt Lee, Susannah Henderson, Elizth Tillman Junr.

TINES, WILLIAM   Apt. 68 Pck. 2439
        Lavina Tines applied for admn, 8 Apr 1782. Citation published in
Meeting 14 Apr 1782, Solomon Thomson.
Bond: Levina Tynes, admx., John Wesbury, Robert Dearington, sec., Wit:
John Bradford, 30 May 1782.
Inventory by Robt Dearington, John Wesbery, John Bradford, 6 June 1782,
Ł 2398 10 00.
Sale 27 June 1782, by Robert Lewis, Vendue Master, (no buyers listed).

TUCKER, RICHARD   Apt. 69 Pck 2479
            Mary Tucker applied for admn, 2 Jan 1783.
Citation published at Richard Stratford's by Joshua Palmer, 12 Jan 1783.
Bond: Mary Tucker, admx., Samuel Luckey, John Motly, sec., 13 Jan 1783,
Wit: Sarah Haynsworth.
Appraisement 29 Mar 1783 by Thos Griffith, Arthur B Ross, Wm Collins.
Sale 23 Apr 1783, Buyers: Saml Luckey, Jeremiah Taylor, Mary Tucker, Robt
Willis, Wm Hughs, Joseph Sims, Jno Smith, Jno Chestnut, Willm Randol,
Isaac Ross, Jas Pery, Wm Hews, Danl Williams.

TUCKER, WOOD SR   Apt. 69 Pck. 2480
            Will of Wood Tucker of the Congarees, 18 Feb 1783...to wife Milley,
four Negroes (two named), and after her decease to my sons David & Robert
Tucker...to Wood Tucker my son, two cows and calves and what he has had

heretofore; unto my son David Tucker, one negro Boy Petter, and my Waggon and Team, whom I constitute my Sole Exr; which waggon & Team is to be kept for the use of the Estate enduring my Wife Milley's living, except the Hogs now claimed by my son Robert;to my daughter Lucy Harper, one negro Girl Peg; to son Robert Tucker negro Boy Bob, & remainder of household furniture to my two sons David & Robert Tucker; Wood Tucker Senr (Seal), Wit: Ludwell Evans, Jno Dicky. Proved 7 May 1784.
Appraisement 10 July 1784, for ₤ 389 8 7½, by Robert Lyell, Thomas Hutchinson, Robt Goodwyn.

TUPPLEY, JOHN   Apt. 69 Pck. 2481
Sale 28 Nov 1786, Buyers: Hugh Mathews, Mrs. Tappley, John Malone, ₤ 14 14 8.   (See estate of John Tappley, p. 58).

TURNER, ALEXANDER   Apt. 69 Pck. 2485
John Turner applied for admn 6 Dec 1783. Citation published at Catholick Congregation 14 Dec 178-, Robt McClintock.
Bond: John Turner, admr., John Bell sec., Wit: Jno Harbirt, 15 Jan 1784.

TURNIPSEED, BEAT   Apt. 69 Pck. 2490
Will of Beat Turnipseed of Camden Dist., Broad River... to my wife, possession of my dwelling house; to my son Hans Beat Turnipseed, 50 A on John Kennerlys Creek adj. to his own 100 A; to son Jacob Turnipseed, 200 A on Austins Mill Creek adj. Woodreds land; to son Zeb(?) Turnipseed, land on Broad River near Cedar Creek, 250 A; to daughter Maria Margrett Turnuseeds, ₤ 150 SC currency besides her child's portion...Beat Turnipseed (Z) (Seal), Wit: Frederick Dubber, Nicholas Wayerf (German Signature), Michal Vogt. Prov. by Michael Voght, 14 Oct 1782.
Warrant of appraisement to Michael Boght, Jacob Buchman, Richard Stroder, John Geiger, Aberhardt Neats, and John Turnipseed, 24 Oct 1782. Inv. 4 Dec 1782 by John Geiger, Jacob Büchman, Michl Vogt. Buyers at sale (no date), Wideto Turnipseed, John Beat Turnipseed, Jacob Turnipseed, Margred Turnipseed, Barny Pope Esqr., John Turnipseed, Christian Kinzler, Felix Turnipseed, Wm Kirklin, John Murff, Widdow, Adam Hemeter, old John Turnipseed, Michael Hoke, John Bur.

TURSDON, ROGER   Apt. 69 Pck. 2491
Bond: David Evans, admr., Henry Hunter, Thomas Baker, sec., 13 Setp 1785. Wit: Benj. Harrison.

TYLER, SPENCE   Apt. 69 Pck. 2496
Marcellus Little-John applied for admn as near of kin, 7 Aug 1782.
Citation published 11 Aug 1782 by Jacob Gibson.
Bond: Mercellus Littlejohn, admr., Henry Hunter, John Pope, sec., 31 Aug 1782, Wit: John Wooton, John Pope.
Inventory by Jas Gray, William McMoris, Jas Kinkead, (no date).

VALENTINE, DOUGAL   Apt. 70 Pck. 2499
Elizabeth Valentine applied for admn as nearest of kin, 11 June 1785. Citation read at Rocky Creek before Congregation 19 June 1785 by Wm Martin.
Bond: Elizabeth Valentine (X), admx., Margaret Downey, sec., 6 July 1785, Wit: James Knox, JP.
Estate appraised by James Crofford, Alexander Kenney, John Carson, for ₤ 28 8 1.

WALKER, ANDREW   Apt. 71 Pck. 2518
Glass Caston applied for admn on estate of Andrew Walker, late of Hanging Rock Settlement, planter, as greatest creditor, 26 May 1787. Citation published by John Cato.
Bond: Glass Caston, admr., Frederick Joiner, Bailey Fleming, sec., 19 July 1787.

WARNEL, WILLIAM   Apt. 71 Pck. 2528
Eleazer Gore applied for admn 8 Apr 1783. Citation published 13 Apr 1783 by Alexr Donald. Citaiton pub 20 Apr 1783 by Thos Duke.

Bond: Eleazer Gore, admr., Joseph Timms, John Ashford Gore, sec.
Warrant of appraisement to John Seley, Churchwell Carter, Jas Gore
& John Pratt.
Inventory 26 May 1783, includes one Negro (not named), by Churchill
Carter, James Gore, John Pratt.

WATSON, DAVID Apt. 71 Pck 2549
Will dated 10 Dec 1776, pro. 4 Feb 1786...wife Hanna, son
James, son Joh, daughter Ann Moffett, son William, daughter Sarah
TEmpleton, son John, son David, son Samuel, Samuel's son Gilbert;
Exors wife Hannah, and son Samuel, Wit: Samuel Watson, Alexander
Carruth, Alexander Kennedy.
Estate appraised by John Venables, Hugh Allison, James McNair (X),
James Watson 6 June 1786, before Jno Moffett, JP of York County.

WATSON, JOHN Apt. 72 Pck. 2552
Joseph Feemster and Samuel Watson applied for admn as near
of kin 5 Apr 1782. Citation read at Bullocks Creek 15 Apr 1782 by
Jos. Alexander, V. D. M.
Bond: Samuel Watson, Joseph Feemster, admrs., James Kirkpatrick, John
Moffett, sec., 30 May 1782, Wit: Wm McCulloch, Mary McCulloch.
Admrs. qualified before Wm McCulloch, JP 22 July 1782.
Warrant of appraisement to William Henry Senr, John Venables, James
Watson, James McCord. Appraisement 12 Aug 1782 by John Venables,
James Watson, James McCord.
Purchasers at sale, 14 Aug 1782: James Templeton, James McNeirs, James
Ross, Samuel Watson, John Moffett, Joseph Patterson, 'Daniel Collins,
Walter Carson, Jas Patterson, Felix Walker, John Patton, John Chambers,
John Peters, Samuel Burns, Francis Kirkpatrick, James Crafford, Isaac
Enlow, Abraham Barron, John Johnston, John Cooper, William Digby,
Alexander Allison, James Smith, Edward Morehead, Nathl Porter, William
Stevenson, Alexander Stuart, Wm McCulloch, Wm Erwin, John Martain,
Jos. Wallis, John Cansler, Samuel Watson, Senr; John Givens, Newberry
STockton, John Willson, John Walker, James McCormick, Peter Patterson,
Wm Ridly, John Jordan, Henry Wright, James Scott, Robert Patterson,
Hugh Allison, Mary Laughlin, Matthew Black.

WAY, MOSES Apt. 72 Pck. 2559
Ann Way, relict of Moses Way, applied for admn 29 Dec 1781.
Citation read in publick meeting by Solomon Thomson. Min.
Bond: 16 Feb 1782, Ann Way, admx., Joseph Hill, John Harvin, Wit:
Nathl Richbourgh.
Inventory 29 Feb 1782 includes Negroes (named), by Isham Moore, John
Harvin, and Matthw Singleton.
Sale 1 May 1782. Buyers not listed.

WEAVER, JACOB Apt. 72 Pck. 2561
Bond: George Slicker, admr., William Slicker, Gasper Slicker,
sec., 15 Dec 1784. Wit: Jno Harbirt.
Warrant of appraisement 15 Dec 1784 to John Arnold Pender, David Morrow,
Amos Richards, John Davis, and Robert Davis.
Sworn by Andw Foster, JP 13 Jan 1785: David Morrow, Amos Richards and
John Arnold Pender.

WERSHING, GEORGE Apt. 72 Pck. 2572
(Apparently the same estate as Gosper Weshing which follows)
Warrant of appraisement to Christian Kinseller, Benjn Grub, Burrel
Fust, Jas Taylor, Jacob Fust, 15 July 1783; Thomas Taylor, admr.
Inventory 14 Aug 1783 by James Taylor, Benjamin Grubb, Christian
Kincsler, includes Negroes (named).

WERSHING, GOSPER Apt. 72 Pck. 2573
Bond: Thomas Taylor, admr., Kemp T. Strother, sec., Wit:
R. Winn, 15 July 1783.

WESTBURY, WILLIAM Apt. 72 Pck. 2588
Mary Westbury applied for admn 9 Feb 1782. Citation read
17 Feb 1782, by Richard Furman. Mary Westbury, and William Wesbury
bonded as admrs. 20 Mar 1782 with Anthony Leigh (X) and John Wesbury,
sec. Wit: Josiah Furman.
Estate appraised 28 Mar 1782 by Robert Dearington, Robt Lewis, John
Wesbury.

Purchasers at sale: Samuel Dwyer, John Wooderson, James Rembert, Mary Westbury, Robert Lewis, Wm Wesbery, John Wesbury, Burrell Brown, John Wheeler, Charles Spain, Jonathan Searth, Aduel Atkinson.

WHEATLEY, JOHN   Apt. 72 Pck. 2590
Richard Perdue applied for admn as a Creditor, 9 Nov 1785.
Citation published by Joseph Rees, 13 Nov 1785.
Bond: Richd Perdue, admr., Francis Goodwyn, sec., 30 Nov 1785. Wit: Andrew Baskin.
Dedimus to Thomas Taylor to admn. oath of admn., 1 Dec 1785.
Warrant of appraisement to James Taylor, Josiah Daniel, Stewart Patterson, Benjamin Grub, and Sterling Clark.
Inventory 6 Dec 1785, by James Taylor, Stuard Patteson, Starling Clark, includes debt due from Constant Harrison.

WHITAKER, JAMES   Apt. 72 Pck. 2593
12 April 1777, Will of James Whitaker of Craven County...to son Willis Whitaker, 300 A adj. Edward Stone and John Stone; to son John Wiggins Whitakers, 250 A on a branch of Two Mile Creek adj. Andrew Hendricks; to son James Whitaker, 250 A on Sampsons Bobs and Joseph Kershaws lines; to son Simon Whitaker, 250 Al to wife Mary, three negroes (named); my seven children: Martha Whitaker, Catherine Whitaker, Willis Whitaker, John Wiggins Whitaker, James Whitaker, Mary Whitaker, and Simon Whitaker...William Whitaker Sr., and Willis Whitaker, Exrs....
James Whitaker; Wit: William Whitaker Jr., Joel Hudson.
Prov. 22 Apr 1782 by Wm Whitaker Jr.
Warrant of appraisement to William Lang, Samuel Boykin, Arthur Brown Ross, William Whitaker Jr., and JOhn Wyly, 22 Apr 1782.
Inventory includes Negroes (named) 15 July 1782, by Wm Lang and Arthur Brown Ross.

WHITAKER, JOHN   Apt. 72 Pck 2595
Willis Whitaker applied for admn, 15 Sept 1784.
Citation read in the Congregation of Camden, 10 Oct 1784, John Logue.
Bond: William Whitaker, admr., Henry Hunter, sec., Wit: Jno Pearson, 13 Nov 1784.

WHITAKER, RICHARD   Apt. 73 Pck 2600
William Whitaker applied for admn as next of kin, 20 Aug 1782.
Citation read in an assembly of people called Quakers near Camden, 25 Augt 1782, certified by Zimri Gaunt, Nebo Gaunt, Samuel Tomlinson, and Sam. Gaunt.
Bond: William Whitaker admr., Willis Whitaker, James Beaty, sec., 21 Nov 1782, Wit; Jno Blanton.
Dedimus to Coll. Joseph Kershaw to admn oath, 21 Nov 1782.

WHITAKER, ROBERT   Apt. 73 Pck. 2602
Letters fo admn, Richland County, to Willis Whitaker and Thomas Whitaker, 21 Aug 1789, Phil Perason, C. C.

WHITE, JOSEPH   Apt. 73 Pck 2609
Will of Joseph White of Craven County, 13 Mar 1784; to my son George 212 A on N side of ye plantation, and one cow and calf and heifer; to sons JOseph and Hugh, the other two parts of my plantation, Joseph to have ye East with the Houses upon it; to son Joseph, one Horse and saddle, etc....to son Hugh, one Bay mare and roan mare, etc....to daughter Issabel Helena, one Cow and Calf & Heifer, etc. and her maintainance on the plantation while she is single; all the rest of effects and negro Bob to be equally divided amongst all my children, that is to say, George, Joseph & Hugh, Isabell Helena, Mary and Joanna...son Joseph and Archibald McCorkle, exrs...Joseph White (X) (Seal), Wit: Andw Foster, Issable helena Foster (X), John Foster. Prov. 28 Jan 1785. Appraisement 9 Feb 1785 by Hugh White, John Foster, John Kennedy.

WHITE, STEPHEN   Apt. 73 Pck 2610
Craven County, April 21, 1780...Will of Stephen White...uncle John Gamble and uncle John White, Exrs...to brother John White, all of plantation...Stephen White (Seal), Wit: John Gamble, Jean Gamble (OO), Provedby <u>Jane</u> Gamble, before Andw Foster, 5 Oct 1785.

Dedimus to Andrew Foster to admn oath of appraisement 12 Oct 1785.
Bond: John White, admr., John Couser, sec., 21 Oct 1785, Wit: Andw
Foster, JP, Wm Nilson, Thos Nilson.
Warrant of appraisement to John Craig, Henry Coffe,, Wm Nelson, John
Crockett, and Thomas Nelson.
Inventory 21 Oct 1785, L 75 13 6 by Henery Coffey, William Nilson, Thos
Nilson.

WILLIAMS, NATHAN   Apt. 73 Pck 2630
    Will of Nathan Williams of Camden District; to wife Sela;
friends Joel Williams and William Nassery, exrs...all estate divided between my wife SEla and my children (not named)...26 Aug 1778...Nathan
Williams (Seal), Wit: Thomas House, Thos Boone, Samuel Woodward (( ),
Michael McCartney (X).   Prov 21 Oct 1782 by Michael McCarty.
Appraisement L 788 19 0.
Bond 1779 due by Albright Averit, Note 1779 Timothy Rieves; dated 1
Dec 1782 by Thomas House, William Killingsworth, Mickel McCarty.

WILSON, JAMES   Apt. 74 Pck. 2637
    Janie Wilson applied for admn as nearest of kin, 28 Apr 1785.
Citation read at Salem Church 5 May 1785 by Thos Reese.
Bond: Jean Wilson, admx., Moses Gordon, Robert Carter, sec., 28 Apr
1785 Wit: James Carter.
Estate appraised by John Armstrong, William Thompson, Henry Cassels
Junr, 11 July 1785, for L 494 14 4.

WILSON, JOHN JR.   Apt. 74 Pck 2640
    Dicksy Ward applied for admn as his wife is the relect of sd.
John Wilson Jr., 15 Feb 1782.
Citation published by Raff (sic) Jones, M. G. in my meeting and congregation 10 March 1782.
Bond: Dicksey Ward (X), admr., Elias Ward, Moses Jordan, sec., 19 Mar
1782, Wit: Josiah Furman.
Warrant of appraisement to James Lawhaugh, Jesse Wilson, William Jones,
Charles Seal and Robert Elkins, 19 Mar 1782.
Inventory (includes box of Shoe makers tools), 18 May 1782 by Jas.
Laughon, Jessee Wilson, William Jones.

WILSON, WILLIAM (Dr.)   Apt. 74 Pck. 2648
    Will of William Wilson, 28 Feb 1776...to wife Marey Willson, all
lands, chattels, etc....Wm Willson (Seal), Wit: William Geiger, Uriah
Goodwyn, Prov. 25 Nov 1785 by Mary Willson before William Meyer.
Bond: Mary Willson, admx., John Marshall and Wm Marshall, sec., 25 Nov
1785, Wit: Jeremiah Juggers, Jonan. Wise.
Dedimus to Wm Myers to prove will 7 Nov 1785.
Warrant of appraisement 23 Mar 1786 to John Marshall, Andrew Patterson,
and Samuel Penny. Inventory (not dated), accts on Malica Howell,
Henry Chappell, Cathrin Blanshad, Nathan Dorch, John Wyche, Drury Wyche,
Hardy Hay, Hicks Chappell, Laban Chappell, Howell Hay, Gilbert Gibson,
Frederick Heath, Jonathan Durgan, James Taylor, Noah Philps, Robt
Leviston, Richard Evans, Joseph Westcoat, Peter Smith, Joseph Martin,
Daniel Tateman, Joel Threewits, John Gauge, Robt Goodwyn, John Geely,
Nazurah Hunter, Capt. William Howell, Olliver Legran, Phillip Pearson,
Gabrel Parker, James Pearce, Collo. William Thomson, John Robertson,
Robt Rives, Henery Papick, Thomas Jefferys, Joseph Tatelin, Ludwell
Evans.

WINN, JOHN   Apt. 74 Pck. 2652
    Will dated 16 Jan 1781; prov. 4 Mar 1782...son John, S side of
tract where I formerly lived in Georgia, adj. Wm Graves, Tennett,
Stevens; son Peter, N side of above tract in Ga.; grandson Thomas Bacon;
nephew Joseph Winn; sons John Winn and Peter Winn and friend Thomas
Baker, Exrs...Wit: Naomi Hampton (X), John Bacon, Henry Wheeler,
Inventory and appraisement by John Wheeler, John Bacon, Henry Wheeler
11 Mar 1782.

WISE, SAMUEL
    Capt. Felix Warley, Capt. John Blake and Richard Andrews Rapley sworn as appraisers of estate of Maj. Samuel Wise, 16 Aug 1782.
Letters testamentary granted by Wm Burrows, Ordy of SC to John James Haig as Exor 14 Jan 1780.
Estate inventoried and appraised at his plantation at the Congarees, 16 Aug 1782, for ₤ 1352 13 6.
Letter found in package, now kept in the safe in office of Judge of Probate:
                                        " Cheraws Novr 19 1783
Sr:
    General Harrington informs me that when Major Wise's Estate was appraised, by mistake several Negroes belonging to the Estate of Mrs. Betty Wise deceased, & several others belonging to Miss Wise in England were included in the appraisement. The General has Bills of Sale & authentic Documents to evince(?) this. It will be therefore necessary to have this matter rectified before the Ordinary & proof made before him of these facts on oath & by exhibiting the Bills of Sale. the Bills of sale are only to be shewn to the Ordinary and not to be left with him. I have the honour to be
                                        Your most obedt. Servt:
                                        Charles Cotesworth Pinckney"
John James Haig Esqr.
[N. B. Samuel Wise was killed in the attack on Savannah, 9 Oct 1779]

WISHER, WALTER Apt. 74 Pck. 2656
    Mary Ranick applied for admn 9 Dec 1784.
Citation read at my house. W. Bratton, Dec. 10, 1784.

WOOD, JOHN Apt. 74 Pck. 2669
    Will of John Wood of St. Marks Parish and Craven County, being in perfect health; to wife Susannah, household goods, debts & moveable effects during her widowhood & afterwards to be equally divided between all her children & my son Samuel Wood and my Daughter Mary Wood; to my sons John Wood & William Wood, all my Houses,Plantations & Lands; reserving to James Huey 50 A where he now lives; to son Archilus Wood, one shilling sterling...Susannah Wood & John Wood, Exrs., 24 Jan 1777... John Wood (Seal), Wit: John Pratt, Winefred Wood, William Wood. Prov. 19 May 1783.
Archilus Wood applied for admn, 29 Aug 1783. Citation published 8 Sept 1783 by Jacob Gibson.
Debts paid by Elizabeth Wood (X), admx. of John Wood decd, 9 Mar 1801.

WOODERSON, JOHN Apt. 75 Pck. 2677
        Ann Wooddison applied for admn, 19 Feb 1784.
Citation read 22 Feb 1784 by Richard Furman, V. D. M.
Bond: Ann Woodison, admx., David Reynolds Junr and Charles McGinney, sec., 27 Apr 1784, Wit: David Rogers, JP, William Sanders.
Dedimus to David Rogers to admn oath 4 Mar 1784.
Warrant of appraisement 4 Mar 1784 to John Wheeler Senr, David Reynolds, Fedrick Adkins, John Melone, and John Saunders.
Inventory 27 Apr 1784 includes Negroes (named), by Jno Wheler Senr, David Reynolds Jr., William Sanders.

WOODWARD, THOMAS Apt. 75 Pck. 2679
        Will of Thomas Woodard of St. Marks Parish, Camden District... 31 Oct 1780, prov. 9 Apr 1782. Sons Thomas, Simon and John; daughters Elizabeth Davis, Martha Allison, Mary Woodard, and Priscilla Woodard; son in law William Davis and Thomas, Simon & John Woodard, exrs... Wit: David Reynolds Senr, David Reynolds Junr, Jno Postell.
Estate appraised by David Rogers, Thos Neal, Isaac Lenoir, 3 June 1782.
Warrant of appraisement to afore-mentioned appraisers and Frederick Atkinson and John Postell.

WOODWARD, WILLIAM Apt. 75 Pck.2680
        Elizabeth Woodward applied for admn, 13 Mar 1784. No return of citation.
Bond: Elizabeth Woodward (X), admx., Samuel Simmons, sec., 1 Apr 1784.
Wit: Jno Harbirt.

Warrant of appraisement to James Hoard, Alexander Brent, Thos Harbirt, Saml Simmons and John Brent; Inventory 24 May 1784 by Thos Harbirt, Saml Simmons, John Brent, for L 47 10 1.

WOOTERS, JACOB   Apt. 75 Pck 2681
    (Package missing from file)

WYCHE, DRURY   Apt. 75 Pck. 2692
    Will of Drury Wyche of Craven County...to wife Sarah Wyche, the Land and two of the Negroes (prince and Juda), together with the stock & furniture lent her by her former husband, also Negroes Roger and Hagr, if she have no issue to my grandson David Hopkins; Executors to buy Negro girl about 5 or 6 years ot age to give to my grandson David Hopkins; my three children Wm Wyche, John Wyche and Mary Wyche; to daughter Alcey Williamson, L 1 s 1 d 9 sterling, together with a proportional part of my part of that Estate of Wm Dancey, Decd., which falls to me after the death of Mrs. Mary Wyche; to son William Wyche, one Bay Mare and two Colts; to sons William Wyche and John Wyche, all my Swamp Land, to be divided when my son Wm comes to the age of 21; my 50 A tract on which I formerly lived at pee hill to be sold; to children, 10 negroes (named)...friends Thomas Taylor, William Meyer Esqr & Joel McLemore, Exrs & Guardians for my Children, 16 Aug 1784...Drury Wyche, Wit: William Hopkins, Abraham Kearslick, Prov. 28 Jan 1785.
Warrant of appraisement to(28 Jan 1785), John Hirons, Green Rives, Henry Rives, Thos Harvil, James Taylor. Estate appraised for L 885 14 10½ (no date).

WYLY, JOHN   Apt. 75 Pck 2695
    William Lang and wife Sarah, William Wylie and Joseph Kershaw applied for admn as next of kin, 11 Jan 1783. Citation read 12 Jan 1783 by Richard Furman.
William Lang, William Wyly, and Joseph Kershaw, bonded 5 Feb 1783, Arthur Brown Ross, sec., Test: Richard Furman.
Estate inventoried 1 Mar 1783.
[Note: John Wyley, Sheriff at Camden, incurred the savage anger of Tarleton by executing some men for treason, and Tarleton determined to put him to death. However, his men mistook his brother Samuel Wyley for him and killed him instead.]

WYLY, SAMUEL   Apt. 75 Pck. 2696
    William Lang applied for admn, 4 Apr 1783. Citation read in congregation at Camden, Sunday 6 Apr 1783 by John Logue.
Bond: William Lang, 4 Feb 1787, admr., John Harker and Thos Brown, sec.
(See above note).

WYLY, WILLIAM   Apt. 75 Pck 2697
    Will of William Wyly of Camden in the District of Camden...13 Nov 1785, prov. 22 Nov 1785...wife Elizabeth, daughter Dinah Wyly; James Willson Lang, Samuel Lang and John Wyly Lang(sons of William and Sarah Lang); sister Sarah Lang, to take care of Dinah Wyly...Eoxrs: William Lang, John Chesnut, and John Millhouse...Negro slave Toney to be freed after my deceased...Wit:Joseph Bulkley, Robt Reed, James Galbraith.
Bond: William Lang, admr., 26 Nov 1785, Arthur Brown Ross, sec.
John Galbraith, John Belton & Thomas Brown sworn appraisers 19 Dec 1785.
George Ganter qualified 2 Jan 1786.

WYLEY, WILLIAM   Apt. 75 Pck 2698
    William Dunn, Jane Wyley and Sarah Wyley applied for admn, 16 Sept 1785. Citation read at New Erection Meeting House [Fishing Creek] in Mr. Simpson's congregation 30 Sept 1785 by Samuel Neely.
Bond: William Dunn, Jane Wyley and Sarah Wyley, admrs.,3 Oct 1785.
William Lewis, Michael Dickson and William Miller sworn as appraisers 16 Nov 1785 by John Adair, JP
Appraisement made 1 Dec 1785 of estate of Wm Wiley, late of Rocky Creek, states" William Willey Departed this Life Septr one 1783" Five heirs (not named). Jane Wyley married Morrow, apparently Joseph Morrow, as the appraisement was received on 22 Dec 1785 from him.

YOUNG, AMOS   Apt. 76 Pck 2702
    Inventory only: 22 Jan 1787 by Andrew Walker, Robert Adams, John Waugh.

YOUNG, LeGROS   Apt. 76 Pck 2712
    William McGrew applied for admn of LeGros Young, late of Congaree, 5 Mar 1787. Citation published by Joseph Rees, 11 Day March 1787.
Dedimus to Richard Hampton to admn oath to Wm McGre 27 Mar 1787
Warrant of appraisement to David Wescott, Benj. Evaret, Wm Taylor, Robt Tweedy and Mathew Howell, 27 Mar 1787.
Swron appraisers 4 Apr 1787, David Wescott, Benjamin Everit, William Taylor.
Inventory, at Congaree, 12 Apr 1787.
Bond: 4 Apr 1787, William McGrew, admr., David Westcott and Wm Taylor, sec.

YOUNG, WILLIAM   Apt. 76 Pck 2717
    Margaret Atkinsons, late widow of Wm Young, applied for admn, 14 Feb 1787.
Citation read at Jackson Creek Church, by Thomas H. McCaule, 15 Feb 1787.
Warrant of appraisement to James Russell, Samuel Gladney, Maruice Weaver, Alexander, Roseborough, Robert Hannan, 16 May 1787.
Inventory 13 Aug 1787 by Robert Hanon, Samuel Gladney, and Alexander Rosborough.

BRUMFIELD, REUBEN Apt. 21 Pck 376
    Robert Lewis applied for admn as one of his creditors, 31 Dec 1781. Citation published in publick meeting, 13 Jan 1782, Solomon Thomson.
Bond: Robert Lewis, admr, John Westbury, William Graham, sec., 22 Jan 1782.
Drury Fletcher applied for admn, 17 Nov 1781. Citation published 18 Nov 1781, Solomon Thomson.
Inventory 14 Mar 1782 by Chas. Spann, William Graham, John Wesberry, includes a Negro Oure.
Sale 22 Mar 1782 (no buyers listed).

MOBBERLY, EDWARD   Apt. 45 Pck. 1593
    William Mobberly applied for admn as next of kin, 14 Aug 1782.
Citation published to a considerable Congregation on Sandy River, 25 Aug 1782, Jas Fowler, V. D. M.
Published at the house of Thomas Duke 18th inst.
Bond: William Mobberly, admr, John Moberly, Henry Rogers, sec., Wit: Josiah Furman, 10 Sept 1782.
Warrant of appraisement 10 Sept 1782 to Benjamin Mobbly, Francis Coleman, Moses Hill, Robert Coleman and David Richardson.
Sworn before Dd. Hopkins, JP, 4 Nov 1782.
Appraisement 10 Nov 1782 by Benjamin Mobberly, Francis Coalman, Robert Coleman.
Sale 20 Nov 1782, purchasers: William Mobberly, Edward Mobberly, Susanna Mobberly, Henry Rogers., money due from Solomon Peters, Wm Philips, William Few.

MONTGOMERY, HENRY   Apt. 45 Pck. 1600
    William Montgomery, James Armstrong, Sylvester Dunn and John Armstrong applied for admn, 8 May 1787. Citation read in my church, Thos Reese.
Dedimus to John Dickey, JP 29 May 1787 to qualify admrs.
Bond: William Montgomery, James Armstrong, Sylvester Dunn, John Armstrong, admrs., Archibald Connor, James Armstrong Jr., John Armstrong, sec., 5 June 1787.
Estate appraised 5 & 6 June 1787 by Samuel Bennett, Henry Blanchard, Isaac Connor.

MONTGOMERY, HUGH   Apt. 45 Pck. 1601
          Marcey Montgomery applied for admn, 14 July 1783
Citation read to his Congregation at Fishing Creek, 17 Augt 1783, by
William Martin, Minister.
Bond: Massey Montgomery (X), admx., Moses Smith, sec., 17 Sept 1783,
Wit: R. Winn at Winnsborough.

THOMSON, NATHAN   Apt 67 Pck 2404
          Bond: Joseph Payne, admr., John Swilly, William Goin, sec., 25
Feb 1785.
Warrant of appraisement 25 Feb 1785 to William Goin, Malachi Murphey,
Nicholas Swilly, George Payne and William Nettles.
Inventory 10 June 1785 by George Payne, Willim Nettel, Niclas Swillea.

RUSSELL, JOHN   Apt. 67 Pck 2402
          William Thompson applied for admn of John Russell, late of
Congree, in right of his wife, Eugenia Thompson, 6 Aug 1785.
Citation published by Joseph Rees, 7 Aug 1785.

ADDENDA:
Estate of Gen. Richard Richardson (Apt. 59 Pck. 2069) should include
   Oath of Extx administered to Dorothy Richardson, 8 Dec 1787 by Wm
McConnico, Clarendon County.

The estate of William Hay (Apt. 30 Pck. 1088) should include
   Mary Hay of Camden District, wife of William Hay send Greeting:
"Whereas sundry unhappy disputes and irreconcilable differences
happened and long subsisted between me the said Mary Hay and my said
husband, and finding it therefore necessary for us to live Separate...
deed of two slaves, Carolina and Jane...and other Negro wench Cloe,
on or before 25 Dec 1777, instrument dated 14 Sept 1776...Mary Hay (X)
Wit: Wm Meyer, Phil Pearson.

The estate of John Cunningham (Apt. Pck. 607) had proceedings which
continued in the probate court of York County. The reference for
those documents is Case 66 File #3144.
Amounts paid 1 Nov 1783:
to Jesse Douglass, to Col. H. Hampton, Ordinary for letters, to Alex
McWhorter, James Blair, James Armstrong, Moses Ferguson, John Pattan
Junr, to Ara Company [Aetna Iron Works], Prudence Hall, John Eakin,
Isaac FAries, James Alexander, John Pursley.
Inventory 24 Sept 1784 by Jas Simral, Alexander McWhorter, Thomas
McMurry, sworn before Wm Hill, JP

N. B. The following 20 estates were located in Sumter records.
Apparently they were transferred from Camden to Sumter at some time.

ATKINSON, JAMES   Apt. 119 Pck. 1
    Will of JAMES ATKINSON of St. Mark's Parish, Craven Co.,
planter...to wife ELIZABETH, the use of the plantation whereon I now
live on Black River and negroes (named)...to son MARMADUKE ATKINSON,
negro Ned...to son SHADRACH ATKINSON, negroes (named)...to son
FEDRICK ATKINSON, negro Simon...to son ADWELL ATKINSON, negro Isaac
...to the heirs of my daughter MARTHA LENOIR deceased....to my daughter LUCY CROSSWELL...to my daughter ELIZABETH MELONE, negro Winney...
to my daughter SYLVIA SPIGHT...money due from JOHN McQUEEN...31 Oct
1785...JAMES ATKINSON (+), Wit: WILLIAM DAVIS, MATHEW CARTER, REDDEN
McCOY. Proved by WILLIAM DAVIS before J. ALEXANDER, J. P.
    Inventory Dec. 5, 1786. Shows notes on JOHN McQUEEN and JOHN
MALONE, made by WILLIAM DAVIS, RICHARD HARVEY, ELIJAH McCOY.
Warrant of appraised 10 Oct 1786 to WILLIAM DAVIS, RICHARD HARVEY,
ELIJAH McCOY, and HENRY CASTLES.
Dedimus to ELIAS DUBOSE to qualify appraisers 28 Apr 1787.
16 Oct 1786, ELIZABETH ATKINSON declines to serve of the Executrix
of the will from age and infirmity.

The following letter was found in this package, but probably belongs
with the estate of JOHN ATKINS (see page 3).
to Col. HENRY HAMPTON, Nov. 8, 1783. I just inform you that at the
request of my relatives some time agow I begged for letters of administration on my father's estate, but after I returned home to
Virginia where I live I understand some of my friends entered a
cavit (sic).... JOSEPH ATKINS.

BARBER, AGNESS   Apt. 119, Pck. 2
    Will of Agness Barber of Watree Creek, Cambden District,
Craven Co., and St. Mark's Parish...to JOHN BARBER, for the use of my
three children ROBERT, JAMES and BETHRIDGE BARBER...JOHN BARBER,
and JOHN CONNER of Watree Creek, Exrs...8 Oct 1784...AGNESS BARBER
(X) (SEAL), Wit: THOS JOHNSTON, CHARLES JOHNSTON (+), JOHN JENKINS
(O). Proven by CHARLES JOHNSTON and JOHN JENKINS, 23 Oct 1784,
before JNO HARBIRT, J. P.
Sale 5 Nov 1784; Buyers: ROBERT EWING, BENJA. HARRISON, JAMES ARNETT,
JOHN SHAINS(?), ELIZABETH LENNOX, JOHN CONNERY, THOS ROBINSON, SAMUEL BARBER, THOS JOHNSTON, ALEXANDER GOYNE, JAMES OWENS, JOHN WINN,
JOHN McKEOWN, JAMES McCREIGHT, JAMES JOHNSTON, CHARLES LEWIS, THOMAS
MILES, JARVIS GIBSON, JOHN WATTS, JOHN BARBER, THOS GOODRAM, ALLEN
GOODRAM, JAMES HOLLIS, EDWARD MORGAN, ISAAC GRAHAM, CHARLES LEWIS,
JOHN JENKINS. Inventory 2 Nov 1784 by SAMUEL ARMSTRONG (O), JOHN
WATTS (X), THOS JOHNSTON.
Warrant of Appraisement to SAMUEL ARMSTRONG, JOHN WATTS, THOMAS
JOHNSTON, MOSES KNIGHTON, and JOHN KING, 23 Oct 1784.
(This estate may have been transferred to Sumter by error; it appears
 that the testator lived in what is now Chester or Fairfield County).

BRADLY, SAMUEL   Apt. 119 Pck. 3
    Will of SAMUEL BRADLY of Black River, Craven County...2 Jan
1778...to my son JAMES BRADLEY, 250 A adj. WILLIAM ROBERTS in a place
called Long branch & Negroes (named)...to son ROGER BRADLEY, 3 negroes
(named), 150 A on a Swamp called Scape Whore, plat dated 12 Sept 1767
...to my daughter MARY CARTER, negroes (named)...to my daughter
JENNET WILSON, 5 negroes (named)...to son SAMUEL BRADLEY, 3 tracts,
2 of 150 A and one of 500 A opposite to tract on which I now live,
when he reaches 21...to son MOSES BRADLEY, tract of 250 A on which my
house stands & 150 A adj. JAMES BRADLY SR., but not to have possession until the decease of my wife, until he reaches 21....to daughter
ELIZABETH, tract adj. to me and JAMES BRADLY, originally JOHN TOMLENSON, now JOHN DICKEY & ROSE LLOYD, between ROBERT ELISON, & negroes
(named), when she becomes 21 or marries...to wife ELIZABETH, tract
on which my house now stands & negroes (named)...L 200 to my neice
ELIZABETH BRADLEY, daughter of ARTHUR BRADLEY...wife ELIZABETH, sons
JAMES & ROGERS & Brothers JAMES & THOMAS BRADLEY, DAVID WILSON &
ROGER WILSON, Exrs...SAMUEL BRADLEY (SEAL), Wit: MOSES GORDON, THOMAS
REESE, JOHN SHAW, JNO DICKEY. Proven by MOSES GORDON 14 Aug 1782,

before ROGER WILSON, J. P. Craven County.
Dedimus to WILLIAM MARTIN to prove will & qualify Exrs., 13 Apr 1784.
Warrant of Appraisement to JOHN ANDERSON, JAMES ARMSTRONG, ROBERT CARTER, WILLIAM THOMPSON & HENRY CASTLES, 17 June 1784. Sworn 17 June 1784.
Inventory made 10 July 1784, by JNO ANDERSON, JAMES ARMSTRONG, HEN. CASSELS, JUNR.

BENBOW, RICHARD   Apt. 119 Pck. 4
       Will of Richard Benbow of Saint Marks Parish, Craven County...
to wife SARAH, Her living on my plantation during her widowhood...to my son JOHN BENBOW, 200 A in the neighborhood where I now live adj. JOHN CASTLES & JOHN DANIELS...land where I now live after my daughter SARAH attains the age of 18, to my three youngest children to be sufficiently educated...to daughters SUSANNAH HUGGINS, MARY BENBOW, ELIZABETH BENBOW, SARAH BENBOW & son ADAM BENBOW...friend WM THOMAS NEWMAN & Brother POWEL BENBOW, trustees for my children...son ADAM & daughter MARY, Exrs...26 Sept 1782...RICHARD BENBOW (SEAL), Wit: DANIEL JEFFORDS, CHARLES BURCH (C), JOHN CASSELS. Proven by JOHN CASSELS 21 Apr 1784, before H. HAMPTON, O. C. D.
Appraisers sworn 4 May 1784: JNO CASSELS, BENJAMIN CASSELS, GEORGE BYRD, before ELIAS DUBOSE, J. P. Appraised 5 May 1784.

COPPLEY, ELIZABETH   Apt. 119 Pck. 5
       Will of ELIZABETH COPPLEY of St. Marks Parish...to eldest daughter CATHRINE, 1/5 of personal estate of the age of 18 or her marriage... to my oldest son ROBERT, 1/5 part of personal estate, when he reaches 21 or marries...to my 2nd son ELY, 1/5 of personal estate...to 3rd son PATRICK, 1/5 of personal estate...to my youngest daughter (not named), 1/5 part of personal estate...ь 350 to be divided between CATHRINE & ROBERT... JAMES FRIERSON, FRANCIS LESSESNE & HUGH WATSON, Exrs...17 Jan 1785... ELIZABETH COPPLY (X) (SEAL), Wit: JAMES BRENTER(JS), GEO: FRYERSON, ABSALOM FRIERSON...Proven by JOHN BRENTER, 12 Mar 1785 before JOHN CANTEY, J.P. "WILLIAM MARTEN Esq. being from home"
(Papers from a Sumter District Equity Suit in the package, suit involving this will 1797-1817.)

CONYERS, JAMES JUNR.   Apt. 119 Pck. 6
       Will of James Conyers Jr. of Camden District, (Gent.)...to wife SUSANNAH, any two Negroes of my property, 2 horses, a woman's saddle... to the eldest son JOHN, 1/3 of estate & he is to be sent to School at 8 years old & to be sent to Colledge (sic)...to my youngest son JAMES, 1/3 of estate, and he is to be sent to school at 8 years old & there continue till he is Master of the Language, and then he is to be initiated into the Continental army if a Commission can be obtained for him & a small sword..wife SUSANNAH, Extx, during her widowhood & no longer, & DANIEL CONYERS, JOHN ANDERSON, THOMAS OSBORN Esqr., JAMES DAVIS, Exrs... 19 Feb 1780....JAS CONYERS JUNR, Wit: WM MARTIN, SUSANNAH DAVIS, JAMES HODGE. Prov. 6 Dec 1783.
Inventory 6 Jan 1784 by JOHN McCAULY, WM. BRUNSON SERN., WM BRUNSON JUNR.
Warrant of appraisement, 6 Dec 1783 to MAJOR JNO GAMBELL (stricken), JNO NELSON (stricken), EDWARD PLOWDEN (stricken), EBENEZER BAGNALL (stricken), & WM BRUNSON SR., WILLIAM BRUNSON JR. & MAJ. JAS McCAULY.
N. B. I do certify that the persons names that is erazed (sic) was at the assembly at the time of appraisement. WM. MARTIN, J. P.

CAMPBELL, ALEXANDER   Apt. 119 Pck. 7
       Will of Alexander Cambell of St. Mark's Parish, Planter...to my sister Mary Hunt during her widowhood & if she married to my nieces Elizabeth and Sarah Hunt, when they arrive to 18 years; Mathew Singleton & John Singleton, Exrs. 19 Oct 1783; Alexr Campbell (Seal), Wit: John James, William Dinkins, Thomas Andrew. Proved by Capt. John James, 11 June 1784 before William Murrell, JP.
Dedimus to William Murrell to prove will 29 Apr 1784.
Warrant of appraisement 29 Apr 1784 to John James, Isham Moore, Peter Molitt, Hubbard Rees and Fd. Pringle. Inventory 14 June 1782(sic) by Isham Moore, Huberd Rees, John James.

COMMANDER, SAMUEL   Apt 119 Pck. 8
       Will of Samuel Commander Senr of St. Mark's Parish...to sons

to sons JAMES and THOMAS COMMANDER, s 5 each and s 5 to each of my deceased children (which I had by my first wife), Likewise to all the children which are married which I had by my last wife (I have given them their part already) & my upper tract of Land I bought of John Egan, 1/2 for son Samuel and 1/2 for son Joseph...plantation, to my wife Mary to live on during her widowhood...my four youngest children: Samuel, Joseph, Jesse and Martha...12 June 1783...Samuel Commander Senr (Seal), Wit: Peter Dubose Senr, Samuel Newman, Deborah Rows (X), Prov. by Peter Dubose 13 May 1784.
Warrant of appraisement to: Thomas Newman, Jonathan Newman, Andrew Dubose, John Norwood, and Peter Dubose, 13 May 1784.
Inventory 23 June 1784, by Andrew Dubose, Peter Dubose Sen, John Norwood, Thomas Newman.

ANDERSON, DAVID Apt. 119 Pck. 9
Will of David Anderson of Camden District, Craven County, planter...to sons John Anderson and William Anderson, all those plantations 1200 A, some of which granted to, other purchased by me in the State of Georgia, in a place called Newport; to son Cooper Anderson and grandson James Cantey, two tracts of 450 A in Newport, State of Georgia; to son John Anderson, negroes (named); to wife Mary Anderson, all the estate she was possessed of at the time of our marriage; to Roger Wilson, son of David Wilson decd, 50 A on Black River, SC, known as the Mill tract; sons John, William, Cooper, grandson James Canty, granddaughters Mary and Sarah; Son John, wife Mary, Thomas Quarterman, and Andrew Walltour, Exrs., 12 Apr 1784...David Anderson (LS), Wit: Wm E. Herring, Mary Gamble (X), Hugh Gamble. Prov. by Hugh Gamble, 5 June 1784.
David Anderson of Midway, State of Georgia, will dated 12 Apr 1784, do ratify the same and give to my nephew John Anderson, 443 A, the tract where he now lives; nephew William Anderson, 257 A on the Barony; the said John to allow his mother Ann Anderson to live on any part; to newphew Joseph Anderson, 200 A on Lynches Creek, 12 Apr 1784...David Anderson (Seal), Wit: Thomas Reese, Hen: Cassels Senr, Mary Wilson.
Prov. by Mary Wilson, 5 June 1784.
Dedimus to Roger Wilson 5 June 1784.
Inventory 12 June 1784 including negroes (named), ₤ 2209 15 0. by Roger Bradley, Richd Cooper, Jno Anderson.

EDWARDS, WILLIAM Apt. 119 Pck. 10
Will of William Edwards...to wife Elisabeth Edward, the Plantation where I leatlie lived on the waters of Black River on Puddling Swamp, 200 A and six negroes(Named)...to James Wootars, son of Jacob Woottars Junr, decd...11 Feb 1782, Wiell: Edwards, Wit: Robert Henderson, Daniel Keils, A true copy taken from the original Will, Chas. Lining, 12 Jan 1784. (original recorded in Charleston).
Elizabeth Edwards applied for admn, 25 Apr 1784. Citation read 27 Mar 1784 in my church at Salem, by Thos: Reese.
Bond: Elizabeth Edwards, John Tomlinson, 23 Mar 1784, Wit: Thos Millis.
Dedimus to Roger Wilson to admn oath 25 Apr 1784.
Warrant of appraisement to CHARLES STORY, ROBERT HENDERSON, WILLIAM MILLS, EDWARD HEVY(?), & Aaron Frierson.
Inventory St. Marks Parish, Craven County, 4 June 1784, by CHARLES STORY, WM HILL, AARON FRIERSON.

JAMES, JOHN Apt. 119 Pck. 11
Dedimus to WM Murrell, 1 Sept 1784.
Warrant of appraisement, 1 Sept 1784 to Isham Moore, Huberd Rees, John Singleton, George Ioor, and Thomas Andrews.
Inventory includes Negroes (named), ₤ 1925 15 -, by Isham Moore, Huberd Rees, Geo. Ioor, 1 Nov 1784.
Will of John James of the Parish of St. Marks, planter...to wife Sarah James, all my Estate real and personal over and above what I shall make mention of; to my daughter Mary Bradford, three Negroes (named); to son John James, the old plantation,known as the high hill tavern, contains in ballance of a part sold to John G. G--gard, 208 A and three Negroes (named), when sd. John Becomes 21; to son Samuel James, 184 A adj. to the old survey, adj. Daniel Hollody up to Mr. Sanders, 200 A, 16 A titled to Nathaniel Moore, ballance 184 A and 3 negroes (named; to daughter Sarah James Junr, two tracts of 100 A each, one Moses Ferguson, the other 100 A at the Epper Eand(sic) of the White Dearpon; to daughter Rebecca James; 346 A on _____ Swamp, part of a 400 A warrant; wife Sarah, Col. Singleton,

and John James, Exrs., 17 July 1778...John James (Seal , Wit: John Holladay, Benjman Holday, William Hollady.

JAMES, SHEARWOOD Apt. 119 Pck. 12
Will of Shearwood James of St. Mark's Parish, Planter...to wife MARTHA JAMES, during her Widowhood, all my Lands & Negroes; to my two sons Talefore and Shearwood James; in case she should marry she shall be cut out of my two son's estates annually for a maintenance during Life; to daughter Martha James, two Negroes, Alse & Tabby and one gray horse; to son Talefero James, tract of 300 A, the tract I formerly lived on and 9 negroes (named); when Talefero becomes of age, remainder of estate to be divided between him and Shearwood; to son Shearwood James, my manor Plantation whereon I now live, 200 A and another tract on Rafting Creek adj. Mr. Robert Darington, 100 A and 9 negroes (named); to grandson William Rees, son of my daughter Mary Rees, a negro Abram formerly lent to my daughter Mary Rees; to grandson Richey, son of my daughter Sarah Rees, negro girl named Luce; to Nancy Brunson, daughter of Peter Brunson, negro Robin; to daughter Elizabeth Singleton, negroes Ben & Sucky; to granddaughter of my daughter Elizabeth Singleton, negro Eve; wife Martha and Joseph Singleton, Exrs, 9 Nov 1782, Shearwood James. Wit: Saml Tynes, William Wood, Richard Singleton, Thomas Andrews. Proved by Wm Wood before Henry Hampton.
Appraisement 1784, by Matthw Singleton, Isham Moore, Joseph Hill.
Warrant of appraisement to Matthew Singleton, Isham Moore, As. Silvester, Joseph Hill, John James, 2 Mar 1784.

HOWARD, JOSEPH Apt. 119 Pck. 13
Will of Joseph Howard of St. Marks Parish, Craven County, Doctor of Physick, being about to take a journey; children shall be schoolled sufficient for any of the Country business on the parts where they dwell; to daughter Jerusha Howard, tract I bought of Hodges Moore that James McCormack formerly dwelt on, granted to John Fletcher and 50 A adj. to it I bought of James Rivers, and negroes (named); to her two brothers Heli Howard and James Howard, tract of land bought of Andrew Alison, granted to John Dargon and negro (named)...my aged father to be provided for... 150 A I bought of John Appell...5 Nov 1773, JOSEPH HWOARD (LS), Wit: Mathew Parrison, William Howard, Asbery Silvester (+). A true copy taken from the records. Dec 29, 1785. Peter Freneau, D. Secry.
(Original in Charleston Will Book TT, pp. 257-258.)

FURMAN, WOOD Apt. 119 Pck. 14
Will of Wood Furman, St. Mark's Parish, Craven County...to wife Rachel Furman, 250 A on both sides Beach(?) Creek, granted to me, cattle etc., and negroes (named); to son Josiah Furman, tract in St. Mark's Parish, purchased of Bernard Bookman, 550 A on Wateree River, adj. to est. of James Postel, and Tennis Tiebont, adj. land I purchased from Samuel Barnet; to daughter Sarah, wife of Henry Haynsworth, 100 A I purchased of Thomas Evans, known as the Duck Pond and tract adj. to Ruben Ross, Robert Green, and Rev. Elisor (500 A, I purchased from Joseph Fogartie) and to her sons Henry and Richard Harynsworth; wife Rachel and sons Josiah and Richard and daughter Sarah, Exrs., 5 Aug 1777, Wit: John Newton Senr, John Newton Jr., Ann Newton (Z). Proved by John Wesbury, 10 Sept 1783. Codicil 24 July 1782, Wit: James Rembert, Jacob Chambers, John Wesbury. Sale 1 Mar 1784, Certified 27 Apr 1784. Inventory 10 & 11 Nov 1783, includes Negroes (named), by Thos Neal, William Hampton, Anthony Lee (A). Warrant of appraisement 16 Sept 1783.

NEILSON, SAMUEL Apt. 119 Pck. 15
Will of Samuel Neilson of St. Mark's Parish, Craven [County]... 18 Dec 1782,; estate to be divided between my wife and three children, Isabella, Mary and Samuel; my slaves not to be divided until my son comes of age; to son Samuel, 400 A; 100 A on S side Santee, 3 miles from Nelsons ferry on the head of Sandy Run be sold...wife, William Little and John Paisley, Exrs., Samuel Neilson (Seal), Wit: Alexdr Colclough, W. Candloss, John Bowman. Proved by John Bowman before John Canty, 11 May 1785.
Dedimus to Canty to prove will, 27 Apr 1785.
Qualified Sarah Neilson as Extx, 11 May 1785.
Inventory including Negroes (named), by Levi Moor, David Anderson, James Gilson.

RICHARDSON, WILLIAM Apt. 119 Pck. 16
    Will of William Richardson of Bloom Hill in the District of
Camden; to wife in lieu of her dower, Ł 1000 sterling; to each of my
daughters (whether born before the date of this will or after), Ł 1000
sterling; to sons, who may survive to the age of 21, my whole real estate,
equally divided the day the youngest attains the age of 22; and as I always
had an aversion to the name of Richardson, I desire and request that my
children would change it for Rich, which is a short easy wrote name...
friends Charles Cotesworth Pinckney, John Pringle, John Smyth and John
Chesnut, Exrs., and all my sons as they attain the age of 21 years...1
Dec 1785...Wm Richardson (Seal), Wit: Eliz. Sley, Joseph Dukes, Rich
Chewning. Proved by Rich Chewning and John Smyth 10 Mar 1786 before
Isaac Alexander.
Ann Richardson qualified as Extx, 19 Apr 1786 by Wm McConnico, JP.
Warrant of appraisement to A. T. Brisbane, Wm Boykin, Douglass Starke,
and Nath Alexander, 19 May 1786.
Warrant of appraisement to Capt. Saml Little, Thos Roche, and George
Ioore. Sworn appraisers 19 Apr 1786.
Inventory of plantation called Bloom Hill, 19 Apr 1786, includes Negroes
Ł 4485 6 1, by S. Little, J. Singleton, Geo. Ioor, Thomas Roche.
Inventory of plantation called Rich Land near Camden, 24 May 1786, includes
Negroes (named), Ł 2859 18 -, by Adam H. Brisbane, William Boykin, Douglas
Starke, Nath. Alexander.
Notes and indents: John McCool, Thomas Brandon, William Henderson, Charles
Sims, Richard Hail, William Cobb, Francis Lesesne, Edward Watts, Mary
Thompson, William Flud, Frederick Kimball, John Adair, William Palmer,
William Hays, Benjamin Shingleton, David Jones, Thos Taylor, John Smyth,
John McCord to Edward Richardson, Fielding Woodroff to James Armstrong,
James Taylor, Benjamin Warring to Thomas Warring, John Rutledge to Hutson,
Continental certificate signed by Tim. Pickering, Isam Moore to John
Postell, Joshua Inglish and John Adamson to Burwell Boykin, William
Whitaker Senr, William Whitaker Jr., Willis Whitaker, John Blanton and
Douglass Stark bond; William Bennet, Robert Carter & Robert Roberts bond;
Lawrence Manning and Richard Richardson; Thomas Charlton, James Love,
Samuel Bennett, Edward Richardson, John Chesnut, Alexander Irvin, Wade
Hamton, Robert Lewis and Seth PettyPool, Darrel Hart (in possession of
Thomas Pinckney), James Turner, Edward Watts, Mathew Gale, Malachi Ford
to John Neilson, Robert McKelvey, Genl Marion order on Thomas Dunbar, John
Newton, Ambrose Gayle, Hubbard Rees to John Rambert, Edward Broughton,
John Winn, John R. Davis, Gersham Kelly, Norwd. Hunter & Daniel Hart,
M. Murphey, James Habersham, William Colwell, John Chisolm, Wade Hampton
order on Col. Lawrence, Frederick Bell and James Purnell; David Platt,
Morgan Sabb, John Hunter, John Lewis Gervais, William Morant.

RAGAN, WILLIAM Apt. 119 Pck. 17
    Will of William Ragan of St. Mark's Parish, Craven County...to wife
Lucey Ragan, use of my Dwelling House; till my daughter Lucey shall get
marryed, all estate sold (except a Negro Sharper); to daughter Elizabeth,
wife of Edward Broughton, one guinea; to daughter Jemimey, wife of William
Griffen, one guinea; to daughter Sarah, wife of William Sanders, 1/3 part
of estate after it is sold and legacies paid; to daughter Frances, wife of
Richard Harvin, one guinea; to son John Ragan, one guinea; to daughter
Lucey Ragan, 1/3 of estate; to son William Ragan, negro Sharper and Ł 220
sterling; to the children of Jemimey Grfffin's as they become 21, Ł 100
and to the children of my daughter Frances Harvin,; to grandsons William
Sanders, son of Sarah Sanders, John Broughton son of my daughter Elizabeth
Broughton; to granddaughter Mary Ragan, daughter of Lucey Ragan, Ł 40 st.
friends John James, Samuel Little and William Sanders, exrs., 15 Jan 1785
...Wit: Josiah Furman, Thomas Casity, Sarah Furman. Proved by Josiah
Furman, 16 Mar 1787. Dedimus to Thomas Roach, 16 Mar 1787 to prove will.
Proved by John James in Clarendon County, before Thomas Roche JP 24 Apr
1787.
Warrant of appraisement not filled out.
Inventory 28 Apr 1787 by Wm McConnico, Wm Little and Thos Maples, including
Negroes (named).

WILSON, DAVID Apt. 119 Pck. 18
    Will of David Wilson, 1 Feb 1779, Craven County, St. Mark's Parish,
to wife Mary, 1/3 of estate after Legacies; to son Robert William Wilson,
tract I now live on at lawfull age; to son David Wilson, tract on SW side

of the North prong of Black River, adj. James Armstrong, Roger Wilson, and land on which I dwell, at lawfull age; to son Roger Wilson, land on Stoney-Run, adj. David Anderson; to daughter Jane Allen Wilson, Ł 1000 at age 21 or marriage; to daughter Margaret Grace, Ł 1000 at lawfull age or marriage; to the Catholick Society, Ł 500 two years after my decease; wife Extx, and James Carte(sic), Matthew Bradley, James wilson Senr and Robert William Wilson, when he is 21....David Wilson (Seal), Wit: Elias Dubose, John Graham, Samuel Bradley, Prov. 13 July 1784 by Elias Dubose before Roger Wilson.
Warrant of appraisement to Robert Carter, James Armstrong Senr, John Armstrong, William Carter, and Thos Wilson, 5 June 1784.
Inventory 4 Augt 1784 including Negroes (named), by Robert Carter, John Armstrong, Robert William Carter.

PEARSON, WILLIAM Apt. 119 Pck. 19 (two estates in one package)
     John Ogilsvee applied for admn, 13 Apr 1784. Citation published 9 May 1784 by Jacob Gibson.
Bond: John Ogilvie, admr., James Ogilvie and Thomas Parrot, sec., 10 May 1784. Wit: Jno Harbirt.
Dedimus to John Harbirt, 10 May 1787 to admr. oath.
Warrant of appraisement to Henry Crumpton, Jacob Gibson Senr, Thos Harbirt, William Rabb, and Thomas Parrott Senr, 10 May 1784.
Inventory 8 June 1784 by Thomas Harbirt, William Rabb (W), Thos Parrot.

Will of William Pearson of Camden District, planter...to wife Dorcas Pearson, negroes (named); to son James Pearson; to my trusty negro fellow Jem of No Carolina his freedom; to son James Pearson, remainder of my estate at age 21 or marriage; if sd. James dies, estate to the children of John Pearson, Robert Pearson, and Mary Pearson of Talbott and Annapolis Counties in Maryland...to Negro Jem, 20 A off West corner of the place where I now live...William Martin Esqr., and John Cantey, Exr. of Camden Dist., Exrs., 24 Feb 1783...William Pearson (X) (seal), Wit: Absalam frierson, William Elmer Barrett (X), Michael Birch.
Proven 6 Dec 1783 by Wm Elmer Barrett before Henry Hampton.
Warrant of appraisement 6 Dec 1783 to Capt. James Davis, Majr. Jno Gambell, Benjamin Davis and David Davis and Capt. James McCauley.
Appraisement includes 13 slaves (not named), Ł 623 19 9, 1 Jan 1784, by James Davis, Benja. Davis, Davd. Davis, James McCauley.

CONYERS, JAMES SR. Apt. 119 Pck 20
     Will of James Conyers of Camden District; to the children of my eldest son James, vizt, John and James Convyers, all that tract where my son James Did live in the fork of Black River, 150;A to son Daniel, 100 A where he now lives; to son Straughan, tract where I now live, 250 A; to daughters Elizabeth and Sarah, a full suit of mourning; to daughter Sarah negro girl Phillis; to Martha Benbow and her four children, onw cow and calf each and three of her children be schooled for one years; to John Webb, Ł 100; to the childrne of my daughter, Mary Gamble, late wife of Hugh Gamble, 1/6 of estate...son in law John Anderson, son Daniel Conyers, and son in law Daniel Carter, Exrs., 5 Mar 1783...James Conyers (X) (Seal) Wit: Willm Gamble, William Grahams, Marthew benbo (X). Proved by William Graham 22 July 1784.
Dedimus to Wm Martin to admr. Exrs. oath, 6 Dec 1783. Oath admrd. 25 Aug 1784.
Warrant of appraisement to John Gambole, William Fuller, John McFadian, Thomas McFadian, and William Graham, 22 July 1784.
Inventory 25 Aug 1784, includes 15 Negroes (not named), Ł 1138 9 4. by Thomas McFaddian, Jno Gambell, John Graham.

In Name of God amen November 26 1775
I Leard Burns of Craven County in y'e province
of South Carolina being in common or perfite health
Mind and Memory taking into Consideration my
Mortality and that it is apointed for all men
to Die Do Constetute this My Last Will and
[testa]Ment as to my worldly Goods with which it ha[th]
pleasd God to bless Me first I order that th[ey] be
Devided in ye manner following that is to say Ifh[?]
order all My Just Debts to be paid of as soon as [they]
can be Don Item I bequith to my Dough[ter?] ...
her husband one Coun Starling Item I bequith to
my Son John one Coun Starling Item I bequith to my
Son James one Coun Starling Item to My three Dough-
ters Janet ann and Martha the three heffers Name[d]
to them before the young Name to Janes is ...
the Loom to ann Item I bequith to My loving wife
the black Meare and her Sadel her ... bed and
furnetur the puter and apot and the third of all my
Moveabel Goods Item I bequith to my Son Leard
two traks of Land I live oppon with this provise
that my wife shall have yarly and every year paid
to her of ye produce of ye place ten buchels of Corn and
five of wheat if she Demand it but not to be paid in
any other with a Convenient Little houe for her to
live in and her fire wood provid the Land on Gilkes Creek
to be Sold and that with the Remender of my Movabel
Goods to be Equilly Devid amongst My Children after
named Janet ann Martha Leard & Learah if Lea[rd]
Dies before he com of age ye Land that is his to be
Devided betwixt John and James further I Do con-
Stetut My Son James and Robert walker Sen of Alexander walker My Executors as witness My hand the
Day and Yare above written   Leard Burns
witness present

Rynehe ? Huster
...
... ? Huster

Will of Leard Burns on whose plantation in Chester County, S. C.
Maj. Gen. Alexander Leslie and his British Army camped Jan. 15-16 1781

December 21th 1784

A memorandum of part of the goods and Cattles of the Estate of Lean Burns and Thomas McCarron Distd as they appeared to us at this present Vandue the Particulars is as follows Viz

	£	s	d
1 pot rack	0	9	0
1 frying pan	0	9	0
1 Cow	0	6	0
1 Lot of Sundries	0	8	0
1 Mear and Colt	2	1	0
1 Lot of Hogs	0	15	0
Total	4	8	0

Robert Walker Cost

July the 16th 1789

A Memorandum of the goods and Cattles Belonging to the Estate of Lean Burns now Decesd

	£	s	d
1 Negro	15	0	0
2 Horses	9	1	0
1 Mear and Colt	7	0	0
3 Cows and Calves	6	6	0
1 Do	1	3	0
1 parcel of Hogs	4	0	0
1 Lot of Sundries	0	17	6
1 Lot of Sundries	0	12	0
3 Lot of Sundries	1	8	0
4 Lot of Sundries	3	8	0
5 Lot of Sundries	7	8	4
1 Saddle	0	9	8
1 Do	0	7	8
Ready money	1	7	4

John Fleming
Joseph Telford
William McCaa
This Inventory is Certifyed by Robert Walker Coust (?)

In the Name of God amen the first day of June in the year of our Lord God one thousand Seven Hundred and Seventy Eight I Alexander Pagan of Fishing Creek in the County of Craven and Province of South Carolina Planter being in Good Health and of perfect mind and Memory thanks be Given unto God therefore Calling while in mind the mortallity of my Body and Knowing that it is appointed for all men once to die to make and ordain this my Last Will and Testament that is to say first of all I Give and Recommend my Soul into the hands of God that Gave it. Not doubting but at the General Resurrection I Shall receive the same again by the mighty Power of God And touching such worldly Estate wherewith it shall Please God to bliss me in this Life I Give devise and Dispose of the same in following manner and form

first I Give and Bequeath to Janet my Dearly Beloved Wife the Third Part of my whole Personal Estate with her Living of the Place during her widow hood. Likewise I Give and Bequeath to my Daughter Agness Pagan the other two thirds of said Estate. Likewise if it should please the providence to Give me a son by my wife Jannet Pagan now being Pregnant, I Give and Bequeath to him my whole Real Estate only Agness to have if Living to the years of Maturity one Hundred Pounds or the Value thereof from said Estate But on the other hand if being a female Child, I Give and devise in form and manner following that is to say my two Daughters to be Coasqual Sharers in the Whole, and if it should Please Providence to Call off one of them in Non Age then the Survivor to be heire and on this Condition as before Willed and Bequeathed the Surviver Shall heire the Deseaseds Estate and Lastly these my Children dying in None Age, I Give and Bequeath my Land to my Brothers James and Archibald Pagan them Paying my wife Jannet Pagan the Sum of two hundred Pound Currancy of said Province of South Carolina Likewise Constitute make and ordain my Loving Uncle Robert Gill and Uncle John Mills my only and sole Executors of this my Last Will and Testament ratifying this and no other to be my Last Will and Testament in Witness whereof I here unto set my hand and seal the day and year above Written in Presence of the Subscribers

Alexd Pagan (seal)

John Lattas
Robert Cooper
John _____

INDEX

Abbeville, S.C. 46
Abbott, John 1
  Winifred 1
Acker, Peter 18
Acre, William 1
Adair, John 10, 21, 66, 73
  William 43
Adams, Abraham 37
  Francis 20, 52
  George 12
  Godfrey 39, 54
  Joel 43, 50, 53, 59
  John 16, 33, 37
  Margaret 37
  Martha 55
  Robert 30, 67
  Thomas 55
Adamson, ___ 15
  John 4, 15, 16, 24, 39, 73
Adderson see Addison
Addis, Richard 14
Addison, Mrs. Esther 1
  Thomas 1
  William 17, 42
Adkins see Atkins
Adkison see Atkinson
Aetna Iron Works 68
Agnew, George 1
  John 1
Aikins see Akins
Aires see Ayres
Akins, Alexander
  Peter 40
  Thomas 39
  Walker 21
Akins see also Atkins
Aldridge, John 43
Aldridge see also Arledge
Alexander, Eleazer 15
  Elir. 49
  Isaac 10, 18, 24, 31, 36, 38
      43, 45, 52, 55, 73
  J. 4, 5, 8, 10, 69
  James 68
  John 20
  Jos. 40, 62
  Joseph 14, 28, 30, 41, 43
  Nathaniel 73
  Rachel (Duncan) 20
Alexander & Brownfield 39
Allen, Beverly 39
  Charles 10
  Ginnins 10
  John 1, 10, 55
  Mrs. Mary 1
Allison, Alexander 62
  Andrew 23, 72
  Hugh 62
  James 39
  Martha 65
  Robert 5, 69
Alston, John 57
Ancrum, George 1
Anderson, Mrs. Ann 71
  Cooper 71
  David 71, 72, 74
  George 2
  John 22, 38, 43, 48, 70, 71, 74

  Joseph 71
  Margaret 2
  Mary 71
  Mrs. Mary 71
  Sarah 71
  William 2, 52, 71
Andras, David 17
Andrews, David 56
  Drury 57
  Edward 56
  Frances 2
  James 10, 17
  James Jr. 56
  John 23, 44
  Thomas 2, 11, 51, 70, 71, 72
  William 31, 56
Annapolis, Md. 74
Antrim, Ireland 16
Appell, John 72
Archer, Alexander 8, 43, 52
Ard, John 2
Arendall, Benjamin 7
Arlage see Arledge
Arledge, Amos 2
  Clement 2
  Isaac 2
  Joseph 2
  William 2
Armstrong, ___ 45
  James 3, 25, 53, 67, 68, 70, 73, 74
  James Jr. 66
  John 20, 30, 64, 67, 74
  Samuel 1, 69
  William 25
Arnett, James 1, 69
  Samuel 1
Arnold, Benjamin 17
  Mary 17
  Moses 17
Arrant, Conrad 2, 3
  Elizabeth 3
  Mrs. Elizabeth 3
  Hannah 3
  Jane 3
  Mary 3
  Peter 3
  Rebecca 3
  William 3
Arrick, Frederick 2
  John 2
Ashford, George 37
Ashley, Osborn 13
Atkins, Elisha 3
  Mrs. Elizabeth 3
  Frederick 65
  John 3, 69
  Joseph 3, 69
  Richard 3
  Samuel 3
Atkins see also Akins
Atkinson, Adwell 63, 69
  Eliza 25
  Elizabeth 69
  Mrs. Elizabeth 69
  Frederick 58, 65, 69
  Henry 3
  James 69
  Lucy 69

Atkinson, Margaret 3
  Mrs. Margaret Young 67
  Marmaduke 69
  Martha 69
  Shadrach 69
  Sylvia 69
August, John Samuel 15
Aulston see Alston
Austin, Betty 3
  Casia 3
  Davies 3
  Drewry 3
  Drury 3
  Mrs. Elizabeth 3
  Nancy 3
  Nathan 3
  William 3
Austin & Moore 39
Austin's Mill Creek 61
Averit see Everit
Ayres, Daniel 1, 55

Bacon, John 64
  Thomas 64
Bagnall, Ebenezer 4, 6, 11, 39, 46, 52, 70
  Ebenezer II 4
  Isaac 4, 46
  John 4, 52
  Martha (Cantey) 11
Bailey, John 4, 10, 34, 56
  Robert 4, 11
Bailey see also Baillie & Bayley
Baillie, Jean 4
  John 4
Baillie see also Bailey & Bayley
Baird, James 13, 53
  William 41, 55
Baker, Jacob 54
  John 3, 31, 38
  Thomas 4, 6, 13, 30, 33, 57, 61, 64
Ball, Isaac 3, 47
Ballard, Thomas 58
Bamberg, J.G. 17
Bankhead, James 4
Baptist Society, Pa. 49
Barber, Agnes 69
  Bethridge 69
  Charles 45
  James 69
  Jesse 47
  John 1, 69
  Robert 69
  Samuel 69
Barclay, ____ 32
  John 18
  Robert 18
  Willie 18
Barden, John 35
  William 36, 51
Barker, Charles 45
Barklame, John 4
Barnett, Ann 4
  Humphrey 8, 30
  Jacob 14
  Mrs. Jane 4
  John 4
  Margaret 4
  Mary 4

Barnett, Michael 4
  Robert 4, 43
  Robert Jr. 43
  Samuel 72
  William 4
  William Jr. 4
Barns, Zachariah 7
Baron see Barron
Barony river (?) Ga. 71
Barr, Nathan 16
  Thomas 5
Barrett, William Elmer 74
Barron, Abraham 40, 62
  Alexander 24
  Archibald 17
  John 24, 58, 59
Barrows, William 56
Barry, Andrew 20
Bartlam, Mrs. 39
Bartley, ____ 6
  Robert 55
Baskins, Andrew 2, 49, 58, 63
Batchelor, Jolly 39
Baxter, Barnaby 58
Bayley, John 34
  Robert 4, 11
Bayley see also Bailey & Baillie
Beach Creek 72
Beam, James 5
Beard, Agnes (Moore) 47
  Hugh 45
  James 11, 13, 14, 37, 41
  Jonas 19
  Ulrich 17
  William 17
Beaty, James 63
Beaumont, H. 2, 4, 5, 14, 54
Beaver Creek 1, 43
Bee, Joseph 32
Beersheba Presbyterian Church 23
Belcher, Thomas 53
Bell, Benjamin 12
  Deborah (Sadler) 54
  Frederick 5, 32, 35, 44, 51, 73
  Harrison 53, 54
  James 54
  John 5, 17, 39, 61
  John II 5
  Mrs. Mary 5
  Penelope 5
  Samuel 42
  Vincent 5
  W.M. 46
  William 41, 46, 54
  William Rasor 5, 35
Belley see Bailey
Bellie see Bely
Belton, John 19, 23, 35, 37, 66
  John Jr. 39
Bely, John 10, 34
Bembridge, Henry 32
Benbow, Adam 70
  Elizabeth 70
  John 70
  Martha 74
  Mary 70
  Powell 70
  Richard 70
  Sarah 70
  Mrs. Sarah 70

Benbow, Susannah 70
Bender, John Arnold 4, 48
Bennet, Hugh 23, 53
   Matthew 23
   Samuel 44, 67, 73
   William 23, 73
Bennington, John 31
Benson, Elizabeth 49
Berkley Co., S.C. 11
Berry, William 17, 31
Bertie Co., N.C. 40
Best, Benedict 50
Bethany, Jacob 33, 34
Beths Meeting House 14, 56
Bettes see Bettis
Bettice see Bettis
Bettis, Francis 31, 38, 46
   James 5
   Lucy 5
Bibbe, John 54
Bierly see Byerly
Biggot, John Sr. 13
Bigham, James 38
Binnicker, Charles 17, 28
Birch see Burch
Bird see Byrd
Bishop, Dorcas 5
   Hannah 5
   Mrs. Hannah 5
   Henry 5
   James 2, 5, 15, 16
   John 5
   Nicholas 5, 20
   Nicholas Jr. 5
   William 5, 26, 29, 36
Bissip, Luke 35
Biswell, John 16
Black, George 17
   Matthew 62
   Thomas 22
Black River 25, 69, 71, 74
Blair, James 26, 31, 39, 68
   Ketris 35
   Thomas 26
Blake, Frances 6
   John 65
   William 5, 6
Blanchard, Cathrin 29, 64
   Henry 67
Blanton, John 63, 73
Blare see Blair
Blayr see Blair
Blear see Blair
Bliss, Henry 6
   John 6
Bloom Hill 73
Bobs (?) Sampson 63
Boggs, Jos. 56
Boggy Gully Plantation 29
Boght see Voght
Bohannon, James 39
Boid see Boyd
Bolding, John 1
Bond, Alcey 6
   Alse 6
   George 6
   Isom 6
   Moses 6
   Mrs. Usly 6
   William 6, 13, 19, 24

Bonner, Henry 56
   Jennet 16
   John 16
Booker, _____ 39
Bookman, Bernard 72
Bookter, Jacob Sr. 17
Boone, Thomas 64
Booser, George 11
Booth, George 6
   Hugh 6
   Mrs. Matthew 6
   Thomas 6
   William 6
   William Jr. 6
Borough, James 51
Bosher, John 48
   Mary 48
   Sarah 48
   Thomas 48
Bostick, Floyd 53
   John 57
   Mrs. Nancy Gooch 28
   William 28, 53
Botetourt Co., Va. 59
Bottace, Francis 46
Bourdeaux, Daniel 39
Bowen, Ann 6
   George 6
   Samuel 17
Bowers, Henry 33
   Mrs. Sarah 33
Bowman, John 72
Box, Edward 10
Boyd, Andrew 4, 39
   Andrew Sr. 4
   David 5, 26
   John 9, 13, 29, 33, 36, 38, 59, 60
   William 3, 10, 33, 44
Boykin, Burl 5, 13, 24, 25, 43, 59
   Burwell 56, 73
   Frances 8
   Francis 24, 39, 42
   John 39, 46, 50, 59
   Samuel 5, 8, 9, 10, 19, 46, 59, 63
   William 10, 36, 39, 73
Bradford, Charles D. 18, 51
   John 60
   Mary (James) 71
   Richard 55
   Thomas 35
Bradley, Arthur 69
   Charity 6
   Elizabeth 69
   Mrs. Elizabeth 69
   James 7, 69
   James Sr. 69
   Jennet 69
   John 59
   Joseph 6, 7
   Joseph Jr. 6
   Margaret 7
   Mary 6, 69
   Matthew 7, 74
   Moses 69
   Roger 7, 69, 71
   Samuel 7, 69, 74
   Samuel Jr. 69
   Sarah 6
   Mrs. Sarah 7
   Sion 6

Bradley, Suky 59
  Mrs. Susannah 6, 7
  Thomas 7, 69
  William 6, 12
Brady, Alexander 2
  John 4
Brailsford, Morton 39
Brandon, Richard 45
  Thomas 45, 73
Branham, Robert 52
Brasey, William 35
Bratton, William 10, 22, 38, 47,
        56, 65
Brazell, Mrs. Averilla 7
  Jacob 7
  William 7
Bready see Brady
Breed, Samuel 39
Breedin, James 43, 47
  Mary 47
  Mrs. Mary 47
Breedlove, William 34
Bremar, Francis 39
Brent, John 37, 66
Brenter, James 70
  John 70
Brevard, Joseph 24
Brewer, William 1
Brewton, Jennet (Griffen) 30
  Mary 14
Brick Chimney tract 29
Bridges, Mrs. Ann 7, 8
  Benjamin 7
  James 7, 28, 59
  John 7, 28
  Joseph 7
  Leady 7
  Lyde 8
  Richard 7, 8
  Sarah 7
  Thomas Sr. 7, 8
  William 7
Brient see Bryant
Briggs, Frederick 6, 10, 39, 50
Brisbane, A.T. 73
  Adam 54
  Adam F. 51
  Adam H. 73
  Foullar 4
Brisno, Francis 13
Brison see Bryson
Bristol, England 38
Broad River 3, 23, 28, 54, 61
Brock, Charles 10
  Patrick 12, 38
Brockett, William 3, 26
Brothers, Thomas 28
Broton see Broughton
Broughton, Edward 21, 56, 73
  Elizabeth (Ragan) 73
  John 73
Brown, Alexander 4, 26
  Anes 8
  Arthur 63
  Burrill 8, 9, 63
  Elijah 9, 16
  Mrs. Elizabeth 8
  Esebel 9
  George 8, 32, 39, 56
  Isaac 25

Brown, James 4, 8, 12, 14, 15, 39,
        40, 48
  James Jr. 8
  Jeremiah 8, 9, 14
  John 8, 25, 26, 31, 41, 46, 52
  John Jr. 8
  John Meredith 16
  Joseph 39, 40
  Mark 8, 9
  Mary 9
  Mrs. Mary 8
  Maryan 9
  Nancy 9
  Mrs. Patience 9, 21
  Reuben 8
  Richard 6, 12, 18
  Robert 8
  Samuel 9, 26
  Sarah 89
  Mrs. Sarah 8
  Shaw 8
  Stewart 43
  Susannah 8
  Thomas 9, 10, 16, 40, 58, 66
  William 8, 9, 14, 21, 27, 28, 54, 58
  William Jr. 9
  William Spiers 9
Brugg, Benjamin 15
Brumfield, Charles 9
  Elizabeth 9
  John 24
  Reuben 67
  Watson 9
Brummett, William 46
Brunson, Ann 9
  Charles 35
  Daniel 9
  David 9
  Isaac 35
  Marthew 9
  Nancy 72
  Peter 6, 35, 51, 52
  William 9, 70
  William Jr. 9, 70
Bryant, James 9, 10, 28
  John 10
Brynam, Robert 33
Bryson, John 38, 41
Buchanan, John 3, 11, 18, 22, 32, 52
Buckhead River, Ga. 3
Buckley, Joseph 46
Buckman, Jacob 41, 61
Buford, William 44
Bulkley, Joseph 10, 24, 66
Bullock's Creek Church 14, 24, 28, 30,
        40, 41, 43, 50, 62
Burns, Ann 10
  Dennis 43
  James 10
  Janet 10
  John 10, 43
  Laird 10
  Laird Jr. 10
  Martha 10
  Mary 10
  Patrick 10
  Samuel 62
  Mrs. Sarah 10
  Thomas 10, 11
Burch, Charles 70

Burch, Michael 53, 74
Burchell, James 52
Burd see Byrd
Burge, Jeremiah 49
  John Rains 49
Burnett, A. 34
  Benjamin 34, 38
  Lucy (Kimball) 40
  Richard 34
Burnson, William Jr. 53
Burr, John 61
Burrace, William 54
Burroughs, James 11
  Mary 11
Burrows, William 6, 12, 30, 65
Bursbey see Busby
Burton, John 48
  Watthal 22
  William 10
  William Allen 47
Busby, Benjamin 13
  Jacob 11
  Mrs. Marget 11
Buser, Casper 11
  Catherine 11
  Christian 11
  Frederick 11
  George 11
  Hannah 11
  Jacob 11
  John Ulrich 11
  Mrs. Margaret 11
  Randolph 11
  Ulrich 11
Bush, David 24
  Elizabeth 55
  Gasper 55
Bush River 54
Butler, Joel 11
  Rachel 51
Byerly, Casper 54
Byers, David 50, 56
  Edward 50
  William 40, 50, 56
Byrd, George 12, 70
  John 40, 46, 53
  Michael 46
  Richard 40
  William 12
Byrns, John 30
  Mrs. Mary 30

Cahune, Margaret 10
Cain, Daniel 15
Cain Creek 37
Caldwell, Henry 17
  John 73
Cahoun, Margaret 10
  Pat. 46
California, Univ. of 42
Callet, Joseph 10
Cambert, John 15
Camden Congregation 4, 11, 19, 23,
    24, 32, 37, 39, 63
Camden District 1, 3-13, 15, 16,
  18-25, 28-32, 37, 40, 42-48, 52-55,
  57-61, 63, 64, 65, 66, 68-74
Cameron, Andrew 44
  James 32, 44
  John 32

Cameron, Joseph 44
  Simon 44
  Susannah 52
  Thomas 32, 52
  William 39
Cammell see Campbell
Camp, Joseph 7, 28, 40, 58, 59
  Moses 8, 59
  Thomas 7, 8, 28, 58, 59
Campbell, Alexander 51, 70
  James 5, 9, 14
  John 15, 70
  Mary 70
  R.M. 12
Campbell Co., Va. 9
Campble see Campbell
Candloss, W. 72
Cansler, John 62
Cantee see Cantey
Canter see Center
Cantey, Arabella (Kelley) 39
  Charles 14
  Elizabeth 12
  James 9, 11, 12, 32, 39, 71
  John 11, 44, 47, 53, 70, 72, 74
  Joseph 11
  Josiah 11, 12, 48
  Martha 11
  Mrs. Martha 11, 12
  Mathew 11
  Samuel 11
  William 11, 12, 18, 21, 56
  William Sr. 12, 52
  Zachariah 10, 11, 21, 32
Caper, Greenburg 51
Carden, Jean (Cason) 12
  Larkin 6
Carey's Saw Mill 20
Carns, David 44, 46, 60
Carr, David 26
  William 30, 40
Carrall see Carroll
Carreal see Carroll
Carrell see Carroll
Carroll, David 34
  Elizabeth 34
  Jacob 17
  Joseph 5, 12
  Margaret 12
  Samuel 12
Carryall, Edmund 60
Carruth, Alexander 62
Carson, John 13, 19, 32, 34, 54, 61
  Samuel 54
  Walter 62
Carter, Mrs. Barbara 12
  Benjamin 12, 24, 32, 44, 48, 58
  Churchill 62
  Daniel 74
  George 12, 32
  Hannah 12
  Mrs. Hannah 12
  Henry 12
  Henry Jr. 12
  Jacob 12
  James 7, 53, 64, 74
  John 12
  Lydia 12
  Martha 12
  Mary 12

Carter, Mary (Bradley) 69
  Mathew 69
  Rachel 12
  Robert 5, 7, 12, 58, 64, 70, 73, 74
  Robert William 74
  William 74
Cary, James 6
  Nathaniel 14
Casity see Cassity
Caskain Creek, Pittsylvania Co. Va. 57
Caskey, Mrs. Ester 12
  Isabel 12
  John 12
  Marey 12
Cason, Anne 12
  Cannon 12, 30
  Cannon Jr. 12
  Jean 12
  Laban 12
  Whitehurst 12
  William 12, 30
  Willis 12
  Winnifred 12
Cassells, Benjamin 70
  Henry 13, 64, 69, 71
  Henry Jr. 53, 70
  John 7, 12, 51, 70
  William 12
Cassells see also Castles
Cassity, Charles 13
  Hugh 13
  James 13
  Mrs. Martha 13
  Naomi 13
  Peter 13, 21
  Robert 13
  Thomas 13, 73
  Thomas Jr. 13
Casson see Cason
Castles, Henry 13, 69, 70
  John 70
Castles see Cassells
Caston, Glass 1, 18, 21, 50, 60, 61
  John 2
Catawba River 55
Cathcart, Joseph 17
Catholic Church 4, 10, 61, 74
Cato, John 56, 60
  William 51
Caves, David 44, 46, 60
Ceall, John 34
Cedar Creek 28, 29, 59, 61
Cedar Creek Church 19
Center, Elizabeth 13
  John 13
  Mrs. Martha 13
  Nathan 13, 29, 33, 36, 51, 59, 60
  Nathan Jr. 13
  William 13
Cereal see Carroll
Cerrall see Carroll
Chambers, Jacob 8, 72
  John 62
Champion, Jacob 19
Chandler, Samuel 13, 47
  Samuel Jr. 13
  Thomas 13, 47
Chapman, Joseph 3

Chappell, Elizabeth 13
  Mrs. Elizabeth 13
  Henry 13, 14, 64
  Hicks 13, 25, 34, 64
  John 13
  Laban 13, 34, 64
  Martha 13
  Robert 13, 34
Charleston, S.C. 4, 12, 15, 16, 32, 41, 54, 71, 76
Charlotte, N.C. 4
Charlotte Co, Va. 45
Charlton, Thomas 24, 73
Cheraw District 24, 35, 65
Cherokee War 14
Cherry, Mrs. Elizabeth 14
  Jacob 7
  Moses 14
Chesney, James 14
  Jennet 14
Chesnut, Jane 14
  John 4, 5, 11, 13, 35, 59, 60, 66, 73
  Samuel 14
Chester District, S.C. 6, 12, 48, 69
Chewning, Rich. 73
Chick, Reuben 14
Chirley see Shirley
Chisolm, John 73
  Thomas 8
Church, Mecal 41
  Michael 41
Cinart see Kinart
Clair, James 31
Claremont Co., S.C. 42
Clarendon Co, S.C. 38, 68, 73
Clark and Clark
  Edward 39
  Mrs. Elizabeth 14
  Henry 9, 51, 59
  Isham 55
  James 8, 9, 14, 55
  Malcolm 12, 54
  Mary 14
  Starling 63
  William 14
Clary, Ethelred 59
Clay, William 32
Clement, John 4
Clements, Arthur 12, 14
  Christian 14
  David 14
  James 14
  Katherine 14
  Martha 14
  Mrs. Martha 14
  Michael 14
  Sarah 14
  William 14
  William Jr. 14
Clements see also Clemmons
Clemmonds see Clemmons
Clemmons, Arthur 12, 14
  Christian 14
  David 14
  James 14
  Katherine 14
  Martha 14
  Mrs. Martha 14
  Michael 14

Clemmons, Sarah 14
  William 14
  William Jr. 14
Clemmons see also Clements
Clendennum, Thomas 39
Clinton, David 56
  Mrs. Frances 14
  James 56
  Peter 14
Cloud, James 34
  William 55
Cloyd, Sally (Nance) 48
Clyne, Peter 12
Coats, Anne 15
  Barton 15
  Benjamin 15
  Mrs. Frances 15
  Mary (Perry) 49
  Polly 15
  Priscilla 15
  William 15
  Wilson 15
Cobb, Samuel 28
  William 73
Cochran, James 23, 24
Cockrell, John 15
Coffey, Henry 64
  Jesse 6
  John 37
Cogdell, Charles 39
Coheron, James 24
Cokely, Alexander 44,
Colclough, Alexander 48, 72
  Mary (Newton) 48
Colcough see Colclough
Cole, Abram 24
  Richard 39
Coleman, Frances 67
  Henry 15, 23
  Robert 67
Coll, Daniel 10
  John 34
Colledon, Martha 14, 15
Collins, Daniel 62
  James 28
  Lewis 7, 9, 36, 43, 56
  William 42, 60
  Zach. 42
Collson, Daniel 27
Colney, Daniel 15
Colonals Creek 20
Colvin, John 15, 30, 54, 58
Colwell see Caldwell
Commander, James 71
  Jesse 71
  Joseph 71
  Martha 71
  Mrs. Mary 71
  Samuel 71
  Samuel Jr. 71
  Thomas 71
Compty, John 40
Coms, Thomas 10
Conaway, John 1
Coner see Conner
Congaree River 29, 33, 36, 37, 45, 51, 54, 55, 57, 60, 65, 67, 68
Conn, George 54
  John 54

Conn, Samuel 54
Conner, 5
  Archibald 6, 67
  Isaac 67
  John 69
Connery, John 1, 69
Conyers, Daniel 9, 70, 74
  Elizabeth 74
  James 70, 74
  James Jr. 70, 74
  James III 70
  John 70, 74
  Martha 74
  Mary 74
  Sarah 74
  Straughan 74
  Mrs. Susannah 70
Cook, Alice 12
  Benjamin 46
  Burrel 34
  Daniel 26, 31
  Elizabeth 8, 15
  Mrs. Elizabeth 15
  James 24, 40
  Jesse 15
  John 8, 13, 15, 25, 29, 39, 43
  John Jr. 15
  Joseph 56
  Levinah (Stallings) 56
  Martha 16
  Mary 15
  Nathan 25
  Reubin 1
  Sarah 25
  William 15
  William Jr. 15
Coombes, William 32
  William Jr. 32
Cooper, Ben Allen 50
  Jacob 16, 59
  Jean 50
  John 62
  Richard 71
  Robert 25, 49, 56
Copeland, John 7, 8
  William 28
  William Sr. 8
Coppley, Catherine 70
  Mrs. Elizabeth 16, 70
  Ely 70
  Patrick 16, 70
  Robert 70
Corbett, Beny 38
  Brinkley 12
  James 38, 55
  Susannah (Jenkins) 38, 55
Core, Elisha 15
Cornelius, Rolle 2, 41
Corry, Samuel 16
Corry see also Curry
Cortna, Robert 8
Cotes see Coats
Coulliette, Elizabeth 12
Coulter, Archibald 12
Courtney, Robert 49, 53, 55
Cousart, Archibald 4, 16, 21
  Catherine 16
  James 16
  Jane 16
  John 16, 64

Cousart, Lettia 16
  Nathaniel 16, 32
  Richard 16 (3)
Couser, John 16, 64
Couturier, Philip 15
Cowden, Robert 15
Cradock, Jacob 41
Crafford, Alexander 4, 59
  James 3, 16, 19, 32, 61, 62
Crage see Craige
Craig sse Craige
Craige, George 26
  James 16, 33, 42, 46
  John 16, 37, 54, 64
  William 16, 32, 58
Craton, Thomas 45
Crane Creek 57
Craven Co., S.C. 2, 3, 6, 8, 11,
  18, 21, 24, 25, 30, 33, 34, 35,
  37, 41, 43, 45, 49, 52, 54, 55,
  57, 59, 63, 65, 66, 69, 70, 71,
  72, 73
Crawford, Alexander 4, 59
  James 3, 16, 19, 26, 32
  Michael 34
  Robert 6, 47
Crenshaw, Jesse 9
  Micajah 57
Crim, Peter 20
  Rachel (Duke) 19
Crocker, James 39
Crockett, John 24, 59, 64
  Robert 21
  Robert Jr. 21
Croft, Abiah 16, 43, 50
  Edward 16
  Elizabeth 16
  Henry 16
  Jesse 16
  John 16
  Moses 16
  Rachel 16
  Rebecca 16
Cromer, Godfrey 41
Crosby, Mrs. Hannah 17
  John 17
  Richard 17
  Thomas 17
  William 17
Crosley, William 32
Croswell, Gilbert 9, 51
  Lucy (Atkinson) 69
Crump, John 10
Crumpton, Henry 10, 11, 51, 54
Cully, Ephraim 32
Culp, Augustin 16
  Benjamin 16, 59
  Henry 16
  Peter 16, 26
Culpepper, Joseph 29
Cumberland Co, Va. 49
Cummins, Francis 5, 12, 14, 48
  Hester 15
Cunningham, Ann 17
  George 31, 56
  James 56
  John 17, 68
Curey see Curry
Curry, Dudley 1, 23
  Jacob 1, 13

Curry, Jane 59
  Peter 23
  Stafford 42
  Stephen 15, 23, 51, 55
Currey see Curry
Cusack, Ann 39

Dabney, James 7
Da Costa, Isaac 24
Daily, Alexander 55
  Mary 13
Dale, Joseph 7
Dampier, William 5
Dampio, William 43
Dampur see Dampier
Dancer, Mrs. 17
  Henry 17
  John 17
  Peter 17
Daniel, James 13
  Jely 8
  Jesse 13
  Josiah 63
  William 13
Dargan, John 72
  Timothy 47
  William 17
Darington see Dearington
Darwin, James 40
Dason, Cornelas 26
Davidson, James 16
Davie, Archibald 59
Davies, David 26
  John 39
Davis, Allen 19
  Amos 5, 17, 18
  Archibald 3
  Benjamin 74
  Mrs. Dacey 18
  David 11, 74
  Mrs. E. 39
  Edward 18
  Elijah 18, 26
  Elizabeth (Woodward) 65
  Elnathan 17
  Ester 18
  Henson 18
  J. 44
  James 18, 32, 35, 44, 70, 74
  Jeremiah 38
  John 8, 17, 18, 35, 56, 62
  John Jr. 18
  John R. 73
  Jonathan 18
  Lucretia 56
  Mason 18
  Mrs. Nelly 17
  Rachel 18
  Robert 19, 62
  Rosher 18
  Rozure 18
  Samuel 18
  Mrs. Sarah 17
  Susannah 70
  Thomas Richard 38
  Wenefor 18
  William 18, 38, 65, 69
  William Ransom 32
Davise see Davis
Davison, George 31

Davison, John 58
  Rebekah 19
  Samuel 19
  William 19, 38
Davison see also Davidson
Davys see Davis
Dawson, Frederick 19
Day, Henson 19
  Rachel (Carter) 12
  Thomas 34
Dayley see Daily
Dean, William 19
Dearington, Robert 9, 51, 60, 62, 72
Deason, Benjamin 38
  Sarah (Johnson) 38
  William 48, 60
Debruell, Godart 57
Debrusk, Andrew 35
  Peter 35
Deep Creek 46
Deeson see Deason
Delap, John 39
Delcore, Peter 4
Denely, James 20
Denison, Robert 10
Denkins see Dinkins
Denly see Denely
Dennis, Richard G. 12, 32, 57
Denny, John 36, 51
Denton, James 1, 2, 19, 22
  Mrs. Mary 19
  Samuel 40
Dervin, James 40, 53
Desachar, Peter 34
Deval, Lewis 10
Dickey, David 24, 50
  George 26, 41
  John 4, 9, 14, 44, 53, 61, 67, 69
Dickson, James 28
  John 9, 12, 27, 28
  Michael 10, 15, 66
  Thomas 35
Dickson see also Dixon
Die see Dye
Dieger, John 57
Dikey see Dickey
Digby, William 62
Dingle, Robert 49
Dinkins, Samuel 5
  William 24, 36, 51, 70
Dirk, Charles 26
Discson see Dickson
Dixon, Elijah 47
Dixon see also Dickson
Dodd, Hugh 26
  John 26
  William 1
Doherty, Bryant 19
Donald, Alexander 61
Dorrity see Dougherty
Dortch, Nathan 64
  William 33
Doty, Isaac 39
  Samuel 39
Dougherty, Jervais 19
  John 8, 22
Douglass, James 56, 58
  Jesse 68

Dowd, Caleb 19
  Susanna 19
Dowdell, Robert 26
Dowden, Michael 29
Downey, John 19
  Margaret 19, 61
Downing, Alexander 26
  John 26, 57
Downs, Ann 19
  Mary 19
  William 19
Doyle, John 44
  Thomas 19
Draden, Wenefor (Davis) 18
Draughon, J. 50
Drawn, Joshua 50
Dry Creek 57
Dubberts, Frederick 19, 61
Dubose, Andrew 71
  Elias 5, 13, 47, 53, 69, 70, 74
  Elias Jr. 13, 47
  Margaret 47
  Peter Sr. 71
Duck Pond 72
Dudley, Arthur 30
  Edward 50
Dugan, Thomas 21
Duglas see Douglas
Duke, Aaron 20
  Ester 49
  Jesse 20
  Joseph 73
  Moses 20
  Mrs. Nancy 20
  Rachel 19
  Robert 19, 20, 22, 23, 49
  Thomas 18, 19, 54, 61, 67
  William 12, 56
Dulles, Joseph 28
Dunbar, Thomas 73
Duncan, James 20, 39
  John 20
  Jonathan 15
  Margaret 20
  Mrs. Margaret 20
  Mary 20
  Patrick 20
  Robert 20
  Thomas 20
  Violet 20
  William 20
Dunkin, Thomas 20
Dunlap, George 48, 60
  John 32, 60
  Lettia (Cousart) 16
  Robert 16, 24, 32, 45, 60
  Samuel 52, 57, 58, 60
  Samuel Jr. 16
  Thomas 60
Dunn, Mrs. Elizabeth 20
  James 26
  Samuel 11, 20
  Sylvester 67
  William 66
Dupree, Elizabeth 39
Durer, John 15
Durgan, Jonathan 64
Durham, Charnal 11, 35
Dutchman's Creek 30
Duven, Monnaca 50

Dwyer, Samuel 63
Dye, John 10, 22, 28, 42, 55
  Sarah 42
  Thomas 22, 42

Eakins, Alexander 5
  John 31, 68
East Florida 54
Ederington, Christopher 28
  James 28
Edmonds, James 4, 19
Edwards, Mrs. Elizabeth 71
  Joshua 32
  William 71
Egan, John 72
Elden, Thomas 20
Eliot see Elliott
Elisor, Rev. 72
Elkins, Ann 20
  David 20
  Nelly (Scoldfield) 55
  Robert 64
  Sarah 20
  William 20
Ellerby, William 39
Elliott, Archibald 26
  Benjamin 26
  Daniel 20
  Elizabeth 26
  James 21, 44
  Jane 21
  Mrs. Jean 21
  John 21, 52
  Mary 21
  Robert 14
  Thomas 21
  William 16, 20, 26, 48
Ellis, Robert 24
Ellison, Robert 5, 69
Ellison see also Allison
England 32, 38, 40, 65
Engleman's old place 18
English, Joshua 23, 73
  Thomas 25
Enlow, Isaac 62
Ensminger, Frederick 21
  Peter 21
Eoff, Peter 5, 42
Errick, John 33
Ervin, Mary 47
  Samuel 2, 10, 15, 45
  William 62
Erving see Ervin, Erwin, Irvin
Erwin, Samuel 2, 10, 15, 45
Esbell see Isbell
Eustace, Thomas 32
Evans, David 61
  Ludwell 25, 29, 33, 34, 59,
      61, 64
  Richard 5, 13, 29, 33, 34
  Thomas 72
Evant, Benjamin 41
Everit, Albright 38, 64
  Benjamin 20, 45, 67
  Richard 34
Ewing, Robert 54, 69
Ezel, John 34

Faile, Lewis 46
Faircheld, John 13

Fairfield Co, SC 10, 16, 17, 18, 30,
  35, 40, 42, 46, 49, 52, 55
Farell see Farrell
Fargison see Ferguson
Farguson see Ferguson
Faries see Faris
Faris, Alexander 26, 31
  Elizabeth 21
  Isaac 68
  James 31
  Jennet (Hall) 31
  John 21
  William 26, 31
Farr, Richard 39
Farrell, Eleanor 21
  Thomas 26
  William 21, 24, 58
Fauson, Francis 32
Feemster, Joseph 41, 62
Felder, Abraham 56
  John 21
Ferguson, Abraham 37
  Arthur 54
  Francis 45
  James 21
  Jene 25
  John 16, 21, 26, 30, 32, 38
  Mrs. Mary 21
  Moses 24, 68, 71
  Poll 26
  Robert 21
  Samuel 21
  William 21, 34, 37
Feris see Faris
Ferrell see Farrell
Fetherstone, William 21
Few, William 67
Fields, John 15, 52
Findley, Robert 4, 23, 31, 43, 48,
      58, 59
Fisher, Mrs. Sarah 21
  William 21, 22
Fishing Creek 20, 21
Fishing Creek Meeting House 1, 5, 10,
  15, 16, 17, 20, 21, 25, 31, 33, 37,
  41, 42, 45, 48, 49, 54, 55, 56, 66,
  68
Fitchett, Jonathan 12
Fitzpatrick, Jacob 60
  Peter 13
Flat Creek Congregation 38
Flat Rock Meeting House 3, 56
Fleming, Alexander 22
  Bailey 57, 61
  Elijah 56
  James 55
  John 22, 53
  Robert 22
  William 22
Flemming see Fleming
Fletchall, Thomas 22
Fletcher, Drury 11, 67
  John 58, 72
Flintham, Joseph 22
Flinton, Jacob 22
Flood, Mrs. Susanna 4
Florida 54
Flowers, Lucia 40
  Thomas 40
Fogartie, Joseph 73

Fondren, John 59
Forbes, Mary (Hawthron) 33
Ford, Daniel 43, 50
  Gardner 55
  Malachi 73
  Mary 22
  Thomas 22
  William 22
Fore, James 15, 30
  Joshua 29, 30
Forgoson see Ferguson
Forgueson see Ferguson
Forster, John 39
Fort, Albert 9
  Jesse 10, 21, 23, 44
Fortune, Mrs. Anne 22
  Elizabeth 22
  Jenny 22
  John 22
  Mark 22
  Mary 22
  Richard 22
  William 22
  William Jr. 22
Fosky, Junk 39
Foster, Andrew 4, 5, 21, 31, 62, 63, 64
  Henry 59, 60
  Isable Helena (White) 63
  John 4, 39, 53, 55, 63
  John Crow 30
  Richard 40
Foust, Burrel 62
  Jacob 7, 15, 23, 62
  John 7, 62
  Margaret (Galman) 23
  Robert 62
Fowler, James 3, 32, 38, 39, 67
  William 22
Fox, William 12
Fraishair, William 28
Franklin, John 21, 22, 23
Free, Adam 11
Freeman, Frederick 23
Frenchman's bond land 29
Freneau, Peter 72
Friday, John 13
Frierson, Aaron 71
  Absalom 70, 74
  George 70
  James 53, 70
  John 32, 44
Fritchell, Stephen 21
Frizzle, Gaal Sr. 38
  Gace Sr. 38
  Thomas 38
Fuller, William 74
Fulton, Mrs. Jane 23
  John 23
  Paul 23
  Rebecka 23
Fullwood, William 23
Furman, Benjamin 23
  John 39
  Josiah 1, 9, 25, 38, 51, 60, 62, 64, 67, 72, 73
  Rachel 2, 20, 31, 52
  Mrs. Rachel 72
  Richard 5, 9, 11, 12, 14, 72
  Sarah 72, 73

Furman, Wood 1, 2, 3, 24, 29, 51, 72
Fust see Foust

G__gard, John G. 71
Gage, Henry 30
  John 64
Gage see also Gouge
Gailey see Galey
Gaither, James 17
  Mrs. Jane 42
  Richard 2, 42
  Thomas 22, 42, 45
Galbraith, J. 35, 46
  James 32, 66
  John 15, 40, 66
Gale, Ambrose 73
  Caleb 51
  Josiah 24
  Josiah Jr. 24
  Matthew 51, 73
  Rebecca 24
Galey, John 64
  Samuel 3, 26, 31
Gallman see Galman
Galloway, Absolam 51
Galman, Henrich 23
  Henry 15, 23
  Mrs. Margaret 23
Galman see also Coleman
Gambell see Gamble
Gambrell, Jane 24
Gamble, Andrew 24
  Elizabeth Sr. 46, 47
  Elizabeth Jr. 47
  Hugh 71, 74
  Mrs. Jane 23, 24, 47, 67
  Mrs. Jean 23, 24, 47, 67
  John 4, 23, 24, 44, 46, 52, 63, 74
  Mary 71
  Mary (Conyers) 74
  Robert 47
  William 24, 74
Gambole see Gamble
Gant see Gaunt
Ganter, George 24, 66
  Michael 24
  Mrs. Sarah 24
Garden, Benjamin 18
Gardiner, Thomas 1, 6, 24
Gardner, Hannah 24
  Jean 24
  John 24, 44
  Martha 24
  Mary 24
  Rebeckah 24
  Mrs. Sarah 24
  Thomas 1, 6, 24
  William 24
Garner, Thomas 23
Garnet, John 32
Garrett, David 32
  Hannah 41
  Thomas 34, 39, 41, 42
Garrison, Capt. 20
  Margaret 32
  Paul 32
Garrot see Garrett
Garter, George 4
Gartman, Daniel 54
Garton, Jenneat 34

Garvan, John 20
  Mary 20
Gaston, Esther 3, 41
  Hugh 43
  John 34, 35, 36
  Joseph 5, 20, 26
  Margaret 34
  Robert 26
  William 41
Gater, James 17
  Thomas 22
Gather see Gaither
Gauge see Gage
Gaulden see Golden
Gaunt, Nebo 25, 63
  Samuel 24, 39, 63
  Zebulon 24, 25, 39
  Zimri 25, 63
Gavier, Charles 2
  Thomas 35
Gayle see Gale
Geally see Galey
Geather see Gaither
Gee, John 25
  Rebecca 25
Geely see Galey
Gegar see Geiger
Geiger, Jacob 41
  John 17, 23, 41, 61
  William 64
Genot, Louslain 8
Georgetown District 14, 44
Georgia 3, 23, 32, 42, 46, 58,
    64, 65, 71
Gerrald, Gabriel 8, 21, 56, 67
Gerreat see Garrett
Gerrot see Garrett
Gervais, John Lewis 73
Getsinger, John 54
Gewin, Christopher 39
Gibbins, Michael 35, 46
Gibbs, Thomas 35
Gibhart, A. 36
Gibson, Abraham 19
  Gilbert 33, 34, 50, 64
  Isaac 2, 35
  Jacob 1, 10, 11, 17, 23, 35, 37,
    38, 44, 50, 61, 65, 74
  Jacob Jr. 2, 51
  James 6, 32, 52, 54, 57, 72
  Jane 25
  Jarvis 69
  John 32, 47
  Jos. 50
  Joseph 50
  Mary 25
  Mrs. Mary 25
  Roger 25
  Samuel 25
  Mrs. Sarah Burns 10
Gidens, Isaac 52
Giger see Geiger
Gilbert, David 36
  William 40
Gilham, Ezekiel 54
  Isaac 54
  James 30
  Thomas 40
  William 9
Gill, Archibald 26

Gill, Mrs. Elizabeth 25
  George 26
  George Jr. 26
  James 29
  John 16, 26, 27, 28
  John Jr. 25, 27
  Robert 25, 26, 27, 49
  Robert Sr. 26
  Thomas 26
Gillam see Gilham
Gills Creek 16
Gilmore, Charles 6, 41
Gilson, James 72
Gindrat, Abraham 25
  Henry 25
  Henry Abraham 25
Givens, Daniel 14
  Isaac (?) 52
  John 62
  William 10
Gladden, Ann 28
  Jesse 31
  John 35
  Mrs. Nancy 27
  Richard 27, 28, 35, 37
  William 28, 42
  William Jr. 28
Gladen see Gladden
Gladin see Gladden
Glading see Gladden
Gladney, Richard 56
  Samuel 56
Glasgow, J. 40
Glass, John 56
Glaze, Gideon 19
  Patrick 19
  Thomas 1, 48
Glenn, James 17
  Samuel 54
Goard, William 6
Godfrey, Mrs. Ann Margaret 28
  John 11, 28
Going, Daniel 35, 57
  William 58, 68
Goins, Drury 14
Golden, James 9, 24
  John 24
  Susanna 9
  Mrs. Susannah 24
Goldin see Golden
Golding see Golden
Gomery, Samuel 5
Gooch, Clabourn 28
  Mrs. Nancy 28
Good, Robert 53
Goodall, Alexander 16
  William 24
Goodram, Allen 69
  Thomas 69
Goodwin, Amy 29
  Angelina 29
  Francis 14, 15, 28, 29, 33, 34, 59,
    60, 63
  Francis Jr. 21, 29, 59
  Howell 28, 29
  James 28
  Jesse 28, 29, 34, 50
  John 28, 29
  John Jr. 29
  John William 28

Goodwin, Kezia 29
  Mrs. Martha 29
  Martha Epps 29
  Mrs. Mary 29
  Rd. 41
  Robert 13, 29, 33, 34, 36, 38, 60, 61, 64
  Thomas 29, 51
  Uriah 14, 28, 29, 33, 36, 64
  W. 57
  William 28, 29
  William Jr. 29
Goodwyn see Goodwin
Goore see Gore
Gordon, Alexander 42
  Moses 7, 53, 64, 69
  William 7
Gore, Davis 29
  Eleazar 29, 48, 54, 61, 62
  Elisha 30
  Mrs. Elizabeth 29, 30
  James 6, 29, 30, 32, 48, 62
  John 29, 30
  John Ashford 29, 54, 62
  Joshua 29
  Michael 30
Gouge, Clayburn 28
  Mrs. Nancy 28
Gouge see also Gage
Gouyen see Goyen
Goyen, Alexander 69
  Amos 30
  Daniel 35
  William 39
Gradick, Richard 57
Gradock, Jacob 41
Graham, Andrew 12
  Charles 35
  David 12
  Isaac 6, 69
  John 12, 14, 50, 74
  Robert 14
  William 67, 74
Grant, James 20
Graves, Mrs. Ann 30
  Elizabeth 30
  Mrs. Elizabeth 30
  James 30
  James Jr. 30
  John 30
  John Jr. 30
  Lucey 30
  William 30, 64
Gray, Jacob 40
  James 61
  John 30, 44
  Sherrod 40
Great Britain 40
Green, Daniel 2, 42, 56, 57
  Isaac 59
  James 3
  John 20, 26
  Robert 22
  Thomas 50
  William 58, 59
Green Hill Plantation 29
Greer, James 3, 38
  Mrs. Mary 30
  William 30
Gregg, John 18, 35

Gregory, Henry 13, 15
Gregory see also McGregory
Grenshaw see Crenshaw
Gresham, John 15
  William 6
Griffen, Benjamin 30
  Jemima (Ragan) 73
  Jennet 30
  Jonas 30, 31
  Jonas Jr. 30
  Major 30
  Robin 30
  William 73
Griffith, Thomas 60
Grimes, ____ 51
  Isaac 35
  James 35
Grisham see Gresham
Gros, Jacob 46
Grubb, Benjamin 13, 15, 23, 62, 63
  Hannah 59
  Nicholas 55
Guernsey Island 32
Guerrey, Legrand 41
  Peter Sr. 40, 41
Guiger see Geiger
Gullock, John 19
  Martha (Davison) 19
Guphill, William 23
Guthrie, Robert 4
Gwinn, Christopher (?) 39
  John 17

Habersham, James 51, 73
Hadden, James 31
  Mrs. Mary 31
  William 31
Hagan see Hogan
Hagood, Buckner 2, 34, 35
Haig, John James 65
Haile, Benjamin 30, 38
  Colon 51
  Ferguson 30, 31
  Richard 73
  Susanna 30
Hakins, William 34
Halfway Swamp Meeting House 21, 56
Hall, Alexander 31
  Brown 31
  Cibila 31
  James 31
  Jennet 31
  John 31
  John Jr. 31
  Josiah 31
  Hyman 46
  Major Temple 31
  Margaret 31
  Prudence 31, 68
  Temple (?) 31
  Thomas 31
  Warren 1
  William 17, 31
Halsell, Benjamin 42
Hambleton, James 53
  Mary 26
  Samuel 26
  William 26
Hames (?), Amos 8
Hamilton, James 43, 53

Hamilton, Jean 31
  John 31, 38, 51, 60
  Mary 31
  Patrick 31
  Rachel 1, 8, 23, 24, 25, 50,
    57, 60
  Robert 7
  Samuel 33
  William 31
Hampton, H. 4, 6, 12, 18, 23, 68,
    70
  Henry 1, 2, 3, 20, 24, 36, 69,
    72, 74
  John 2, 3
  Martha Epps (Howell) 36
  Naomi 64
  Richard 28, 45, 67
  Susannah 56
  Wade 28, 45, 57, 73
  William 72
Hancock, Edward 31
  Elizabeth 31
  George 31
  George Jr. 31
  Judith 31
  Mary 31
  Mrs. Rachel 31
  Robert 18
Hane & Birk 39
Hanging Rock 19, 21, 49, 61
Hanging Rock, Battle of 43
Hanlin, William 32
Hanna, Capt. 56
  James 4
  James Br. 56
  William 56
Hannon, Robert 67
Harben see Harbin
Harbin, John 1, 17
  Nathaniel 17, 18
  William 17
Harbirt, John 1, 4, 5, 12, 19, 20,
    21, 23, 30, 31, 32, 34, 36, 37,
    42, 43, 46, 48, 50, 54, 58, 61,
    62, 65, 66, 69, 74
  Thomas 12, 13, 37, 74
Harbison, Ann 31, 32
  James 34
  William 31, 32
Harddick see Hardwick
Harden, Elizabeth 32
  Henry 32
Hardgrove, Jean 26
Hardis, ___ 51
Hardwick, Richard 5
  William 25
Hargreaves, Joshua 39
Harker, John 19, 24, 40, 58, 66
Harlewood, William 32
Harnin, John 24
Harper, Arthur 16
  James 32, 49
  Lucy (Tucker) 61
  Robert 32
Harrell, Holladay 1
  Mary (Allen) 1
Harrington see Herrington
Harris, Charles 32
  James 3
  James Hartimer 32

Harris, James Mortimer 32
  John 3, 26
  John George 32
Harrison, Benjamin 57, 61, 69
  Constant 63
  Ephraim 32
  George 17
  James 30, 43, 59
  John 54
  Reuben 10, 28, 43
  William 39, 43, 44
  Willaby 10
Harssom see Harrison
Hart, Daniel 73
  Darrell 12, 73
  Jacob 33
  James 57
  Margaret 32
Harvey, James 10
  Richard 64
Harvil, Thomas 66
Harvin, Frances (Ragan) 73
  John 62
  Richard 73
Hatcher, William 39
Hatfield, Samuel 51
Hause see House
Haven, John 17
Havis, John 35
Hawthorne, Adam 32
  Benjamin 32
  Elizabeth 32
  Mrs. Elizabeth 32
  James 20, 32, 49
  James Jr. 32
  John 32, 52
  John Jr. 32
  Joseph 32
  Margaret 32
  Mary 32
  Robert 32
Hay, David 33, 57
  Dortch 33, 50
  Elizabeth 33, 34
  Hardy 29, 33, 64
  Howell 34, 64
  James 33, 17
  Lucy 32
  Mary 29
  Mrs. Mary 68
  William 33, 68, 73
  William Howell 33
Hayes, Elizabeth 34
  Jesse 56
Haynam, James 3
Haynsworth, Henry 72
  Henry Jr. 72
  Richard 72
  Sarah 60
  Sarah (Furman) 72
Hays see Hay and Hayes
Heath, Elizabeth 34
  Etham 13
  Ethel 25, 29
  Frederick 13, 34, 64
  Thomas 32
Heatly, Andrew 28
  William 28
  William Jr. 28, 54
Heeth see Heath

Hegood see Hagood
Heighs see Hayes
Hemeter, Adam 61
  John 41
Hemphill, Andrew 2, 10, 34, 42, 57
  James 57
Henderson ____ 20
  Anne 34
  Archabal 34
  Edward 6
  Edward John 34
  Elizabeth 34
  Eswar 32
  Frances 34
  Francis 37
  James 34
  John 56
  Nathaniel 14, 34
  Nathaniel Jr. 34
  Pattane 34
  Richard 34
  Robert 48, 71
  Sherod 34
  Susannah 60
  Tyre 34
  William 18, 34, 73
  Wilson 34
Hendley, William 28
Hendricks, Andrew 63
Hening, James 3
Henry, Alexander 5, 12, 28
  Robert 16
  William 12
  William Sr. 62
Henson see Hinson
Herbison see Harbison
Heris see Harris
Hermon, Andrew 34
  Robert 34
  Steven 34
Heron, John 15
  Mary 34
  William 25, 34
Herring, William E. 71
Herrington, Gen. 65
  Susannah 6
  Zilpha 6
Hetherington, James 3, 10, 54
Hevy, Edward 71
Hews see Hughes
Heylegar & Benners 39
Heywood, Buckner 12, 34
Hicklin, John 34
  William 34
Hicks, Angelina (Goodwyn) 29
Hiers, ____ 16
Higgs, Humphrey 35
  Isaac 32, 35
  James 32
High, James 17
High Hill Meeting House 8
High Hill Tavern 71
High Hills of Santee 1, 2, 55
Hikes, John 34
Hill, Capt. 35
  Edward 56
  John 28, 40
  Joseph 62, 72
  Moses 67
  Robert 23

Hill, Thomas 2
  William 17, 20, 31, 68, 71
Hillhouse, James 41
Hilton, Andrew 56
  Jesse 14
  John 56
  Joshua 14
Hinson, Archibald 36, 51
  Bartlett 2, 35
  Benjamin 35
  Charles 35
  Isham 35
  John 35
  Kenianna 35
  Mrs. Mary 35
  Obediah 35
  Philip 35
  William 35
Hirons, John 53, 59, 66
Hitchcock, John 15, 30, 32
Hixon, John 47
Hixons, Mary 16
Hoard, James 66
Hodge, James 70
Hoff, James 14
Hogan, John 4
  Michael 59
  William 17, 18
Hoge, James 26
  Mary 27
Hoke, Michael 61
Hollan, John 27
Hollbrook, J. 40
Holley, Jacob 17
  John 37
Holliday, Benjamin 35
  Daniel 35, 71
  Daniel Jr. 35
  Elliott 35
  John 35
  Letty 35
  William 35
Hollis, James 35, 46, 69
  James Jr. 35
  John 27, 35
  John Jr. 35
  Moses 31, 35, 37
  Nottley 35
  Stasey 35
Holloway, Benjamin 51
  Taylor 32
Holms, John 10
Holzendorf, John 6, 16, 21
Homes, William 8
Honeywood, Arthur 39
Hood, John 50
  Robert 43
Hope, Mrs. Ann 35
  John 30, 35, 36
Hopkins, David 6, 22, 36, 38, 47, 66, 67
  John 15, 34, 36
  Solomon 59
  William 14, 29, 66
Horton, ____ 49
  Amos 1
  Daniel 1
  Harry 1
  Henry 56
  John 1

House, Christian 11
  James 22
  Reuben 43, 50
  Thomas 8, 9, 14, 64
Houston, John 6
Houston see also Huston
Houze see House
Howard, Buckner 4
  Heli 36, 47, 72
  James 36, 72
  Jerusha 72
  Joseph 72
  Richard 28
  Sarah 36
  William 72
Howe, Joseph 14
Howell, Arthur 15, 38
  Grace 36
  James 36
  Mrs. Lucy 13, 36
  Malachi 29, 36, 38, 64
  Martha-Epps 36
  Mathew 45, 67
  Robert 36, 37, 38
  Thomas 28, 29, 36
  William 9, 29, 36, 38, 59, 60, 64
  William Jr. 36
Howell's Ferry 36
Hoy see Hay
Hoyle, Jonathan 10
Hudleson, John 44
Hudson, ___ 73
  David 6
  James 36
  Joel 63
  John 4
  Lodwick 36, 37
  Samuel 36
Huey, Alexander 37
  Arculeas 37
  Arculeas Jr. 37
  Mrs. Cattrin 37
  Eleasebeth 37
  Hercules 37
  James 22, 37, 65
  John 37
  Margret 37
  Mary 37
Huey see also Hughes
Huffman, Jacob 26
Hugar, Daniel 39
Huggins, John 7, 47
  Susannah (Benbow) 70
Hughes, Cattren 37
  Mrs. Elizabeth 37
  John 6, 37
  Josiah 37
  William 60
Hughes see also Huey
Hughey see Huey
Hull, Hartwell 46
Humphries, Charles 6
  Thomas 6, 48
Hunt, Lawyer 1
  Elizabeth 70
  Joseph 37
  Mary (Campbell) 70
  Sarah 70
Hunter, Archibald 37
  Caffield (?) 37

Hunter, David 5, 31
  Davin 5
  Elizabeth 37
  Mrs. Fanny 37
  H. 56
  Henry 3, 17, 23, 37, 61, 63
  Henry Jr. 37
  Henry Starke 3
  John 23, 39, 73
  Mary 37
  Nazurah 64
  Norwood 73
  Sarah 37
  Mrs. Sarah 37
  Thomas 37, 41
Hush, Isaac 5
  Jacob 5
Huston, Agness 10
  Mrs. Eleanor 37
  Henry 10
  William 37
Huston see also Houston
Hutcheson see Hutchinson
Hutchinson, Rebecca (Rives) 53
  Thomas 14, 25, 29, 36, 43, 61
Hute, ___ 3
Hutson see Hudson
Hux, William 50
Hyett, ___ 32

Imball, Frederick 21
Indian Land Meeting House 43
Inglish see English
Ioore, George 71, 73
Ireland 4, 16, 37 (?)
Irvin, Alexander 24, 73
Irvin see also Ervin
Isbell, Elizabeth 57
  Kinhappuck 57
  Littleton 42, 57
Ivey, Reubin 20

Jack, James 26
Jacks Creek 13
Jackson, Ambrose 37
  Elizabeth 13
  Isaac 1, 9, 51
  Isaac Jr. 52
  Reuben 52
  Richard 33
  Thomas 52
Jackson Creek 3, 17, 21, 22
Jackson Creek Church 67
Jagar see Jaggers
Jaggers, Jeremiah 35, 64
  Nathan 17
James, Elizabeth 72
  John 24, 51, 53, 56, 70, 71, 72, 73
  John Jr. 71, 72
  Martha 72
  Mrs. Martha 72
  Mary 71, 72
  Rebecca 71
  Samuel 71
  Sarah 71
  Mrs. Sarah 71
  Shearwood 72
  Shearwood Jr. 48, 72
  Talefore 72
Jameson, Mary 26

Jameson, Robert 32
Jefferson Co, Va. 59
Jeffreys, Thomas 34, 64
Jeffords, Daniel 70
Jenkins, Anne 38
  Caroline 38
  Mrs. Catherine 38
  Elizabeth 38
  John 6, 69
  Mary 38
  Richard 6, 38
  Sarah 38
  Susannah 38
  Thomas 22, 47
  Thomas William 38, 52, 56
  Walter 38
  William 38
Jennings, John 9, 35
Jewel, Joseph 20
Jinnings see Jennings
John Kennerly Creek 61
Johnson, Charles 35, 46
  James 14, 26, 30
  Lawed 38
  Nealy 38
  Stephen 22
  William 54, 56
Johnson see also Johnston
Johnston, Brick 39
  Charles 35, 69
  James 14, 26, 30, 45, 69
  John 37, 62
  Margaret (Hawthorn) 32
  Parmenas 10
  Thomas 46, 69
  William 14
Joiner see Joyner
Jonston see Johnson & Johnston
Jones, Darling 19
  David 42, 73
  Jesse 10
  John 38, 39, 46
  Jonathan 26, 56
  Judy 38
  Ralph 2, 5, 12, 16, 17, 19, 20, 21, 22, 28, 30, 31, 33, 35, 36, 39, 41, 42, 44, 46, 48, 53, 60, 64
  Rolfe 33
  Thomas 40, 53
  William 5, 40, 64
Jordan, John 62
  Moses 64
Joyner, David 12
  Frederick 61
  John 60
  Joseph 12
Juggers see Jaggers

Kearslick, Abraham 66
Keils, Daniel 71
Kell, Archibald 38
  James 38, 39
  John 37
  Matthew 38, 39
Kelley see Kelly
Kelly, Arabrilla 38
  Mrs. Arabrella 38
  Elijah 39
  Gersham 73

Kelly, James 38, 39, 48
  James Jr. 38
  Jane 39
  John 39
  Josh. M. 13
  Mary 25, 39
  Rebecca 39
  Samuel 38
  William 39
Kelsey, George 26
  Samuel 49
  Samuel Jr. 26
Kelton, Richard 1
Kemp, Moses 28, 58
  Solomon 59
Kenge see King
Kennedy, Alexander 62
  Mrs. Ann 39
  Felix 39
  Gilbert 39
  James 39, 40
  John 4, 31, 39, 63
  Margaret 39
  Robert 24
  S. 46
  Samuel 16
  William 39, 45
Kennerly, John 61
  Joseph 17, 61
Kenney, Alexander 61
  John 39
Kennington, John 38
Kensler see Kinsler
Kentucky 61
Kerr, James 20
  Jean (Duncan) 20
Kershaw, Ely 39
  Joseph 4, 18, 24, 40, 63, 66
  Mrs. Priscilla 40
  Sarah 39
  William 39, 40
Kershaw & Ridley 39
Kershaw, McRa & Co. 39
Kerswell, Andrew 26
Kerthland, William 41
Kerving, Timothy 41
Key, John 50
Killingsworth, William 64
Kimball, Col. 48
  Benjamin 40
  Benjamin Jr. 40
  Charles 40
  Elizabeth 40
  Elizabeth (Moore) 47
  Fanny 40
  Frederick 1, 15, 20, 21, 30, 34, 38, 40, 41
  John 40
  Jos. 36
  Lucy 40
  Mary 40
Kimbrell, Charles 51
Kinart, Josof 34
Kincaid, James 13, 61
  Joseph 16
King, Ann 40
  Catherine 40
  Elizabeth 40
  Esbelle 40
  Francis 40

King, George 39, 40
  Hannah 40
  Mrs. Hannah 40
  Henry 40, 41, 48
  Isabel 34, 40
  Mrs. Isbell 40
  James 4
  John 6, 35, 40, 46, 51, 69
  John Jr. 40
  Joseph 40
  Judah 40
  Mary 40
  Mrs. Mary 55
  Michael 40
  Michael Jr. 40
  Nathaniel 40, 41
  Penelope 40
  Mrs. Priscilla 40
  Richard 16, 40
  Robert 41
  Sarah 40
  Thomas 40
King Street store 39
Kinge see King
Kingswood, Jacob 12
Kinkead see Kincaid
Kinseller see Kinsler
Kinsler, Christian 15, 17, 41, 57, 61, 62
  Elizabeth 41
  Herman 41
  John 20
  Mary 41
Kinzler see Kinsler
Kirk, Peter 15
  Thomas 6, 26
Kirkland, Joseph 4,
  William 33, 34, 57, 61
Kirklin see Kirkland
Kirkpatrick, Agnes 41
  Ann 41
  Francis 41, 62
  James 41, 62
  James Jr. 41
  Jane 41
  John 41
  Margaret 41
  Rebecca 41
  Mrs. Rebecca 41
  Robert 41
  Robert II 41
  Samuel 41
  Thomas 41
  William 41
Kitchen, Ann 41
  Charles 41, 42
  Charles Jr. 41
  Ely 41, 42
  James 41, 42
  Jane 42
  Mrs. Jane 41
  John 18, 22, 41, 42, 55
  Mary 41
  Priscilla 41
  William 2, 41
  Zachariah 10, 41
Knight, John 5
  William 42
Knighton, Alexander 46
  Isaac 46, 51

Knighton, Moses 6, 35, 46, 50, 51, 69
  Sarah 46
  Thomas 46
Knox, Doctor 5
  Hugh 5, 27
  James 3, 14, 16, 19, 26, 39, 42, 59, 61
  Janet 42
  John 34
  Robert 26, 42
  Samuel 5
Konnold, John 34
Kuhn, Casper 11, 17
Kulp see Culp
Kuns, Adam 11
  Casper 11, 17

Labon, James 23
Lacey, Edward 3, 6, 10, 21, 25
  Easter (Sadler) 54
  Reuben 3, 54
Lacy see Lacey
Ladd, Benjamin 3
  Benjamin Sr. 38
Ladenham, William 42
Lafferty, John 9
Lage, Henry 30
Lahaffe, John 39
Lake, John 50
Lambright, William 25
Lamont, Martha 25
Lancaster Co., S.C. 9, 18, 24, 30, 31, 38, 40, 43, 49, 52, 57, 58
Land, Elliner 42
  James 42
  John 42
  Mary 42
  Thomas 42
Lane, Edward 11, 51
  Maryan 11
Lang, James William 66
  John Wyley 66
  Samuel 66
  Sarah 66
  Sarah (Wyley) 66
  William 19, 54, 58, 63, 66
Lang see also Long
Lanoir see Lenoir
Latham, Andrew 39
Lathrum, William 6
Latta, John 26, 49
  John Jr. 26
  Priscilla 55
Laughlin, Mary 62
Laughon, James 56, 64
Lavender, Robert 46
  Robert Holt 46
Lawhaugh, James 64
Lawrence, ___ 73
Lawson, John 44
Lawton, William 57
Leaney, Isaac 26
Leasley see Lesley
Lentham see Latham
Leavonder see Lavendar
LeCont, John 42
  Joseph 42
  William 39, 42
  William Jr. 42
Lee, Agnes 42

Lee, Agnes (Harper) 32
  Anthony 9, 62, 72
  Elizabeth 42
  Francis 42
  Francis S. 48
  John 13, 42
  John Jr. 42
  Joseph 16, 21, 32, 35
  Mrs. Mary 42
  Rachel 42
  Rebecca 42
  Robert 2, 9, 58, 60
  Rosana 42
  Sarah 42
  Solomon 41
  Stephen 42
Leech, David 47, 54
Lefleur, Charles 51
Legare, Joseph 39
Legge, Maddox 17
Legran, Oliver 64
Leigh see Lee
Lennox, Elizabeth 69
Lenoir, Isaac 58, 65
  Martha (Atkinson) 69
  Thomas 24
Lesesne, Francis 73
  Frederick 44
Lesley, Edward 9
  John 24
Lessesne see Lesesne
Lester, Andrew 19
Leviston, James 36
  Moses 54
  Robert 64
Lewelling, Jonathan 49
Lewis, Charles 5, 6, 19, 22, 35,
  46, 51, 69
  Jacob 17, 23
  James 7
  John 35, 50
  Mary (Bradley) 6
  Robert 13, 35, 51, 53, 60, 62,
  63, 67, 73
  Thomas 17
  Warner 35
  William 16, 35, 66
Lick Creek 49
Liles, Aromanus 28
Liles see also Lyle
Lindley, James 10
Lindsay, James 53
  Samuel 42
Lining, Charles 71
Linn, John 49
Lion see Lyon
Lithrow, Robert 1
Little, Samuel 32, 44, 73
  William 38, 44, 72, 73
Little Lynches' River 18
Little River 42, 46, 52
Littlejohn Marcellus 61
  Samuel 42
Livingston, Duncan 43
  Elizabeth 43
  James 43
  Lucy 43
Lloyd, Joseph 60
  Rose 69
Lockhart, Aaron 1

Lockhart, Andrew 59
  John 31
  Patrick 60
  Robert 31
Loewis see Lewis
Logan, John 28
Logue, Jane 45
  John 4, 11, 18, 19, 23, 24, 32, 37,
  45, 57, 58, 63, 66
  Samuel 45
Lohon, James 56
London, England 32, 38
Long, John Jr. 32
Long see also Lang
Long branch 69
Lott, John 22
Love, Benjamin 6
  Hezekiah 44
  Isaac 10, 12, 13, 19, 20, 43, 45
  Jacob 43
  James 2, 41, 56, 73
  Jane (Cousart) 16
  John 10, 14, 15
  Maglen 43
  Mary 43
  Robert 19, 43
  William 56
Loving, Christopher 6
Lowrie see Lowry
Lowry, John 8, 9, 19, 21, 28
  William 16
Loyal, Robert 23, 51, 60
Luckey, Samuel 60
Lundy, Daniel 39
Lusk, Jane 20
  Mary (Duncan) 20
  Robert 26
Lyal see Lyell
Lyall see Lyell
Lyda, John 22
Lyell, Robert 5, 9, 14, 23, 25, 28,
  29, 33, 36, 38, 51, 59, 60, 61
  Lyle, Robert 28
Lynch's Creek 13, 18, 35, 54, 56
Lyon, Guthridge 39
  Mordecai 26
Lysle, Robert 14
Lysle see also Liles

McAdoo, William 44
McAdow see McAdoo
McAuley see McCaule & McCauley
McBee, Vardrey 14
McBrayer, Martha 7
  William 7, 8
McBrier see McBrayer
McBryer see McBrayer
McCain, John 10
  Patrick 18
McCalla, David 4
  Thomas 4, 34
McCalluch see McCulloch
McCalley, David 4
  Thomas 4
McCallum, Mrs. Ann 43
  Henry 43
  Henry Jr. 43
  James 43
  Jean 43
  John 38, 43

McCallum, Sarah 43
McCambridge, John 4, 39
McCammon see McCamon
McCamon, James 27, 31
  John 16
  Thomas 27
  William 31
McCance, Samuel 16
McCants, Andrew 27
  Thomas 27
McCartney, Michael 64
McCarty, Michael 64
McCaule, Thomas H. 13, 14, 15,
  17, 21, 23, 24, 67
McCauley, James 44, 53, 57, 74
  John 70
  Thomas 21, 24
McCaw, James 56
  William 10
McCay, John 10
  Joseph 10, 55
McCay see also McCoy
McClanchan, Finy 3
  Phineas 3
McClaren, Daniel 28
McCleave, Robert 54
McClelan, Elizabeth 8
  James 8
  Robert 7
  Samuel 22
McCleland, Samuel 68
McClenahan, John 4, 38
McClendon, Dennis 43, 47
  Martha 43
  William 47
McClintock, Robert 1, 2, 45, 48, 61
McCluer see McClure
McClure, Hugh 16, 43
  James 43
  John 43
  Margaret 43
  Mrs. Mary 43
  Mary Jr. 43
McColclough, Alexander 44
McCollom see McCallum
McCollugh see McCulloch
McCollum see McCallum
McConnel, John 54
McConnico, William 11, 56, 68, 73
McCool, Adam 45
  Jean 45
  John 73
McCord, James 62
  John 39, 73
  Joseph 12, 28
McCorkill see McCorkle
McCorkle, Abraham 31
  Andrew 31
  Archibald 63
  Elizabeth 43
  James 43
  Jean 43
  Robert 43
  William 43
McGowan, Joseph 44, 57
  Lydia 44
  Mary 44
  William 44
McGowen see McGowan
McGragh, David 23

McGraugh, Edward 1, 44
McGraw, Mrs. Aimey 44
  Arthur 44
  Benjamin 44
  David 10
  David Jr. 10
  Dorcas 44
  Edward 1, 44
  Edward Jr. 44
  Elizabeth 44
  Enoch 44
  Jacob 44
  James 44
  Janet 44
  John 44
  Mary 44
  Obedience Lucy Martha Patience 44
  Priscilla 44
  Sarah 44
  Solomon 44
  William 44
McGray, Edward 17
  Jacob 1
  John 12
  William 20
McGregory, George Malcolm 39
McGrew, Alexander 20, 45
  Alexander Jr. 45
  Mrs. Margaret 45
  Peter 41
  William 45, 67
McGriff, Patrick 6, 10
McGuire, Merry 14
McIlwain, Andrew 55
McKaime, John 51
McKain see McCain
McKee, John 58
  Samuel 46
  William 45
McKelvey, Robert 15, 73
McKenney see McKinney
McKeon see McGowan
McKinnie's plantation 39
McKinnie see also McKinney
McKinney, Mrs. Ann Hope 35
  Charles 24, 35, 36, 37, 65
  George 4
  Jacob 7
  John 10, 16, 55
  Samuel 27
  William 16, 41
McKnight, Andrew 10
  John 39
McKown see McGowan
McKray see McGray
McLaclen, Mary (McNeese) 45
McLane, Daniel 20
McLemore, Joel 14, 28, 34, 53, 66
McLendon see McClendon
McLennan, Andrew 45
McMaan see McMan
McMan, Elizabeth 45
  Joseph 45
  Rachel (Rogers) 53
  Thomas 45
McManos, James 1
McMeen see McMan
McMichael, John 17, 31, 56
McMoris, William 61
McMullen, Agnes 46, 47

McMullen, James 47
  John 46, 47
  Mary (Erwin) 47
  Sarah 46, 47
McMurray, Thomas 17, 68
McNabb, John 50
McNair, James 62
McNamore, Joel 59
McNeal see Neel
McNease see McNeese
McNeal, James 6, 54
McNeese, Henry 10
  James 45
  Jean 45
  John 45
  Margaret 45
  Mary 45
  Mrs. Mary 45
McNeirs, James 62
McNight see McKnight
McNise see McNeese
McPherson, James 9
McQueen, John 69
McQuiston, David 12
McRa, Duncan 39
McWatters, John 4
McWhorter, Alexander 17, 31, 67
  Benjamin 7
  George 53
  John 16

Machie, James 42
Mackey, Mary (Kitchen) 41
Mackie & Potts 34
Mahaffey, Robert 1
Maham, Hezekiah 44
Malone, Elizabeth (Atkinson) 69
  John 13, 58, 61, 65, 69
Mane, James 44
Manley, Peter 46
Mann, Luke 46
Manning, Laurence 73
Maples, Thomas 38, 73
Marchasl, John 45, 46, 60
Marchel, Elizabeth (Lee) 42
  William 42
Marion, Francis 73
  John 45
  John Jr. 45
  Martha Wickam 45
  Mary 45
  Nathaniel Wickam 45
Markel, John 45, 46, 60
Marley, John 24
Marlow, Elizabeth 34
  William 34, 41
Mars Bluff, S.C. 53
Marshall, A. 48
  Christian (Moore) 47
  Elizabeth (Lee) ? 42
  James 49
  John 1, 2, 3, 31, 33, 39, 40, 45, 48, 49, 58, 64
  Robert 58
  William 52, 64
Martain see Martin
Martin, Andrew 46
  Ann 55
  Benjamin 46
  David 7

Martin, Edward 43
  J. 29
  James 29, 46, 48
  James Jr. 46
  Jane 46
  Jean (McNeece) 45
  John 7, 46, 62
  John C. 39
  Joseph 64
  Nathaniel 33
  Nicholas 46
  Noah 48
  Rebecca 4, 46
  Robert 10, 16, 21, 34, 55
  William 2, 5-11, 14, 19, 21, 22, 32, 34, 37, 46, 47, 49, 52, 55, 57, 61, 67, 70, 74
Maryland 74
Mascall, Henry 15
  Mary (Cook) 65
Mason, James 52
  William 39
Masters, John 3
Mathias, Samuel 4, 39
Mathis, Israel 8, 36
  Samuel 4, 32, 39, 40
Mattecks, Elizabeth 12
Meknzay 12
Matthews, Mrs. Catherine Jenkins 38
  Hugh 61
  James 10, 38
  Peter 50
  Samuel 32
Maxwell, John 58
May, Benjamin 2
  John 13, 15, 23, 29
  Thomas 11, 42, 51
Mayfield, Abraham 18
  John 6
Meek, Adam 14, 50
  James 50
Mehon, Patrick 10
Mellet, Peter 53
Melone see Malone
Mertin see Martin
Meyers see Myers
Mickle, Joseph 12, 43
Middleton, Henry 57
  Richard 49
  William 54
Midway, Georgia 71
Midwood, Samuel 39
Miers see Myers
Miles, James 10
  John 10, 13, 27, 51
  Thomas 46, 69
  William 54
Milhouse, John 25, 39, 54, 56, 66
Milican's branch 56
Mill Creek 29, 33
Mill tract 71
Millen, John 27
  Robert 27
Miller, Abram 22
  Alexander 27
  Ann 12, 46
  Charles 12
  Charles Jr. 21
  Elizabeth 30
  George 1, 58

Miller, Hannah 5
  Hugh 17
  James 48, 57, 58
  John 27, 48
  John David 32
  Mary 46
  Mrs. Mary 46
  Michael 3
  Morris 46
  Nathaniel 36, 37
  Robert 42 (27?)
  Samuel 46
  William 12, 27, 33, 46, 53, 66
Millet, John 36
Milligan, Joseph 46
Milling, Hugh 44
  John 1, 3, 15, 17, 46
Millis, Thomas 71
Mills, John 25, 33, 49, 54, 57
  John Jr. 57
  Sarah 21
  Sarah (Smith) 21
  Susannah (Brown) 8
  William 71
Millwee, John 46
  William 46, 47
  William II 46
Mily see Myley
Minick, Barbara 11
  John Adam 11
Mintz, Marget 11
Mitchell, James 3, 39, 47
  Nimrod 16, 23, 56
Mixon, Elizabeth 47
  Frances 47
  George 47
  Prudence 47
  Sabra 47
  William 47
Mixson see Mixon
Mobberly, Benjamin 67
  Edward 67
  John 38, 67
  Susanna 67
  William 38, 67
Mobly, Sarah (McCallum) 43
Moffett, Ann (Watson) 62
  John 62
  William 14
Molit, Peter 70
Moncks, Isaac 9
Monmouth Co., Wales 38
Montgomery, David 23
  Henry 67
  Hugh 23, 68
  J. 40
  James 24, 27
  John 6, 53
  Marcey 68
  Massey 67
  Ninen 24
  Robert 16, 24, 37, 55, 59
  Samuel 4, 6, 46
  William 4, 44, 67
Moody, Burril 47
  Humphrey 47
  Louisa 47
  Mary 47
  Slomon 47
  Slomon Jr. 47

Moon, Samuel 8
Moore, Agnes 47
  Charles 20
  Christian 47
  Elinor 47
  Elizabeth 47
  Elizabeth (Scoldfield) 55
  Hodges 72
  Israel 47
  Israel Jr. 47
  Isham 25, 39, 51, 53, 60, 62, 70, 71, 72, 73
  James 47, 55
  Jane 47
  John 4, 14, 24, 25, 28, 29, 33, 35, 36, 47
  Lazarus 48
  Levi 6, 12, 72
  Mary 6
  Morris 29
  Nathan 5
  Nathaniel 51, 71
  Philip 32
  Samuel 3, 47
  Sarah 48
  Thomas 47
  William 5, 51
Moorhead see Morehead
Mooses see Moses
Morant, William 73
More see Moore
Morise see Morris
Morray see Murray
Morries see Morris
Morgan, Edward 69
Morris, Benjamin 22, 34
  George 34
  James 22
  John 27, 34
  Miller White 46
  Robert 39
  Thomas 42, 46
Morrison, Robert 15
Morrow, David 27, 62
  Jane (Wyley) 66
  Joseph 5, 27, 66
Mortimer, Edward 16
Morton, Thomas 39
Moses, Myer 6
  Robert 9, 51
Moses & Miner 39
Mothershead, Francis 48
  John Jet 48
  Peter 48
Motley, John 60
Motte, Agnes 48
  David 48
Mountgomery see Montgomery
Mucklevein, Henry 48
Muldoon, James 27
Munson, Robert 19
Murff see Murph
Murph, John 41, 61
Murphey see Murphy
Murphy, Godfrey 41
  John 38
  M. 73
  Malachi 24, 59, 68
  Moses 39
Murray, David 37

Murrell, William 36, 70, 71
Muse, Thomas 20
Myddleton see Middleton
Myers, Christopher 48
  Conrod 48
  Elijah 28
  Thomas 30
  William 9, 14, 15, 29, 33, 36, 38, 50, 64, 66, 67
  Winney 38
Myley, Henry 7, 19
  Robert 7

Nailey, B. 1
Nance, Elizabeth 6
  Mrs. Elizabeth 48
  Elizabeth Mary Ann 48
  Ellenor 48
  Johannah 48
  John 48
  Pattie 48
  Peter 48
  Richard 48
  Sally Cloyd 48
  William 48
Narramore, Edward 40
  William 1
Nasury, William 64
Neal, David 51
  Henry 40, 49
  Thomas 14, 65, 72
Neats, Aberhardt 61
Neel see Neal
Neely, Catharine 48
  Elizabith 48
  George 16
  Hugh 27, 34
  Mary 48
  Mrs. Mary 48
  Matthew 27
  Robert 27
  Samuel 48, 66
  Thomas 27
  William 48
  William Jr. 48
Neilson, David 24, 36
  Isabella 72
  John 73
  Mary 72
  Samuel Jr. 72
  Sarah 72
Nelson, David 36
  James 51
  John 9, 17, 70
  Reason 40
  Thomas 64
  William 11, 35, 53, 64
Nelson's Ferry 72
Nephew, Peter 49
Nettles, William 7, 18, 24, 68
  Zachariah 10, 20, 55
Nevile, Thomas 10
New Erection Meeting House 66
Newman, Jonathan 5, 32, 47, 71
  Richard 38
  Samuel 71
  Thomas 32, 71
  William Thomas 70
Newport, Georgia 71
Newsmith, Nathaniel 57

Newton, Ann 72
  Jane 48, 49
  Jean 48, 49
  John 4, 19, 72, 73
  John Jr. 72
  Mary 48
Nichols, James 12
Nilson see Nelson
Nipper, James 41
Ninety Six, S.C. 20, 45, 48, 52
Nix, Ambrose 23, 38
Norman, John 71
North Carolina 9, 33, 37, 40, 74
Norton, Daniel 52
Nutt, Catherine (Cousart) 16
  William 43
Nuttawell, William 11

O'Bannon, Elizabeth (Kimball) 40
O'Quinn see Quinn
Obstant, John 6
Oglivie, James 11, 18, 33, 41, 51, 74
  John 11, 18, 35, 51, 74
Osborn, Thomas 70
Osgood, John 23
  Peter 16
Oster, Peter 54
Ostrin, Maria 54
Otter's Creek 54
Owen and Owens
  Mrs. Abigail 49
  Benjamin 17, 42
  James 34, 42, 69
  John 17
  Joseph 31
  Lewis 11
  Mary 34
  Samuel 49
  Thomas 49
Owen's Creek 22
Owin see Owen
Oyns see Owens

Pace, Nathaniel 36
Pacolet, S.C. 52
Padian see Peden
Pagan, Agnes 49
  Alexander 25, 49
  Archibald 49
  James 5, 27, 49
  Mrs. Janet 49
Page, Anne (Cason) 12
  Henry 30
Pagen see Pagan
Paisley, John 72
Palmer, ___ 12
  Joshua 8, 35, 36, 45, 49, 56, 60
  William 73
Papick, Henry 64
Pardue see Purdue
Paris, Robert 10
Park, Hugh 34
Parker, Gabriel 50, 64
Parnel, James 35
Parrison, Matthew 72
Parrott, Thomas 11, 18, 35, 50, 51, 74
  Thomas Jr. 35, 51
Parson, Philip 22
Patrick, Henry 11, 13
  John 40

Patrick, William 5
Partridge, John 25, 50
  Philip 16
Paterson see Patterson
Patridge see Partridge
Patterson, Andrew 17, 64
  David 54
  James 62
  John 31
  Joseph 5, 62
  Peter 62
  Robert 62
  Stewart 63
Patteson see Patterson
Patton, John 62
  John Jr. 68
  Robert 3, 38, 40, 41
Paul, Archibald 21
Payne, Joseph 68
Pearce, Hugh 27
  James 64
Pearce see also Pierce
Pearson, Mrs. Dorcas 74
  J. 35
  James 18, 24, 74
  John 49, 51, 63, 74
  Mary 38, 74
  Philip 18, 29, 32, 49, 51, 63, 64, 67
  Robert 74
  Samuel Sr. 54
  Thomas 7
  William 11, 74
Peary see Perry
Peay, Elizabeth 37
  George 37, 49
  Nicholas 43
Peden, James 4, 10, 34, 42, 44
Pedin see Peden
Pee see Peay
Pee hill 66
Peebles, Henry 38
Peedee, S.C. 46
Peeples, Henry 38
Pegan see Pagan
Pegues, William 35
Pender, John Arnold 4, 48, 62
Pennsylvania 14, 32, 49
Penny, Samuel 64
Perdice see Perdue
Perkins, David 49
  Lewis 49
  Lydia 49
  Peter 57
Permon, Joshua 35
Perry, Benjamin 2, 49
  Benjamin Jr. 49
  Elizabeth 49
  Esther 49, 50
  Jacob 49
  James 9, 27, 28, 60
  Jesse 49
  Job 50
  Joseph 50
  Mrs. Judith 49
  Lamuel 49
  Lewis 49, 50
  Mary 49
  Mrs. Mary 49
  Patience 49

Perry, Rigdon 49
  Ruth 49
  Sarah 49
  Mrs. Sarah 49
  Silas 49
  Wineford 49
  Zedick 60
Petegrew, James 57
Peters, Elijah 50
  Jesse 50
  John 62
  Mrs. Sarah 50
  Solomon 13, 50, 67
Peterson, Matthew 51
Petty, Luke 50
Pettypool, Abraham 11
  Abraham Jr. 11
  Ephraim 6, 51
  Philip 51
  Seth 73
Phelps, Noah 25, 64
Philadelphia, Pa. 32
Phillips, Cornel John 3
  John 3
  William 63
Pickens, Gabriel 40
  Thomas 50
Pickering, Tim. 73
Pickett, Charles 2, 6, 19, 35, 46, 50, 51, 55
  Elisabeth 50
  Frankey 50
  James 50
  John 50
  Micajah 1, 46, 50
  Ruben 50
  Mrs. Susanna 50
Pidgeon, Isaac 6, 7, 54
  Samuel 54
Pierce, James 50
  Mrs. Naomi 50
Pierce see also Pearce
Pierly see Byerly
Pierson see Pearson
Pigg, Edward 8
Pinckney, Charles Cotesworth 40, 65, 73
  Thomas 73
  William 15
Piniger, Charles 17
Pittsylvania Co., Va. 57
Platt, David 8, 73
  Hezekiah 50
  John 8, 16, 50
  Philip 39
Pledger, Joseph 24
Plowden, Edward 70
Pool, Ephraim 2, 9, 60
  Philip 51
Pope, Barnaby 1, 2, 13, 23, 30, 31, 37, 41, 50, 51, 61
  Mrs. Jemima 42
  John 61
  Lewis 1, 13, 23
Porter, Agnes 50
  Alexander 39
  Ann 50
  David 20, 22, 27, 33, 50
  James 30, 50
  John 5, 20, 27, 42

Porter, Josiah 27
  Matthew 50
  Nathaniel 50, 62
  Rebeckah 50
  Ruth 50
  Samuel 16
  Mrs. Sarah 50
  Violet 50
Postell, James 72
  John 65, 73
Poupard, Mrs. 32
Powell, Ann 51
  Elizabeth 51
  James 40, 46
  Josiah 46
  Leonard 11, 36, 51
  Penelope 51
  William 50, 51
Powers, Paul 7
Pratt, James 6, 15, 22, 30
  John 54, 62, 65
Presbyterian Church 21, 23
Prescott, Aaron 48
  Ephraim 7, 12, 13
Price, Charles 43
  Daniel 22
Prince William Parish 18
Pringle, Francis 3, 15, 44
  Fd. 70
  John 73
Printer, James 49
Pritchard, Ann 51, 59
  David 51
Pritchett, Stephen 22
Proctor, Samuel 35, 50, 51
Puddling swamp 71
Purdue, Richard 29, 34, 63
Purnell, James 73
Pursley, John 68
Purvis, Alexander 44

Quakers 25, 63
Quarterman, Thomas 71
Quinn, Daniel 19, 39
  Peter 58, 59

Rabb, Mrs. Hannah 52
  James 52
  Robert 2, 11, 13, 18
  William 11, 51, 74
Raegon see Ragan
Raely see Rayly
Rafe, Zachariah 22
Raffield see Rafield
Rafield, Ebenezer 6
  Jean 47
  Mrs. Jean 47
  John 6, 47, 52
Raford see Raiford
Rafting Creek 13, 72
Ragan, Elizabeth 73
  Frances 73
  Jemima 73
  John 21, 73
  Lucey 73
  Mrs. Lucey 73
  Mary 73
  Sarah 73
  William 56, 73
Ragg, Robert 3

Ragon see Ragan
Raiford, Isaac 15, 38
  Mary (Hancock) 31
  Phillip 17
Rainey, Robert 39
  Samuel 3, 47
  Thomas 3, 54
Rambert see Rembert
Ramer see Reamer
Ramsey, Willis 51
Randoll, William 57, 60
Ranick, Mary 65
Rapley, Richard Andrews 65
Ratchford, Joseph 20
  William 20
Ratcliff, James 51
  Mrs. Prudence 51
  Samuel 47, 51
  Susanna 51
Ratton, John 42
Rawlinson, Benjamin 29
Rawls, Gabriel 23
Rayly, Bryant 1, 2, 22, 23
Rea, William 38, 39
Reamer, John 41
Reany see Rainey
Reaves see Reeves
Reed see Reid
Rees see Reese
Reese, Edwin 51
  Elizabeth 51
  Ephraim 29
  Huberd 51, 60, 70, 71, 73
  Hugh 51
  Isham 51
  John 51
  Joseph 14, 15, 34, 36, 50, 57, 63, 67, 68
  Mrs. Mary 51
  Mary (James) 72
  Richey 72
  Sally 51
  Sarah 51
  Sarah (James) 72
  Thomas 7, 9, 13, 44, 51, 53, 64, 67, 69, 71
  William 51, 72
Reeves, Timothy 17, 19
  William 34
Reid, Alexander 9
  James 9
  John 28
  Robert 21, 32, 39, 44, 66
Reily, Bryant 23, 41
  Patrick 10
  Robert 52
  Samuel 47, 52
Rembert, Abijah 51
  James 8, 63, 72
  John 73
Rennington, John 31
Revolutionary soldiers 20, 25, 38, 39, 42, 47, 52, 65, 66, 70, 73
Reyly see Rayly
Reynolds, David 65
  David Jr. 65
Rice, Isaac 28
  Samuel 28
Rich, ___ 73
  Frederick 54

Richards, Amos 62
Richardson, grandson 52
  Ann 73
  Arthur 52
  Charles 5, 52
  Daniel 67
  Mrs. Dorothy 52, 68
  Edward 52, 73
  Hannah 52
  James Burchell 52
  Jennett 52
  John 52
  Margaret 52
  Mrs. Margaret 52
  Mary 52
  Peter 52
  Richard 52, 68, 73
  Richard Jr. 38, 52
  Robert 52
  Samuel 52
  Susannah 52
  Thomas 52
  Thomas Jr. 52
  William 52, 73
Richbrough, Henry 32
  James 32
  John 32
  Nathaniel 62
  William 12, 47
Richburg see Richbrough
Richland, S.C. 63
Richland plantation 73
Richman, Jacob 17
  John 1
Richmond see Richman
Rickard, Thomas 33
Ricketts, Zachariah 20
Riddell see Riddle
Riddle, George 52
  James 52
  John 52
  John Jr. 52
  Mrs. Mary 52
  Patrick 52
  William 39
Ridly, William 62
Ridwell, Peter 51
Ridgell, John 14, 47
  Mary 46, 47
  Richard 8, 47
  Robert 46
  William 56
  William Jr. 47
Riley see Reily
Rish, Frederick 54
Risk, Mary 28
River swamp 11, 44
Rivers, James 72
Rives, Charlotte 13
  Green 14, 25, 29, 38, 52, 53, 66
  Henry 34, 52, 53, 66
  John 53
  Mrs. Lucy 52, 53
  Priscilla 53
  Rebecca 53
  Robert 64
  Silas 52, 53
  Timothy 13, 15, 19, 25, 28, 29, 53, 57
  William 33, 52, 53, 59

Rives, William Jr. 53
Roach, Thomas 1, 73
Roades see Rodes
Roanoke River, N.C. 37
Robbins, Thomas 43
Roberson, Fanny (Kimball) 40
  John 23, 53
  Mary (Kimball) 40
Roberts, Mary (Marion) 45
  Robert 51, 53, 73
  Susannah 53
  William 53, 69
Robertson, John 3, 23, 42, 64
  Peter 27
  William 17, 53
Robeson, Charles 53
  James 27
Robinson, Alexander 11, 53
  Alexander Jr. 44
  David 43
  Frederick 16
  James 3
  John 31, 53
  Joseph 22
  Margaret 44
  N. 58
  N.S. 18
  Nicholas 16, 18
  Mrs. Sarah 53
  Thomas 69
  William 41, 53
Roche, Thomas 1, 73
Rochel, Lovel 49
Rocky Creek congregation 2, 5, 10, 15, 18, 19, 21, 22, 32, 34, 37, 41, 42, 48, 53, 55, 57, 61, 66
Roden, John 6
  William 30
Rodes, Alse 49
  Henry 49
  Peary 49
Rodgers, Mrs. Elizabeth 53
  John 53
Rodgers see also Rogers
Rogers, Ann (McNeese) 45
  Clayton 43, 53
  David 65
  Edith 53
  Edward 58
  Henry 38, 67
  Hugh 39
  John 10, 39
  Joseph 58
  Margaret 53
  Margaret (McNeese) 45
  Margery 53
  Mathew 43
  Rachel 53
  Ralph 53
  William 28, 53
Rogers see also Rodgers
Ronder, John 34
Rosborough, Alexander 21, 44, 67
  Alexander Sr. 27
Rose, Nathaniel 34
Roseborough see Rosborough
Ross, A. Brown 42
  Arthur Brown 7, 35, 39, 42, 60, 63, 66
  Brown 7

Ross, Elizabeth 25, 53, 54
  Euphany 25
  Hugh 53, 54
  Isaac 5, 25, 60
  Isaac Jr. 25
  James 62
  Jane 25
  John 40
  Mary 25
  Mary (Gibson) 25
  Ruben 72
  William 54
Rossel see Russell
Rottonbury, William 13
Rowan, Samuel 17
Rowe, Thomas 32
Rows, Deborah 71
Rugeley, Mrs. Elizabeth 15
  Henry 15, 30, 39, 44
Rush, Abarilla 54
  David 39
  Frederick 54
  Jacob 54
  Mrs. Mary 54
Rusk, Mary 20
Russell, Ann 54
  David 58
  Elizabeth 54
  Eugenia (Thompson) 68
  Grace 36
  Hannah 54
  John 54, 68
  Olive 54
  Mrs. Rosannah 54
  Samuel 54
  Samuel Jr. 54
  William 34
Rutherford, Robert 9
Rutledge, Hugh 19
  John 1, 73
Ryley see Reily

Sabb, Morgan 73
Sadler, Deborah 54
  Easter 54
  George 54
  John 6, 54
  Mrs. Mary 54
  Richard 43, 54
St. Augustine, Fla. 54
St. David's parish 5
St. Mark's parish 4, 6, 9, 11, 12, 16, 18, 21, 23, 25, 32, 34, 35, 37, 38, 44, 45, 47, 51, 65, 69, 70, 71, 72, 73
Salem Church 7, 9, 13, 53, 64, 71
Saluda River 11
Sanders, ____ 71
  Ester 54
  Henry 35
  Hester 68
  John 64
  Nathan 35
  Philip 48
  Sarah (Ragan) 73
  William 13, 22, 24, 54, 65, 73
  William Jr. 73
Sandiford, Philip 3
  William 34
Sandy River 18, 22, 38, 72

Sandy River congregation 67
Sandy Run 32
Sangster, John 16
Sant, Thomas 31, 44
Santee Meeting House 44
Santee River 11, 15, 55, 72
Sarvis, John 54
Satterfield, James 7, 8
Saunders, Ester 54
  John 64
  William 22, 24
Saunders see also Sanders
Savage, William 22
Savannah, Ga. 32, 65
Sawney's Creek 20
Saxagotha township 11, 55
Scape whore swamp 69
Scarborough, Addison 51
Scarth, Jonathan 23
Scent, Thomas 57
Scheurer, Barbara 54
  Mrs. Elizabeth 54
  Jesias 54
  John Martin 54
Scheurer see also Shearer
Schmidt, Paul 46
Schmidt see also Smith
Scoldfield, Elizabeth 55
  Hannah 55
  Nancy 55
  Nelly 55
  Philip 55
  William 55
Scoofel see Scoldfield
Scott, George 56
  James 19, 56, 59, 62
  John 24, 27, 48, 54
  Jonathan 54
  Joseph 50
  Josiah 7, 39
  R. H. 21
  William 13, 16, 24, 43, 50
Scrugg, William 24
Scurry, Gideon 55
  Thomas 55
Seal, Charles 64
Sealey, Job 6
  John 32, 62
  Peter 22, 38
Searth, Jonathan 63
Sely see Sealey
Service, John 15
Seymore, Israel 18
Shains, John 69
Sharon Meeting House 21, 37, 55
Sharp, Eleazer 5
Sharpton, Sarah (McGraw) 44
Shaw, John 69
Shearer, Archible 14
Shearer see also Scheurer
Sheldon, S.C. 18
Shelton, George 55
Sheppard, George 55
Shirley, George 4
Shropshire, Walter 1, 45, 50
Shum, Conrod 39
Sibley, William 17, 34
Simeral, James 17, 31, 68
Simmerly, Mrs. Christiana 55
  John Philip 55

Simmerly, Philip 55
Simmons, John 10
  Mary 10
  Samuel 37, 65, 66
  William 6, 7, 17, 20, 22, 56
Simms, ___ 39
Simon, Charles 18
  Maurice 45
Simons, John 18
  William 17, 23
Simonton, John 24
Simpson, Elizabeth 55
  Hugh 48
  James 1, 2, 45, 55, 58
  Jane 55
  John 1, 3, 10, 15, 16, 17, 20,
    21, 22, 25, 27, 31, 32, 33, 37,
    41, 42, 43, 47, 48, 49, 55,
    59, 66
  Mary 55
  Mrs. Mary 55
  Sarah 55
  Thomas 31, 46
  William 49, 55
  William Jr. 56
Sims, ___ 39
  Charles 73
  Joseph 60
Simson see Simpson
Sinclair, James 39
  Peter 52
Singleton, Benjamin 73
  Elizabeth 50
  Elizabeth (James) 72
  J. 25, 73
  John 70, 71
  Joseph 72
  Matthew 53, 62, 70, 72
  Richard 9, 12, 72
Singleton's Creek 47, 56
Sinkler see Sinclair
Skinner, ___ 51
Skipper, Elizabeth 39
Slaves mentioned and/or named:
  3, 6, 11, 12, 13, 15, 16, 18,
  20, 25, 28-33, 35, 37, 39, 40,
  41, 44, 45, 46, 48, 49, 51, 55,
  56, 57, 59, 60, 61, 62, 65, 66,
  69, 71, 72
Sley, Elizabeth 73
Slicker, Gasper 62
  George 62
  William 62
Smart, Alexander 36
Smiley, William 16, 17, 42
Smith, Abraham 7, 40
  Alexander 25
  Catherine 21
  Henry 21, 23, 36, 40
  Hugh 44, 46, 54
  James 5, 24, 62
  James Jr. 18
  Jane 31
  Jane (Gibson) 25
  Jemima 8
  John 8, 22, 30, 40, 60, 73
  John Jr. 39
  Joseph 56
  Levy 6
  Mrs. Mary 21

Smith, Matthew 20
  Moses 30, 68
  Paul 24, 46
  Peter 9, 64
  Robert 59
  Samuel 27
  Sarah 21
  William 8, 30, 40, 48
Smyley see Smiley
Smyth, John 73
Sneade, Elizabeth (Chappell) 13
Snell, Adam 21
  Adam Jr. 21
  Roger 40
Snidder see Snyder
Snyder, John 10
Sojourner, John 20
Sojourner see also Surgener
Somerville see Summerville
Spain, Charles 63, 67
  George 9, 51
Spann, Charles 63, 67
  George 9, 51
Spartanburg Co., S.C. 30
Spears, Charles 13
Speed, John 39
Speikerman, Lewis 41
Spight, Sylvia (Atkinson) 69
Spivey, William 43
Spradley, Ann (Brown) 8
  Polly 8
Spradlin, Agnes 55
  Ann 55
  Charles 55, 56
  Charles Jr. 55
  David 55
  Mrs. Martha 55
Stallings, James 56
  John 56
  John Jr. 56
  Mrs. Mary 56
  Silas 56
Stallions see Stallings
Stanford, George 34
  Marey 4
  Thomas 4, 11, 34
Stansbury, Solomon 10
Starke, Ann (Coats) 15
  Douglas 5, 36, 37, 56, 59, 73
  John 37
  Keziah 56
  Reuben 56
  Thomas 6, 56
Steedman, John 16
Steel, Archibald 22, 38
  John 34
  Thomas 4
Steen, William 40
Stenson see Stinson
Stephenson, Andrew 37
Stevens, ___ 64
  William 57
Stevenson, Andrew 39
  David 54
  James 2
  William 62
Steward see Stewart
Stewart, Alexander 19
  Daniel 21
  Mrs. Elizabeth 57

Stewart, Robert 22, 57
  Robin 21
  Thomas 39
  William 1, 57
Stewart see also Stuart
Stinson, James 2
  William 57
Stockman, Angel 13
Stockton, David 2
  Newbury 40, 62
Stoggler, Benjamin 56
Stogner, Benjamin 56
Stokes, John 48
Stone, Edward 63
  John 43, 63
  Joshua 56
  Martha (McClinton) 43
  Mary 56
  Thomas 6, 35
Stoney run 74
Storer, Robert 32
Storman, John 2, 22
  William 22
Stormond see Storman
Story, Charles 23, 71
Stow, John 6
Strain, James 31
Strange, Charles 56
  Comfort 56
  Edmund 34, 42
  Nancy 56
Stratford, Richard 24, 60
Strean, David 5
Street, Mrs. 34
Straight, Christopher 25
Stroder, Richard 61
Strong, Charles 56, 57
  Christopher 4, 11, 20, 27, 56
  James 4, 14, 27
  Mrs. Jennet 27, 56
  Lettya 56
  Margaret 56
  Robert 4, 14, 56
Strother, Catharine 57
  Mrs. Catherine 57
  John Dargan 57
  Kemp Talaferro 17, 57, 62
  Richard 24, 57
  William 57
  William Jr. 57
Stroud, Ellinor 42
  Hampton 55
  Hugh 6
  Morris 46
  Thomas 22, 34
  William 34, 35, 56
Strowd see Stroud
Stuart, Alexander 62
  Ann 57
  Mrs. Elizabeth 57
  Esther 57
  Isaac 57
  John 34, 57
  Robert 2
  Sarah 57
  Mrs. Sarah 57
  Stacey 57
  William 57
  William Jr. 57
Streart see also Stewart

Stuckey, Penelope (Bell) 5
Suiley, Samuel 27, 28
Sullavent, Hampton 47
Sullivan, John 16
Summerford, Jane 41
  William 41
Summerlin see Summerville
Summerville, George 57, 58
  Hugh 57, 58
  Martha 57, 58
  Mrs. Rachel 58
Sumter, ___ 39
  Thomas 56
Sumter, S.C. 69, 70
Surgeoner see Surginer
Surginal see Surginer
Surginer, John 17, 20, 45
Sutton, Jacob 27
  William 7
Swan, Adam 58
Swechart, Jacob 57
Swelly, John 68
  Nicholas 68
  Samuel 27, 28
Swetman, Augusten 53
Swift, Richard 6, 14
Swift Creek Meetinghouse 6, 14, 39
Swillea see Swelly
Swilly see Swelly
Sylvester, Asberry 31, 51, 72

Tabb, Robert 17
Talbert, Mathew 15, 33
Talbott Co. Maryland 74
Taleman, Ann 41
  Daniel 41
  David 41
Tanner, Lodovick 58
Tapley, John 58, 61
  Mrs. Mary 58
Tappley see Tapley
Tarleton, ___ 60
Tate, Mrs. Elizabeth 58, 59
  Fanny 58
  Frances 59
  James 24, 27, 58
  Robert 58
  Thomas 58, 59
  Thomas Jr. 58
  William 16, 24
Tatelin, Joseph 64
Tateman, Daniel 64
Tatum, Joseph 36, 59
Taylor, ___ 57
  Jacob 59
  James 5, 15, 17, 25, 34, 36, 50,
    51, 59, 60, 62, 63, 64, 66, 73
  Jeremiah 60
  John 1, 36, 50, 59
  John Jr. 59
  Mary 59
  Mrs. Sarah 59
  Simeon 59
  Thomas 5, 23, 36, 45, 50, 51, 53,
    57, 59, 62, 63, 66, 73
  William 20, 45, 59, 67
Taylors & Rea 39
Telford, Joseph 10, 32
Templeton, James 62
  Sarah (Watson) 62

Tennett, ___ 64
Terrell, John 32
  William 3
Terry, John 6, 32, 48, 54
  Joseph 8, 21, 52
  Stephen 59
Thames, Amos 8
Tharp, Jesse 43
  John Allen 43
Therel see Terrell
Theus, Christian 5, 9, 11, 20, 22,
  29, 34, 59, 60
Thomas, Adam 1
  Anderson 17
  Elizabeth (Hunter) 37
  George 59
  James 17, 59
  John Jr. 20
  Mrs. Mildred 59
  R. 60
  Richard 59, 60
  Sarah 59
Thomason, Betty 59
Thompson, Capt. 20
  Benjamin 60
  Eleanor 60
  Eugenia (Russell) 68
  James 24, 45, 58
  John 19, 30, 39, 60
  Joseph 2
  Mary 60
  Moses 60
  Robert 8, 31, 39
  Solomon 51
  Thomas 40, 58
  William 64, 67, 70
Thomson, Adam 58
  Alexander 32, 55
  Eleanor 60
  James 24, 45, 48
  John 19, 30, 39, 60
  Nathan 68
  Robert 8, 31, 39
  Solomon 8, 9, 11, 24, 51, 52,
    54, 55, 56, 58, 60, 62, 67
  Thomas 40, 58
  William 14, 54, 58, 64
Thorn, David 39
  Sophia 39
Threewits, Joel 60, 64
  John 25, 29
  Mary 34, 60
Thropshire see Shropshire
Thruits see Threewits
Tidwell, Leah 46
Tiebont, Tennis 72
Tillinghast, Henry H. 1
Tillman, Elizabeth Sr. 60
  Elizabeth Jr. 60
  Jesse 2, 34, 41, 46
  William 60
  William Jr. 66
Timmons, Samuel 45
Timms see Tims
Tims, Amos 48
  Hollis 48
  Joseph 6, 48, 54
  Pattie (Nance) 48
Tindall, Robert 48
Tines, Fleming 51

Tines, Lavina 60
  Samuel 24, 72
  William 60
Tobias, Thomas 4
Toby, Mary 14
Toccaw swamp 32
Todd, John 60
Tolen, James 30
Tolbert, Matthew 15, 33
Tomb, Alexander 41
Tomkins, Francis 35
  Stephen 35
Tomlinson, Bridget (Gee) 25
  James 6
  John 69, 71
  Navil Gee 25
  Rebecca 25
  Samuel 25, 63
  William 39
Tonym, Patrick 54
Torbert, Samuel 14
Torley, Peter 45
Townsend, Henry 27
  Repentance 27
  Samuel 27
  Thomas 27
Trussell, William 15, 33
Tucker, David 60, 61
  Lucy 61
  Mrs. Martha 59
  Mary 60
  Mrs. Milley 60, 61
  Richard 60
  Robert 60, 61
  Wood Sr. 5, 34, 36, 38, 51, 60, 61
  Wood Jr. 5, 59, 60
  Zilpah 51
Tuppley see Taply
Turkey Creek 54, 57
Turner, Alexander 61
  Henry 37
  James 42, 73
  John 3, 40, 42, 51, 53, 61
  Sarah (Hunter) 37
Turnipseed, Beat 61
  Felix 41, 61
  Hans Beat 61
  Jacob 61
  John 17, 41, 61
  John Sr. 61
  Maria Margrett 61
  Wideto 61
  Zeb 61
Tursden, Roger 61
Twaddle, Elizabeth 58
  William 45, 52
Tweedy, Robert 67
Twelve Mile Creek 21
Twenty Five Mile Creek 20, 23
Two Mile Creek 63
Tyler, Spence 61
Tynes see Tines

Usk, Wales 38

Valentine, Dougal 61
  Elizabeth 61
Vass, Reuben 25
Vaughan, Elizabeth 17
  Thomas 19, 20, 56

Vawn see Vaughan
Venables, John 5, 12, 62
Vertee, John 6, 52
Viningham, William 3
Virginia 9, 14, 25, 45, 53, 57, 59, 69
Voght, Michael 61

Wade, George 1, 20, 21, 22, 39, 40, 41, 62
  Thomas 39
Waistcoat see Westcott
Wake Co, N.C. 9
Waldrop 45
Wales 38
Walker, Alexander 10, 34
  Andrew 30, 61, 67
  Charles 30
  Felix 62
  James 10
  Jane 48
  John 2, 3, 20, 37, 39, 48, 62
  Joseph 27
  Philip 2, 10, 12, 16, 20, 32, 33, 34, 37, 48, 55, 56
  Robert 10, 21, 27
Wallace, John 3, 54
Wallis, Benjamin 11, 60
  Charles 5
  John 3, 4, 5, 54
  Jos. 62
Walter, John 49
Waltour, Andrew 71
Ward, Mrs. ___ Wilson 64
  Dickey 64
  Elias 64
Warley, Felix 65
Warnel, William 61, 62
Warren, Joseph 51
  Joseph Jr. 51
Warring, Benjamin 73
  Thomas 73
Warshing see Wershing
Wateree River 5, 14, 16, 24, 43, 44, 46, 47, 54, 59, 69, 72
Waters, P. 21
Watson, Ann 62
  Archibald 24
  David 62
  David Jr. 62
  Francis 47
  Gilbert 62
  Mrs. Hannah 62
  Hugh 70
  James 62
  Jean (McCallum) 43
  Job 62
  John 16, 41, 62
  Robert 47
  Samuel 20, 62
  Samuel Sr. 62
  Sarah 62
  William 20, 51, 62
Watts, Edward 73
  George 7, 49, 50
  John 6, 35, 49, 61, 69
  Ruth (Perry) 49
  Sarah 49
  Thomas 23, 49, 51
  William 30

Waugh, John 30, 67
Waxhaw Congregation 4, 19, 23, 31, 32, 43, 48, 58, 59
Way, Ann 62
  Moses 62
Wayerf, Nicholas 61
Wear, John 37
  Samuel 27
Weaver, Widow 28
  Joseph 62
  Maurice 67
Webb, John 9, 74
  Nancy (Scoldfield) 55
Weer see Wear
Weir see Wear
Welch, William 30, 40, 48
Welch see also Welsh
Weldon, William 34
Wells, Henry 13
Welsh, William Jr. 30, 40, 48
Welsh see also Welch
Wershing, Gasper 23, 62
  George 62
Wesbury see Westbury
West, Robert 40
  Robert Jr. 40
Westbury, John 8, 9, 53, 60, 62, 63, 67, 72
  Mary 62, 63
  William 62, 63
  William Jr. 62
Westcoat, Joseph 64
Westcott, David 5, 29, 45, 67
Weston, Robert 12, 37
  William 16
Wheatley, John 63
Wheeler, Henry 51
  John 13, 36, 63, 65
  John Jr. 9, 68
  William 53
Whitaker, Catherine 63
  James 63
  James Jr. 63
  John 63
  John Wiggins 63
  Martha 63
  Mary 63
  Mrs. Mary 63
  Richard 63
  Robert 40, 63
  Simon 63
  Thomas 63
  William 25, 39, 63, 73
  William Jr. 63, 73
  Willis 5, 63, 73
White, Arthur 4, 46, 52
  Ezekiel 56
  George 4, 63
  Hugh 3, 25, 27, 32, 63
  Issabel Helena 63
  Joanna 63
  John 3, 16, 63, 64
  John Jr. 24
  Joseph 33
  Joseph Jr. 63
  Mary 63
  Robert 8, 39
  Stephen 63, 64
  William 8, 54
White Deer Pond 71

Whitehead, Nazarous 50, 54
Whiteside, Hugh 5, 25, 27, 49
  William 27
Whitted, Ann 50
  Nazarus 50, 54
Whorter see McWhorter
Wiley see Wyly
Williams, Christopher 40
  Daniel 60
  James 16
  Joel 64
  Membrance 9
  Nathan 64
  Philip 44
  Roling 5
  Mrs. Sela 64
  Thomas 22, 43, 50
  William 9, 47
Williamsburg, S.C. 46
Williamson, Adam 47
  Mrs. Alcey (Wyche) 36, 66
  Elijah 10
  Rowland 6, 36, 57, 59, 60
  Samuel 32
Willie, Eillean 34
Willingham, Joseph 39
  Thomas 51
  William 13, 56
Willis, Robert 60
Willson see Wilson
Wilson, David 69, 71, 73, 74
  David Jr. 73
  James 8, 58, 59, 64, 74
  Jane 64
  Jane Allen 74
  Jean 64
  Jennet (Bradley) 69
  Jesse 56, 64
  John 14, 23, 43, 55, 56, 62
  John Jr. 64
  Margaret Grace 74
  Mary 49, 71
  Mrs. Mary 64, 73
  Richard 28, 29
  Robert William 73, 74
  Roger 7, 13, 23, 47, 69, 70, 71, 74
  Thomas 7, 59, 74
  William 13, 29, 64
Wimberly, Abraham 1, 50
  William 9
Wimpey, Henry 35, 48
Winborne, Demsey 56
  Jesse 56
  Winney (Stallings) 56
Windham, Amos 51
Windsor, Ann 36
Winn, James 42
  John 3, 13, 15, 17, 22, 28, 31, 41, 46, 52, 64, 69, 73
  John Jr. 64
  Joseph 64
  Minor 1, 17, 28, 33
  Peter 64
  R. 20, 60, 62, 68
  Richard 6, 17, 18, 19, 28, 30, 31, 39, 48, 59, 60
Winnsborough Congregation 1, 2, 48, 68
Winsley, Sally 49

Wise, Miss 65
  Mrs. Betty 65
  Jonathan 64
  Samuel 65
Wisher, Walter 65
Witherspoon, John 30, 43
Wolf, Francis 40
Wood, Archilus 65
  Elizabeth 11
  John 65
  John Jr. 65
  Mary 65
  Samuel 65
  Sarah 59
  Mrs. Susannah 65
  William 65, 72
  Winefred 65
Woodard see Woodward
Wooderson, Ann 65
  John 63, 65
Woodison see Wooderson
Woodred see Woodward
Woodroof, Fielding 14, 15, 24, 57, 73
Woods, Andrew 43
  Edith (Rogers) 53
  Frame 14, 28, 53, 54
  John 35
  Jonas 14
  Sarah 59
  Thomas 14
Woodward, ____ 61
  Mrs. 56
  Elizabeth 65
  John 17, 3_, 58, 65
  Martha 65
  Mary 65
  Priscilla 65
  Samuel 64
  Simon 58, 65
  Thomas 65
  Thomas Jr. 65
  William 2, 10, 65, 66
Wooten, David 10, 51
  John 51, 61
Wooters, Jacob 66
  Jacob Jr. 71
  James 71
Word, Thomas 14
Wrandor, Mary (McGraw) 44
Wren, James 59
  John 2
Wrice see Rice
Wright, Dr. 51
  Abraham 5
  Henry 62
  John 56
  Joseph 20
  Thomas 36
  William 24, 36
Wyche, Alcey 66
  Drury 59, 64, 66
  John 64, 66
  Mary 66
  Mrs. Mary 66
  Mrs. Sarah 66
  William 66
Wyley see Wyly
Wylie see Wyly
Wyly, Dinah 66
  Mrs. Elizabeth 66

Wyly, Frances 27
  James 27, 43
  Jane 66
  John 39, 54, 63, 66
  Samuel 66
  Sarah 66
  Mrs. Sarah (Lang) 66
  William 12, 19, 21, 27, 37, 46, 54, 66
  William Jr. 27
Wyn see Winn

Yarborough, James 6
  Major 51
  Richard 10
Yates, David 54
  George 9
Yeats see Yates
York Co., S.C. 20, 23, 30, 41, 58, 62, 68
Young, Amos 67
  Andrew 16
  Hugh 45
  John 51, 56
  Lagrove 20
  Legros 20, 67
  Mrs. Margaret 67
  Mary (McNeese) 45
  William 67

Zuber, Conrad 54

www.ingramcontent.com/pod-product-compliance
Lightning Source LLC
Chambersburg PA
CBHW020658300426
44112CB00007B/433